For Gaby   The Muses garden with Pedantique
weedes O'rspred, was purg'd by thee

Preface

This may seem a peculiar book at first, concentrating as it does on a body of work most of which Pound abandoned over the years—the contents of *A Lume Spento* (his first printed collection, 1908), the original *Personae* and *Exultations* of 1909, with occasional excursions into *Canzoni* (1911) and a few later volumes. But the book embodies a more interesting peculiarity than this, in that a properly conducted scrutiny of these early poems enables us to catch Pound in the very process of forming his own poetics, a system of thought curiously complete almost from the very beginning. It is safe to say that the thematic and technical interests evinced in those first books and examined in this one remain important and operative down to Pound's most recent work.

Of those parts of the book touching upon Pound's ties with earlier poets, some explanation is in order. I have given fairly short shrift to the Browning question because I think that the relationship is, in critical terms, not so important as it sometimes seems. Browning is simply not the key to very much Pound, as I hope the reader will agree after reading the later parts of the first chapter. In speaking of the 1890s, I have fixed upon one or two key figures (from the point of view of a student of Pound's work) and on what seem the central issues. I have also used the words "Pre-Raphaelite" and "Rossetti" more or less interchangeably, since for Pound Rossetti is the epitome of the movement and the only truly "germinal" artist of the group. I have excluded William Morris from my conception of Pound's Pre-Raphaelite pantheon, for example, on the grounds that his effect on Pound was limited to fairly superficial areas. He stirred Pound's interest in legend and myth and in a rather romanticized Middle Ages, and no doubt his energetic efforts at public betterment find an echo in Pound's sometimes wrong-(and sometimes right-)headed excursions into social and cultural reform;

but his medievalism was not Cavalcanti's, and for Pound the difference is crucial.

The question of which texts to use offers some minor difficulties in a study of Pound's early work. In his earliest collections it is not always easy to tell a misprint from a poetic miscalculation, though the actual textual questions involved are not vital. I have in general used the earliest sound texts, including those of *A Lume Spento* whenever possible, but freely adopting the typographical alterations in the first *Personae*, in *Exultations*, and in *Canzoni*, for the first book was full of errors. In one place I have silently accepted an emendation offered by the recent re-edition of *A Lume Spento*: "you allow / That 'tis not need we *know* our every thought" for "you allow / That this not need." The latter, in both *A Lume Spento* and the 1909 *Personae*, seems fairly clearly a stubborn misprint or an author's mistake. Publications later than *Exultations* are less problem-laden, despite the typographical goblins that have pursued Pound since the beginning of his career (goblins that transformed *Bertran de Born* into *de Bom* in one essay and the artist's *primary pigment* into *primary figment* in another).

By and large, the citations direct the reader to reliable texts he has some hope of being able to find. With the same end in view, I have used the revised edition (1952) of Pound's *Spirit of Romance*. The revisions consist principally of the incorporation of certain footnotes into the text and the addition as a new chapter of the highly interesting "Psychology and Troubadours" (also very slightly altered from its original form), which was originally published in G.R.S. Mead's spiritualist periodical, *The Quest*, in 1912.

Portions of this book first saw the light of day as a doctoral dissertation at Yale University under the direction of Cleanth Brooks. The material has traveled a long road since then, but I am happy to acknowledge my debt to his friendly guidance. The general subject was originally suggested by Louis Martz, but my obligations to him go far beyond the confines of this particular topic. During the composition of the book, Charles Feidelson's ungentle criticisms of that dissertation proved highly relevant. I owe a great deal, too, to Hugh Kenner, in whose classroom these many years ago I first made close contact with Pound's work; my mild disagreements with him, stated and implied, must not be allowed to obscure my obligation both to him and to his book on Pound.

A leave of absence, made possible by a grant from the Old Dominion Fund at the Massachusetts Institute of Technology, enabled me to put the book into its final shape and also made possible the gathering of useful material concerning the Pre-Raphaelites. The M.I.T. Humanities Department and Brandeis University generously allocated funds for typing and other clerical costs.

Wellesley, Massachusetts   T. H. J.
April 1968

Acknowledgments

Permission to reprint quotations from the following works of Ezra Pound has been granted by New Directions Publishing Corporation and Faber and Faber Ltd.: Ezra Pound, *Personae*, copyright 1926, 1954 by Ezra Pound; *A Lume Spento and Other Early Poems*, copyright 1965 by Ezra Pound and New Directions Publishing Corporation; *The Cantos*, copyright 1934, 1937, 1940, 1948, 1956 by Ezra Pound; *Literary Essays, Guide to Kulchur, Gaudier-Brzeska*, and *The Spirit of Romance*, all rights reserved; *Translations*, copyright 1926, 1954 by Ezra Pound.

Permission to reprint passages from *The Letters of Ezra Pound*, edited by D. D. Paige (copyright 1950 by Harcourt, Brace, and World) has been granted by Harcourt, Brace, and World and by Faber and Faber Ltd.

Permission to reprint passages from W. B. Yeats's *Mythologies, Essays and Introductions*, and *Collected Poems* has been granted by Mr. M. B. Yeats and the Macmillan Companies.

Contents

The Early Poetry of Ezra Pound

Abstract

Abbreviations

ALS   *A Lume Spento.* Venice: A. Antonini, 1908.

ALSO *A Lume Spento and Other Early Poems.* New York: New Directions, 1965.

E   *Exultations.* London: Elkin Mathews, 1909.

GB   *Gaudier-Brzeska: A Memoir.* London: John Lane, Bodley Head, 1916.

GK   *Guide to Kulchur.* Norfolk: New Directions [1938].

L   *The Letters of Ezra Pound, 1907–1941,* ed. D. D. Paige. New York: Harcourt, Brace and Co., 1950.

LE   *Literary Essays of Ezra Pound,* ed. T. S. Eliot. Norfolk: New Directions [1954].

NA   *The New Age: A Weekly Review of Politics, Literature, and Art.*

P 1   *Personae.* London: Elkin Mathews, 1909.

P 2   *Personae: The Collected Poems of Ezra Pound.* Norfolk: New Directions [1949].

PD   *Pavannes and Divisions.* New York: Alfred A. Knopf, 1918.

PD 2 *Pavannes and Divagations.* Norfolk: New Directions, 1958.

PE   *Polite Essays.* London: Faber and Faber, 1937.

SR   *The Spirit of Romance* (1910), rev. ed. Norfolk: New Directions [1952].

T   *The Translations of Ezra Pound.* New York: New Directions [1954].

YL   Yale Letters; a collection of Pound's unpublished letters (gathered by D. D. Paige for his edition of *Letters*) in the American Literature Collection, Yale University Library.

I

The Poetic Moment:
Sources, Analogues,
Distinctions

FEW POETS have been so doggedly—so mechanically—experimental as Ezra Pound, and few so deliberatively derivative, at least in work presented to public view. In his introduction to the 1928 London edition of Pound's *Selected Poems*, T. S. Eliot wrote:

> The earliest of the poems in the present volume show that the first strong influences upon Pound, at the moment when his verse was taking direction, were those of Browning and Yeats. In the background are the 'Nineties in general, and behind the 'Nineties, of course, Swinburne and William Morris. I suspect that the latter influences were much more visible in whatever Mr. Pound wrote before the first of his published verse; they linger in some of his later work more as an emotional attitude than in the technique of versification: the shades of Dowson, Lionel Johnson and Fiona flit about. (p. ix)

Eliot seems to have been thinking chiefly of manner and style, but his remark does go far toward defining the matrix of admirations and aspirations from which Pound's early work grew. It is a statement peculiarly applicable to the young Pound.

One result is that it can be highly profitable to examine Pound's early work in the light suggested here by Eliot. It is

3

possible by considering this poetry in relation to that of earlier writers who influenced him to turn up some interesting facts about Pound's poetic theory, his work, and his struggle for style. The point is not to go source hunting, but to clarify our reading of Pound by making the right distinctions between what he did and what other poets did with similar devices and to place Pound in the history of more recent poetry.

i

The question of Pound's relationship to Robert Browning is a good example to begin with. Even a sketchy survey, limited to the broad topics of style, common themes, and formal borrowings, uncovers important basic facts about Pound—facts by no means confined to his "indebtedness." Certainly his early poems often enough proclaim their Browningian ancestry. When we read the early monologue, "Cino," there can be no doubt where Pound went to school. When Cino imagines his women speaking, they speak Browning's English:

> "Cino?" "Oh, eh, Cino Polnesi
> The singer is't you mean?"
> "Ah yes, passed once our way,
> A saucy fellow, but . . .
> (Oh they are all one these vagabonds),
> Peste! 'tis his own songs?
> Or some other's that he sings?
> But *you*, My Lord, how with your city?"

The ancestry of "Famam Librosque Cano" is equally obvious:

> A book is known by them that read
> That same. Thy public in my screed
> Is listed. Well! Some score years hence
> Behold mine audience,
> As we had seen him yesterday.

And, to take one more example, the voice of Arnaut in "Marvoil," describing the result of an intrigue, is basically the voice of Browning:

> Aragon cursing in Aragon, Beziers busy at Beziers—
> Bored to an inch of extinction,
> Tibors all tongue and temper at Mont-Ausier,
> Me! in this damn'd inn of Avignon,
> Stringing long verse for the Burlatz;
> All for one half-bald, knock-knee'd king of the Aragonese,
> Alfonso, Quattro, poke-nose.

There are numerous thematic parallels as well, all tracing the role of the artistically minded misfit in ordinary-minded society. Browning's thought-burdened, often outcast, solitaries, of whom Sordello is perhaps the prototype and who include Fra Lippo Lippi and the dead scholar of "A Grammarian's Funeral," have close relatives in Pound: the speaker in his early "In Durance" constantly feels his kinship with a world of Beauty foreign to the tedious and colorless world of everyday; "Piere Vidal Old" is another dour solitary who knows what other men do not. It remained for the *Cantos* to utilize this motif thoroughly. There we have a whole gallery of such figures—Sigismundo Malatesta, Acoetes, John Adams, Confucius. But it exists in the early work, too—even, perhaps, in the beleaguered comrades of "A Villonaud: Ballad of the Gibbet," with its query, "These that we loved shall God love less / And smite always at their faibleness?"

This tendency to worry the subject of art and its significance for the artist and the world, which emerges in Browning's "Abt Vogler" and "A Toccata of Galuppi's," formed a large part of the thematic material in Pound's early collections—indeed, if *A Lume Spento* and the *Personae* of 1909 can be said to center on a predominant theme, that theme is precisely the nature and significance of art. Loosely speaking, the various themes converge for both poets into a concern over the creative spirit—whether it be embodied in an artist, a philosopher, a politician, or a lover—beleaguered original genius striving to make its mark upon the world against negative forces from within and without. Though for Pound the theme, put just this way, does not enter into the poetry very much until the *Cantos*, it is clearly taking form in his earlier work.

In *A Lume Spento* Pound's "Fifine Answers" (his answer to the question asked by Don Juan in Browning's *Fifine at the Fair*— "Why is it that, disgraced, they seem to relish life the more?") uses just this theme and gives not so much an answer as an affirmation of the state of mind by which Browning's Juan is struck—a kind of grim joy in the freedom afforded by the performer's life, freedom of one sort afforded by living outside society and freedom of another afforded by the pursuit of art. And there is a similarly grim satisfaction at making the sacrifices that art demands:

> Sharing his exile that hath borne the flame,
> Joining his freedom that hath drunk the shame
> And known the torture of the Skull-place hours
> Free and so bound, that mingled with the powers
> Of air and sea and light his soul's far reach
> Yet strictured did the body-lips beseech
> "To drink" "I thirst". And then the sponge of gall.

This frank linking of the criminal-artist-outcast with Christ is insisted upon in Fifine's later assertions that she and her fellows are "sharers in his drink" and that "spite your carping still the thing is done / With some deep sanction." Her ideology is not much different from that of Browning's Fifine, who, to the puzzlement of Don Juan, is willing to forgo the rewards of respectability and regular employment in order to respond to what Pound's poem calls "the grey road's call," a mysterious call that "Doth master and make slaves and yet make free." Pound's closing "Call! eh bye! the little door at twelve! / I meet you there myself" is but a more obvious version of the suggestion of assignation on which Browning's poem closes. Pound is deliberately vague about what "thing" it is that is "done with some deep sanction"—vague, that is, about whether a sexual act or an artistic act is meant. In both poems Fifine is an artist—a gypsy dancer—and undertakes services, in the several senses implied, abjured by others. More specifically, she undertakes to fill needs inherent in man's nature but for which society makes little respectable provision; in her consequent spiritual status she thus assumes the moral burden of humanity, in the same sense, though for a different reason, that Christ assumed the burden of man's sins.

There is a difference, however. For Browning, Fifine embodies a characteristic moral and philosophical ambiguity about the status of the creative act. *Is* what the artist gains worth the sacrifices he makes? Does he merely prostitute himself when he presents his wares to the public? Pound asks these same questions in "Fifine Answers," but answers more readily "yes"—and goes on, as we see, to join the artist-prostitute with Christ so that the artist's sin is pre-redeemed, perhaps, by her sacrifice of self (and partly by the fact that, like Christ's, the artist's *real* self is unsullied in these encounters with the world—compare Pound's "In Durance": "'These sell our pictures!' Oh well, / They reach me not, touch me some edge or that, / But reach me not and all my life's become / One flame."). Pound's blunt insistence on the performer's self-immolation is surely only a version, openly stated, of what is implicit in Browning's recourse to the dramatic lyric: the creative process uncovers Truth, as distinct from personal idiosyncracy, by means of the artist's "destruction" of self.

This takes us to an aspect of the Browning question beyond the issues of style and theme, the use of the dramatic lyric. Again, here is a debt Pound has never concealed. As late as 1917 he could write, in a review of *Prufrock and Other Observations*, "The form of Browning's *Men and Women* is more alive than the epistolary form of the *Heroides*," and "The most interesting poems in Victorian English are Browning's *Men and Women*, or, if that statement is too absolute, let me contend that the form of these poems is the most vital form of that period of English" (*LE* 419). Pound's use of the form can, at least in part, be traced to the same poetic considerations as Browning's.

If we look first at the more exterior attractions, the biographical and mechanical, we may note that both poets' Fifines make much of the importance of the brassy and flamboyant showman's mask as a protection for a private and anguished heart. In anticipation of Elvire's possibly remarking that the Fifines of the world cannot feel slings and arrows so keenly as decent women can, Don Juan says that Fifine's stoic demeanor only means to plead for privacy. "Know all of me outside," she says,

> the rest be emptiness
> For such as you! I call attention to my dress,
> Coiffure, outlandish features, lithe memorable limbs,
> Piquant entreaty, all that eye-glance overskims,
> Does this give pleasure? Then repay the pleasure, put
> Its price i' the tambourine! Do you seek further? Tut!
> I'm just my instrument,—sound hollow: mere smooth
>   skin
> Stretched o'er gilt framework.
>
> *(Fifine at the Fair, st. 32)*

This seems to have been an important issue for Browning and, for him as for Pound, a major consideration in his choice of the dramatic lyric as his favorite poetic vehicle.[1] In an early poem called "Masks" (in *A Lume Spento*), Pound is even more insistent than Browning on the significance of the poetic mask as a means of defense:

> These tales of old disguisings, are they not
> Strange myths of souls that found themselves among

Unwonted folk that spake a hostile tongue,
Some soul from all the rest who'd not forgot
The star-span acres of a former lot
Where boundless mid the clouds his course he swung
Or carnate with his elder brothers sung
Ere ballad makers lisped of Camelot?

Later Pound was to write, "I believe that Greek myth arose when someone having passed through a delightful psychic experience tried to communicate it to others and found it necessary to screen himself from persecution" (*SR* 92). He said almost the same thing still later: "After bitter experience, perceiving that no one could understand what he meant when he said that he 'turned into a tree,' [the first poet] made a myth—a work of art that is—an impersonal or objective story" woven out of his own emotion ("Arnold Dolmetsch," *LE* 431). Perhaps the "persecution" takes the form of ridicule, for like Browning's artists—at least his Fifine and his Shakespeare—Pound's Fifine hopes to conceal or deny any emotional or spiritual commitment to the creative act:

you allow
That 'tis not need we *know* our every thought
Or see the work shop where each mask is wrought
Wherefrom we view the world of box and pit,
Careless of wear, just so the mask shall fit
And serve our jape's turn for a night or two.

Obviously this is a piece of romantic irony, the artist undercutting her own position to avoid being detected holding one.

A different aspect of self-defense is suggested by that quotation about the poet who said that he had turned into a tree—the matter of objectifying a highly subjective experience. The conviction that it is somehow necessary for the poet to separate himself from any fanciful content in his poetry (a characteristic of a naively scientific age, perhaps, and certainly a condition Browning had to face) might be an interesting subject for historical speculation; at any rate, the idea colors these last remarks of Pound's. For both him and Browning the specifically dramatic poem bestows objective credibility on the emotions expressed— hence the poem "Masks," just quoted. For Pound, figures like Cino or Bertran de Born ostensibly undergo experiences that the poet cannot claim for himself without seeming fanciful. By attributing the experience to a character in an implied drama, the poet avoids responsibility—to take one potential source of criticism—for transgressing against reason.

Pound's work with dramatic lyrics had at least one other more or less mechanical kind of usefulness. The dramatic monologue demands of its writer a convincing display of the connection of the speaking voice to the experience in the poem. The poet must be able to suppress every characteristic of style or "personality" that might disturb the fitness of voice to event, with the result that the poet is actually driven to refine and discipline his control of language.

But considerations so strictly pragmatic as these would hardly lead Pound to call the dramatic monologue the most important poetic form in the Victorian period: there are more important factors, most of which come under the heading of *exploration*. When Browning turned from the manner of *Pauline* to more objective forms, he was in a way turning from its matter as well. His gaze would no longer be morbidly inward, but would concentrate upon the world without—although in a special sense. Though his "invention" of the dramatic lyric may have been an attempt to reconcile the demands of subjective poetry—lyric and expressive—with the demands of objective poetry— dramatic and descriptive—there can be little doubt about which horn of this dilemma he preferred, or what he was hoping to preserve by means of the new form; it is the subjective poet, according to Browning's essay on Shelley, who, "gifted like the objective poet with the fuller perception of nature and man, is

impelled to embody the thing he perceives, not so much with
reference to the many below as to the One above him . . . an
ultimate view ever aspired to . . . by the poet's own soul. Not
what man sees, but what God sees—the Ideas of Plato, seeds
of creation lying burningly on the Divine Hand—it is toward
these that he struggles."[2] To some degree these remarks account
for Browning's high-handed "use" of history—the tendency
to alter facts when that helped his poetry—to which Pound
objects in Canto III. In his role as a poet, Browning conceived of
himself as a genius who could perceive the Truth in events,
and his succession of dramatic monologues furnished him with a
stage on which to carry out his search or to act out his findings.
This seems fairly similar to the role of the poet in Pound's
Cantos, though doubtless the similarity is due to the generality
of the concept: we could say something similar about Words-
worth's idea of the poet. But Browning actually does, in a great
deal of his poetry, utilize the dramatic lyric for purposes of
exploration—to explore history in search of Truth, whether that
be Platonic Ideas or the seeds of creation. And this use of the
dramatic lyric is a permanent fixture in Browning's career.

Pound, too, found the dramatic lyric a useful exploratory
device. He wrote in September 1914, in the *Fortnightly Review*:

> In the "search for oneself," in the search for "sincere
> self-expression," one gropes, one finds some seeming
> verity. One says "I am" this, that, or the other, and with
> the words scarcely uttered one ceases to be that thing.
>
> I began this search for the real in a book called *Per-
> sonae*, casting off, as it were, complete masks of the self
> in each poem.   ("Vorticism," *GB* 98)

This passage will have to receive closer scrutiny later. For the
moment we only need note its striking similarity to another
passage in Browning's essay on Shelley: the subjective poet,
"whose study has been himself, appealing through himself to

the absolute Divine mind, prefers to dwell upon those external scenic appearances which strike out most abundantly and uninterruptedly his inner light and power, selects that silence of the earth and sea in which he can best hear the beating of his individual heart." By the time Browning gets to the dramatic lyric—after the inadequacy of *Pauline* and after ten years of trying to write plays—he is past this stage: he is done with himself as the center of poetic interest. He is not describing himself, then, but that last remark does describe the young Ezra Pound. Pound, that is to say, turns to the dramatic lyric, the "mask," to structure and rationalize moments in the lyrical record of an exploration of self rather than of history. Nor is it only himself as such; he searches, he says, for *the real*, which is not too different from Browning's "absolute Divine mind"— some kind of fundamental reality the poet is uniquely equipped to find and formulate. But the form that was for Browning a mainstay of his career is for Pound a tool and, by implication, of temporary usefulness.

Another function of this tool for Pound was to test the validity of inner experience, perhaps of the sort alluded to in those accounts of the origin of poetry quoted above. Pound implies a process of trial and error in one's saying "I am a given thing" and then finding out immediately that one is not, or is no longer: it is doubtless a matter of finding out what emotions one is "really" capable of feeling as opposed to what one can fake. There are subordinate considerations, therefore, in this process: striving for successful dramatic lyrics is a means of ridding oneself of the drag of kinds of experience one cannot write about very well or convincingly, and it is also a kind of imaginative athleticism that may enlarge the range of experience with which the poet is able to deal. Hugh Kenner, Pound's earliest systematic critic, put it well when he said of the personae of the early years that

> self-nourishment through exploring the experiences of other men and ages leads to a purgation of the con-

tingencies of a personality partly private (Hailey, Idaho; Hamilton College), partly public (the legacy of Rossetti, the emotional climate of 1900–1912) but in any case irrelevant to the fullness of poetic achievement . . . [The personae] are deliberate dramatizations which extend the modes of thinking and feeling accessible to the quotidian inhabitant of a given London decade.[3]

These remarks underscore the significance of the dramatic lyric as a means to an end. Indeed, though in the three areas of style, theme, and form Browning seems to have presided over the inception of Pound's development as a poet, his influence very early met with some important solvents—the examples of other poets whose techniques presented more promising possibilities than Browning's did. Pound's complaint to Iris Barry in 1917 that he had caught Browning's manner as if it were a disease arose from more than a poet's longing for originality. The fact is that stylistic or structural tricks modeled too closely upon Browning were not adequate to the ends Pound pursued—or, better, to the kinds of experience in which he was interested. The early poem "Mesmerism," a more or less bantering assessment of Browning's achievement (the poem dates from the period of *A Lume Spento*), suggests part of what was involved, both in praise and in blame. At one point Pound expostulates,

> You wheeze as a head-cold long-tonsilled Calliope,
> But God! what a sight you ha' got o' our in'ards,
>
> . . . . .
>
> Heart that was big as the bowels of Vesuvius,
> Words that were wing'd as her sparks in eruption,
> Eagled and thundered as Jupiter Pluvius,
> Sound in your wind past all signs o' corruption.

> Here's to you, Old Hippety-Hop o' the accents,
> True to the Truth's sake and crafty dissector,
> You grabbed at the gold sure; had no need to pack cents
> Into your versicles.
>   Clear sight's elector!

Words wing'd as the sparks of a volcanic eruption are glorious enough and doubtless have their uses, but they are not likely to be polished and filed, and the last stanza reveals where Pound thought Browning's strength lay. Although the abrupt change of meter in the final stanza conveys affectionate admiration for the boldness and success of Browning's metrical practices, the poem does suggest that, when the "crafty dissector" succeeded in expressing his considerable insights into mankind, it was by main force.

Even "Mesmerism," then, which dates from a time when Browning's influence on Pound was in certain areas truly immense, expresses a qualified admiration and some attempt at dispassionate evaluation. And in spite of Pound's frequent and emphatic assertions of indebtedness, his use of the dramatic lyric is from the beginning unlike Browning's. The differences between the two, considerably more important than the similarities, begin to emerge as soon as we consider the characteristic occasion of a poem by Pound and the particular form his dramatic lyrics take. The poem to which he currently gives pride of place in his *Personae* is "The Tree," which presents a moment of magical transfiguration. The lovely "Ballatetta" from the 1911 *Canzoni* depicts another, the advent of some ethereal, goddess-like Lady who inspires artists to create. So with the Yeatsian "White Stag," "Francesca," and "A Virginal," all of which deal with precarious moments of special—ambiguously mystical—emotional experience. Nearly all these poems stress, in one way or another, the brevity of the experience that is their starting point. The final stanza of the since-excised "Camaraderie" (in *ALS*) is a good example:

> . . . on still evenings when the rain falls close
> There comes a tremor in the drops, and fast
> My pulses run, knowing thy thought hath passed
> That beareth thee as doth the wind a rose.

Trying to explain the strategy of *A Lume Spento* to William Carlos Williams, Pound told him: "To me the short so-called dramatic lyric—at any rate the sort of thing I do—is the poetic part of a drama the rest of which (to me the prose part) is left to the reader's imagination or implied or set in a short note. I catch the character I happen to be interested in at the moment he interests me, usually a moment of song, self-analysis, or sudden understanding or revelation. And the rest of the play would bore me and presumably the reader" (*L* 3–4).

On the face of it, these words might serve as an explanation of Browning's use of the dramatic lyric as well as Pound's. But the real core of the passage and certainly of the poetic strategy Pound is describing is the idea again of the *moment*, and of all the ideas touched upon here that is probably the least applicable to the poetry of Browning. Pound's remark describes a poetry more purely "expressive" than Browning's. In Pound's early work the moments of "self-analysis" to which he refers are few and far between; he is more concerned with fleeting emotional states than with the narrative disclosures characteristic of Browning. Whereas even in "My Last Duchess" or "A Face," in which he comes as close as he ever does to Pound's kind of significant moment, Browning aims at the revelation of a total dramatic character and the events impinging upon that character's experience, · Pound never presents whole personalities. Much less analytic, he never turns to the past in search of masks behind which to explore various moral or psychological problems or situations; nor does he repeat Browning's attempt to revive a total past age or to make historical or quasihistorical figures perform before us as in their own age. Moreover, his distinction between the poetic (that is, expressive) part of his

> is the natural outcome of [the] fitful and unnatural
> ambition of our disunited forerunners. Our impetuous
> hope was to replace this mere egotistical whim for art by
> a patriotic enthusiasm. (I, 138)

One might pass over this as only coincidentally similar to some
of Pound's disgruntled remarks about the failure of English and
American society to take art seriously were it not that Pound had
to argue, or at any rate felt called upon to argue, precisely
this issue again and again.[5]

A few pages further on in Hunt's book is a statement which
says rather more than at first glance it seems to: "Despite differences, we both agreed that a man's work must be the reflex
of a living image in his own mind, not the icy double of the
facts themselves" (I, 150). What this Coleridgean dictum may
have meant for Hunt, whose frigid paintings rarely live up to
the hopeful dramaticism of their titles, we need not ask. What
it meant for Rossetti, who pressed it to an extreme, was an entire
technique of painting and poetry. His paintings are always
visionary; no matter what the subject—literary, historical,
religious—Rossetti's images come to us like visitations from
some private world. Their very preoccupation with detail
and their sometimes arbitrary arrangement give them the quality
of highly subjective experiences the like of which will never
occur again. His poems are often the same: precariously arrested
moments caught by the poet and peculiar to him. Pound, on his
part, would readily agree with Hunt's assertion. He himself
felt that the artist "should *depend*, of course, on the creative,
not upon the mimetic or representational part in his work. It
is the same in writing poems, the author must use his *image* because he sees it or feels it" ("Vorticism," *GB* 99). In a general
way, any poet would agree with Hunt, but in Pound, as in Rossetti, the theory issues in art of an unusually thoroughgoing
subjectivity.

Pound himself has acknowledged his heavy indebtedness to

Rossetti (as in the introduction to his translations of Cavalcanti), and much of his early work reveals important connections with Pre-Raphaelite art in general. The quality in Rossetti which links him with Pound is suggested by Nicolette Gray in an interesting little book on Rossetti's paintings, *Rossetti, Dante and Ourselves.* It is the same quality that separates Pound from Browning. Miss Gray says of Rossetti's paintings and drawings that they "present a fragment of life, he has concentrated on presenting the reality of the image he saw with the greatest possible intensity, the most vivid images at moments of most complete awareness, isolated, everything directed inwards, the space confined, colour opaque, picture surface crowded."[6] *Moments of most complete awareness* recalls Pound's moment of "sudden understanding or revelation." To speak of such moments is to define the occasion of nearly all of Rossetti's paintings: "What Rossetti is painting all the time is not the tenseness of a moment of drama, but the tenseness of a moment of realisation, the whole being of a man absorbed into his consciousness, man as he seems most completely alive and himself."[7] This last statement, however, is too sweeping, for Rossetti's moment often is one of drama as well as awareness.

Perhaps the best example of the image as a moment of awareness—that is, the example least infected by the mawkishness that mars so many of Rossetti's drawings—is "Rachel and Leah"; the two figures, in both posture and facial expression, seem to epitomize a feeling of profound inner peace. In "How They Met Themselves," whatever awareness was aimed at is overcome by the drama of the scene—here as nearly everywhere Rossetti's pictorial work has a good deal of essentially literary content. Yet, if we may risk a troublesome distinction, the drama of these moments is not theatrical, not a drama of peripeteia, but rather a drama arising from a quick concentration of tensions upon a single scene—the moment before peripeteia, perhaps. Each painting is a fleeting, intensely perceived detail in an implied narrative; the paintings are tautly poised, more so than

Rossetti, "How They Met Themselves"
(Reproduced by permission of the Syndics
of the Fitzwilliam Museum, Cambridge)

"A moment . . . of drama as well as awareness . . .
the moment before peripeteia" (p. 19).

Rossetti, "Hamlet and Ophelia"
British Museum

"A quick concentration of tensions upon a single scene . . .
a kind of fugacious drama" (pp. 19, 22).

the luckiest action photograph. Thus the pose of Hamlet in the ink drawing, "Hamlet and Ophelia," suggests that in another fraction of a second he would have changed his facial expression, would have closed or moved his outstretched left hand.

This kind of fugacious drama cannot, of course, be duplicated in poetry, where action must perforce unfold much more slowly, but it has an analogue in the "moments" of many of Rossetti's poems. "Dawn on the Night-Journey" is basically a moment of this kind, a sudden awareness of or exposure to the intense emotional content of a momentarily but vividly perceived gesture, scene, or object—or, for that matter, a seizure by any intense emotion.

> Till dawn the wind drove round me. It is past
> And still, and leaves the air to lisp of bird,
> And to the quiet that is almost heard
> Of the new-risen day, as yet bound fast
> In the first warmth of sunrise. When the last
> Of the sun's hours to-day shall be fulfilled,
> There shall another breath of time be stilled
>
> . . . . .
>
> . . . On the newborn air
> The moth quivers in silence. It is vast,
> Yea, even beyond the hills upon the sea,
>   The day whose end shall give this hour as sheer
> As chaos to the irrevocable Past. [8]

In the brief early-morning stillness, in a delicately poised moment of awareness, the speaker is overtaken by an emotionally defined apprehension of the meaning of "Past." To the speaker's sensibility the silence of the morning is filled with emotional implications, and the poem objectifies both the implications and the events which arouse the poet to an awareness of it. The intensity of the experience is much better handled than in the paintings:

here every detail is clearly relevant to the mood of the speaker—
an achievement to which there is rarely any parallel in Rossetti's
visual art.

Rossetti's aim here is related to the same preoccupation with
heightened moments which differentiates Pound's dramatic
lyrics from Browning's. Not all of Pound's moments involve
the suddenness he speaks of in that letter to Williams. The very
early "In Tempore Senectutis," for example, presents the qualities of precarious poise and intensity found in Rossetti's paintings: an old woman is moved to speech by her keen awareness of
the approach of death, her awareness of the meaning of death
and the significance of the past and her relationship with the
other speaker in the poem. "Camaraderie" is rather closer to
"Dawn on the Night-Journey" in its description of sudden onsets
of an almost mystical emotional experience, but like Rossetti's
"Three Shadows," it recounts a cluster of specifically past experiences and therefore loses some of the emotional immediacy that
characterizes most of Pound's dramatic experiences. "Nel
Biancheggiar," which dates from Pound's early days in Venice,
presents directly a moment of awareness in a poet subjectively
impelled to speech, speaking to no one.

> Blue-grey, and white, and white-of-rose,
> The flowers of the West's fore-dawn unclose.
> I feel the dusky softness whirr
> Of color, as upon a dulcimer
> "Her" dreaming fingers lay between the tunes,
> As when the living music swoons
> But dies not quite . . .

Here is the "moment of song" and the moment of sudden
revelation, when sensory perceptions suddenly lock into an
emotionally coherent unity.

This mood pervades Pound's first collection: among the poems
preserved in the current *Personae*, "On His Own Face in a Glass"

attains no similarly definite "vision" and no such intelligible resolution, but its mood is of a piece with the heightened awareness of "Camaraderie," "Nel Biancheggiar," and "De Aegypto," and so is the mood of "The Tree." Pound's interest in this kind of experience certainly did not end with *A Lume Spento* or the *Quinzaine for This Yule*. His commitment to such moments becomes more, not less, prominent in his later work; it can be followed easily through *Ripostes* of 1912 (in the current *Personae*, poems like "A Girl," "Apparuit," and "A Virginal"), through *Lustra* ("Heather" and "April"), until in the *Cantos* it becomes

> that the body of light come forth
> from the body of fire
> And that your eyes come to the surface
> from the deep wherein they were sunken
>
> . . . . .
>
> That your eyes come forth from their caves
> (Canto XCI)

Thus the poetic occasion for Pound tends to be a moment of private epiphany, of intense emotional or spiritual significance. The detailed implications of this fact will occupy us later. For now we may note that it is part of a thematic orientation which was bound to make the very shape of Pound's dramatic lyrics less like Browning's and more like Rossetti's.

One of the concomitants of this concern with fleeting surges of significant emotion is a feeling of allusiveness: the presented moments imply an emotional context outside the poem. This quality is less pervasive and less important in Rossetti's poetry than in his painting, but it is present—in many of the sonnets of *The House of Life*, for example, and in the poem "Song and Music," which begins *in medias res* and conveys its very action by allusion:

O leave your hand where it lies cool
  Upon the eyes whose lids are hot:
Its rosy shade is bountiful
  Of silence, and assuages thought,
O lay your lips against your hand
  And let me feel your breath through it,
While through the sense your song shall fit
  The soul to understand . . .

There are many parallels in Pound's more Browning-like poems: in "Cino," for example, and "Famam Librosque Cano," the first line of which is a response to a question asked before the poem begins. The technique is certainly related to Browning's dramatic lyrics, but Pound and Rossetti, uninterested in narrative verisimilitude, stress the brevity of the experience and heighten its ostensible emotional intensity by presenting the moment as a distillation of some longer, less significant, and therefore dispensable context. Pound's "Threnos" is a more sophisticated example than those other two poems. Here he attains intensity by giving to allusion the work of narrative and forcing the reader more or less to participate in the gradual unfolding of meaning:

No more for us the little sighing,
No more the winds at twilight trouble us.

Lo the fair dead!

No more do I burn.
No more for us the fluttering of wings
That whirred in the air above us.

    . . . . .

No more desire flayeth me,
No more for us the trembling
At the meeting of hands.

Lo the fair dead!
. . . . .

No more the torrent,
No more for us the meeting-place
(Lo the fair dead!)
Tintagoel.

The first stanza alludes to fairly definite experiences better known to the persona than to the reader; the second stanza ends on an allusion to a more particular experience still more private. The relationship between the speaker and the "fair dead" of the otherwise vague refrain emerges from these two stanzas without any appeal to narrative devices, and the poem continues to develop by means of details ostensibly specific for the speaker but only general for the reader. The first two lines of the final stanza withdraw even this gesture toward the presentation of information and concentrate upon the suggestiveness of certain places the reader cannot possibly know. The referent for the entire poem is revealed in the last line, but of course there is considerably more to the Tristan myth than what is covered in the poem. The poem itself presents only the emotional core—we should probably not be far wrong if we read it as an experiment in seeing how much can be expressed without narrative.

The allusiveness of "Threnos" furnishes a working model of what Pound, in his early years at least, thought poetry should be. In the 1910 introduction to his translations of Cavalcanti, Pound says that "Dante's commentators in their endless search for exact correspondences, seem never to suspect him of poetical innuendo, of calling into the spectrum of the reader's mind associated things which form no exact allegory" (*T* 22–23). Apropos of *Le Cid*, he wrote in *The Spirit of Romance* (published some five months before the date of the Cavalcanti introduction): "As in the Greek, or, indeed, as in most moving poetry, the simple lines demand from us who read, a completion of the detail, a fulfilment or crystallization of beauty implied" (p. 68). The note, "Very dangerous statement," which Pound appends to this remark in the current edition of the book is not a retraction, and in fact even the technique of the *Cantos*—juxtaposing without comment significantly similar or contrasting images—demands of the reader a "completion of the detail" and an effort to assess "associated things which form no exact allegory." The creative procedure implied here (Dante transformed into a Yeatsian symbolist!), and by the allusive poems expressive of special moments, is closely related to Pound's plainly un-Browning-like attitude toward "narrative": though the procedure calls for whatever devices of suggestion the poet can control, it *requires* the total exclusion of all elements of expression and "content" which do not function immediately in the delineation of the crucial moment. It even affects the mechanics of language, for it leads ultimately to the severest possible limitation on the poet's use of relational or structuring words, those words which in a line like "When the Hounds of Spring are on Winter's traces" take up one third of the room but carry none of the emotional weight.

Not that Pound is everywhere successful in these poems. The allusiveness of "De Aegypto" or "In Morte De" at best contributes to an atmosphere of strangeness and creates the often uselessly pointed impression that less is being told than could be. So the final effect in these and many other early poems is often a hint of "wonder," to which the sensational imagery (flames, sapphires, tremblings) and the strained diction also contribute. But this very fact only confirms the claim that Pound's early expressive aims are not like Browning's—he deals very deliberately in a kind of suggestiveness irrelevant to the substance of Browning's work. He *wants* the "wonder," though without the vagueness and without the mawkishness.

We shall not be wrong, then, if we think of Pound as using Rossetti's techniques as a stepping stone away from Browning—

he told one interviewer, though speaking of verbal style, "I first had Browningese, and then I had Rossetti-itis"[9]—toward a means of presentation more suitable to his own less narrative orientation. We can detect the next step in this move away from Browning (it was not, of course, neatly chronological) in his emulation of Rossetti's later admirers, the English Decadents.

iii

There are personal, technical, and ideological resemblances between Pound's work and the Decadents'. He knew the work of the 1890s poets and wrote for Elkin Mathews' edition of the poetry of Lionel Johnson an introduction in which he confesses an early admiration for Fiona MacLeod, Dowson, and Symons. He knew Victor Plarr well enough to exchange Dowson anecdotes with him; he knew T. Sturge Moore and Selwyn Image; and *The Spirit of Romance* was published with the help of Ernest Rhys in 1910. In Pound's youth the Decadents were still the most recent generation of famous poets, and the young Pound worked up several personal quirks that seem to ape them. Certainly their ideas on the artistic life accorded with his, or became his—the professionalism that insisted on being poet and only poet, the idea of the artist as a man apart, and an uncompromising insistence on the transcendent importance of art.

But what is important for my purposes is the connection between Pound and the Decadents regarding the typical poetic occasion. For the Decadents cultivated "moments" even more determinedly than Rossetti did. They had been told by Walter Pater:

> A counted number of pulses only is given to us of a variegated, dramatic life. How may we see in them all that is to be seen in them by the finest senses? How shall we pass most swiftly from point to point,

and be present always at the focus where the greatest
number of vital forces unite in their purest energy? . . .
While all melts under our feet, we may well
catch at any exquisite passion, or any contribution
to knowledge that seems by a lifted horizon to set
the spirit free for a moment, or any stirring of
the senses, strange dyes, strange colours, and curious
odors, or work of the artist's hands, or the face of
one's friend.[10]

As Arthur Symons rephrased them, Pater's words about the focus
of vital forces become: "Art begins when a man wishes to
immortalize the most vivid moment he has ever lived. Life has
already, to one not an artist, become art in that moment. And the
making of one's life into art is after all the first duty and privilege of every man." [11] Here, then, is a more or less clarion call
for just such a poetry of moments as we find in Pound's early
work and in Rossetti—moments in which the poet can snatch
an experience of "beauty" from the jaws of time and decay.
And the poetry appeared; the surcharged moment upon which
Dowson's "Terre Promise" opens is closely reminiscent of
Pound's "Camaraderie":

> Even now the fragrant darkness of her hair
> Had brushed my cheek; and once, in passing by,
> Her hand upon my hand lay tranquilly:
> What things unspoken trembled in the air!

Symons' poetry, too, often turns upon a kind of aesthetic epiphany: "Pastel," for example, from *Silhouettes*—or the wretched
poem "Rain on the Down," which seems, with its charged
details and its delight in momentary stasis, an anticipation
of Pound's "Francesca"—or perhaps a bad proto-Imagist
poem with the narrative still in it:

> Night, and the down by the sea,
> And the veil of rain on the down;
> And she came through the mist and the rain to me
> From the safe warm lights of the town.
>
> The rain shone in her hair,
> And her face gleam'd in the rain
> And only the night and the rain were there
> As she came to me out of the rain.

Symons' early collections especially are heavy with this moment of either aesthetic revelation or aesthetic enjoyment.[12]

But Pater speaks of the "splendour of our experience" as well as "its awful brevity," and we do not need a multitude of examples to remind us of his disciples' close attention to strange dyes and curious odors. One of the things Pater was stressing was the revitalization of perception in the service of joy. "The service of philosophy, of speculative culture, towards the human spirit," he said at the end of *The Renaissance*,

> is to rouse, to startle it into sharp and eager observation. Every moment some form grows perfect in hand or face; some tone on the hills or on the sea is choicer than the rest; some mood of passion or insight or intellectual excitement is irresistibly real and attractive to us— for that moment only ... In a sense it might even be said that our failure is to form habits; for, after all, habit is relative to a stereotyped world, and meantime it is only the roughness of the eye that makes any two persons, things, situations, seem alike.

This is not far removed from a remark of Pound's in an article describing Vorticism (that ill-fated attempt to develop Imagism into something more than a penchant for writing short poems). Since the advent of Vorticist art, he wrote, "I have a double or treble or tenfold set of stimulae in going from my home to Piccadilly. What was a dull row of houses is become a magazine of forms." [13] The context of this quotation is the power of Vorticist art to revitalize perception and thereby to supply a vital sustenance that habituated perception cannot furnish. As stated in a later essay, "the function of literature . . . is precisely that it does incite humanity to continue living; that it eases the mind of strain, and feeds it, I mean definitely as *nutrition of impulse*" ("How To Read," *LE* 20). The central principle is a renewed precision of observation: Pound's early discussions of the creative process and of the job the proper artist must do seem singularly free of such terms as *invention, creation,* and even *inspiration;* his terminology, especially after his joining people like Ford, Hulme, and the London literary set in general, tends to center upon the ideas of *perception* and *exactitude.* The truly "donative" artist, he says, "discovers, or better, he 'discriminates.' We advance by discriminations, by discerning that things hitherto deemed identical or similar are dissimilar; that things hitherto deemed dissimilar, mutually foreign, antagonistic, are similar and harmonic." [14]

These comments, Pound's and the others', and the poems tend to place the poetic experience rather than the creative act at the core of artistic production. Certainly the public utility of art adumbrated here is to hand on to others the delightful experiences to which poets are peculiarly subject, and this general orientation is a concomitant of a further area of agreement between Pound and the nineties: that exploitation of personality, that special kind of self-dramatization, which always seems to characterize very young poets. A systematic preoccupation with perceptions felt to be unique naturally shades over into a preoccupation with the chosen vessel to which the perceptions come, and a poetic personality becomes a very valuable attainment, indeed—note again that Symons credits a vivid moment of experience with the power to make one's life Art. As for Pound, the idea of expanding the potentialities of the personality is exceedingly important and is a basic motive behind his early collection. Nor has he ever made the mistake of believing that true art, which is impersonal, can be produced by anything but a strong personality.

His poetic moments share the essential subjectivity of Symons'. Pound's designation of the first work of art as "an impersonal or objective story woven out of his own emotion" is comparable—and surely related—to Symons' identification of the source of his poems: "The moods of men! There I find my subject, there the region over which art rules; and whatever has once been a mood of mine . . . I claim the right to render, if I can, in verse." Speaking here, in his preface, of *London Nights*, Symons adds, "I do not profess that any poem in this book is the record of an actual fact," but each poem is a "sincere attempt to render a particular mood which has once been mine, and to render it as if, for the moment, there were no other mood for me in the world" (*Studies*, 284–285). There is a certain amount of apologetic Nietzscheism in such a remark, for it implies that whatever the poet feels very strongly for a moment becomes a kind of fact. Again, Pound is affected by this train of thought. Throughout his first four or five collections of verse, he attempts to pry loose—ostensibly from history but more especially from his own imagination—a procession of special sensibilities, a procession mounted in the course of what he calls, as we have seen, the "search for oneself" and at the same time a "search for the real." What he means by the "real" in this context he suggests in another early essay:

> The soul of each man is compounded of all the elements in the cosmos, but in each soul there is some one element which predominates, which is in some peculiar and intense way the quality or *virtù* of the individual; in no two souls is this the same. It is by reason of this *virtù* that we have one Catullus, one Villon . . . It is the artist's business to find his own *virtù*.[15]

The real that the poet discovers in himself is the self's true and unique contents, and it would seem to follow that the value of art is its discovery and revelation of these "realities."

Behind all this lies a conception of art as the chronicle of the human spirit as manifested in the unique sensibilities of individual artists. "The arts give us a great percentage of the lasting and unassailable data regarding the nature of man, of immaterial man, of man considered as a thinking and sentient creature" ("The Serious Artist," *LE* 42). "Carrying on from Balzac's *Louis Lambert,* Symons [in *Spiritual Adventures*] gave us a series of studies in special sensibility . . . As culture this book is worth all the freudian tosh in existence" (*GK* 71). Such ideas are a direct carryover from the nineteenth century. Compare the eminently nineteenth-century Taine: "It was perceived by historians that a work of literature is not a mere play of imagination, a solitary caprice of a heated brain, but a transcript of contemporary manners, a type of a certain kind of mind. It was concluded that one might retrace, from the monuments of literature, the style of man's feelings and thoughts for centuries back." As for *virtù,* Taine assures us that there is a particular inner system which makes each kind of man, and that each "has its moral history and its special structure, with some governing disposition and some dominant feature." [16] It is interesting to know that Pound read and approved of Taine (*YL* 22, January 1905), but the *History of English Literature* was not the only place where he could have found such ideas. There was also W. B. Yeats, saying through Owen Aherne in "The Tables of the Law": "I understood that I could not sin, because I had discovered the law of my being." [17] And Arthur Symons, a man much more permanently committed to the ideals of the nineties than Yeats: "In his escape from the world, one man chooses religion, and seems to find himself; another, choosing love, may seem also to find himself; and may not another, coming to art as to a religion and as to a woman, seem to find himself not less effectually?" ("Choice," *Studies,* 290).

Now the Decadents' exploitation of self and the poetic moments that were at once its modus and its reward were not necessarily an emotional version of art for art's sake. Symons presents art as an alternative to love or religion, and he may be dead serious when he claims that to turn one's life into art is a duty as well as a privilege. In fact, to that latter remark in "The Choice" he added the assertion that to make one's life into art "is to escape into whatever form of ecstasy is our own form of spiritual existence." He speaks disapprovingly of the Decadent tendency to emulate Huysmans' prototypical decadent hero, Des Esseintes, in "Worshipping colour, sound, perfume, for their own sakes, and not for their ministrations to a more divine beauty." Even Huysmans, he says, has realized "that the great choice, the choice between the world and something which is not visible in the world, but out of which the world is made, does not lie in the mere contrast of the subtler and grosser senses." The best choice, he concludes, is a flight to art as to love and religion. The young Yeats, as we might expect, concurred, though with a different emphasis; the decadence of his confreres and their flight into art constituted a phenomenon that was important, he thought,

> because it comes to us at the moment when we are beginning to be interested in many things which positive science, the interpreter of exterior law, has always denied . . . We are, it may be, at a crowning crisis of the world, at the moment when man is about to ascend, with the wealth he has so long been gathering upon his shoulders, the stairway he has been descending from the first days.[18]

The statement is Yeats's alone, but though he was not necessarily speaking for all his fellow artists, he was at least only exaggerating tendencies that were certainly present and at work in the Decadents.

Their militant self-orientation is akin to Rossetti's in being an attempt to exist in a world stripped of any apparent vitalism by the new ways of thinking that attended upon the intellectual developments of the nineteenth century. During the period of the English decadence, the fears of the Pre-Raphaelites were confirmed and their hopes betrayed. The pernicious emphasis that the Victorian mind tended to place upon the fact that poetry does not bake bread or cast pig iron is only part of the story. The Pre-Raphaelites were late romantics, attempting to revitalize everyday life with something of the wonder and aesthetic appeal they believed essential, and their antiacademism in art strove to replace mechanical conventionality with imaginative spontaneity—to see the thing as it "is" instead of through prescribed modes of perception and expression. Hunt and Millais posed as realists at first, but the "truth to nature" the Brotherhood sought in art was nonethless, as Hunt's remark about "the icy double of the facts" implies, an imaginative truth (especially for Rossetti); their effort to revive "imagination" found successors in the Decadents, in Yeats, and again in Pound. Poetry to them was as much a state of mind as it was an art, and it was the conception of poetry as a *valuable* state of mind that they sought to revive. The same issue underlies Pound's call for poetry "that a grown man could read without groans of ennui, or without having to have it cooed into his ear by a flapper" (*L* 103) and his insistence that poetry "feeds the mind."

Humphry House remarked that "one of the big problems for the Pre-Raphaelites and for all their generation was to try to see the daily life of Victorian England . . . as having an equivalent spiritual and human significance to that which medieval life had in all its details for medieval poets and painters . . . There seemed to be an irreparable cleavage between the facts of modern society and the depths it was recognized poetry ought to touch." [19] Even after the Middle Ages the hierarchical view of physical reality (whose abandonment we now call the Renaissance) gave to the material content of daily life a continuing significance in the universal scheme of things.

By the nineteenth century, this feeling and outlook were long gone. It may be that the shortsighted pragmatism of nineteenth-century and especially Victorian thinking, based as it seemed to be on a kind of Baconian dualism that posited separate mental faculties for poetic and for analytic intellection, made it difficult for poetry to perform its customary explorations of the relationship between inner and outer life, between psyche and surroundings, by denying to poetry any "real" (practical) value. But it seems likelier that as English industry made the English landscape uglier and uglier—as Coketown grew and grew—"outer" became less and less relevant to "inner," and the artist seeking "beauty" sooner or later had to abandon "outer" altogether. Victorian art was trapped by the secularization of thought and the industrialization of life.

The Decadents and their immediate predecessors and successors certainly felt the aridity of a universe evaluated in utilitarian, and defined in scientific, terms. The temporarily decadent Yeats wrote mournfully of it in "The Song of the Happy Shepherd"—the woods of Arcady dead, the world no longer nourished by dream but condemned to "toy" with a drab Newtonian "Truth."

But the focus where the most articulate anxieties on this score unite in their purest energy is again Walter Pater. In his elegant prose he confronts a dead universe, composed, however lovely it may seem, of "processes":

> To regard all things and principles of things as inconstant modes or fashions has more and more become the tendency of modern thought. Let us begin with that which is without—our physical life. Fix upon it in one of its more exquisite intervals, the moment, for instance, of delicious recoil from the flood of water in summer heat. What is the whole physical life in that moment but a combination of natural elements to which science gives their names? But those elements . . . are present

not in the human body alone: we detect them in places most remote from it. Our physical life is a perpetual motion of them—the passage of the blood, the waste . . . the modification of the tissues of the brain under every ray of light and sound—processes which science reduces to simpler and more elementary forces . . . birth and gesture and death and the springing of violets from the grave are but a few out of ten thousand resultant combinations.

"This at least of flamelike our life has," he adds, "that it is but the concurrence, renewed from moment to moment, of forces parting sooner or later on their ways." To this way of thinking man and his interesting inner life become lucky cosmological accidents.

In the presence of such truths, perhaps the best one could do was to seize the moment, as Pater advises, and poetic experience, however illusory or private, must be snatched where one can find it. Though some of the Decadents turned to religion as one route of escape from the "clanging space" of Yeats's "Song of the Happy Shepherd," not everyone could or would accept it ("But coɴfound it," said Yeats to Pound, "in my country the Church ɪs Babbitt!" [GK 155]). We have instead Symons' flight "to art as to a religion and as to a woman." Symons' notion that art begins when we wish to immortalize our most vivid moment, along with the vast number of delicately perceptive Decadent poems of which his phrase seems the summary, is clearly a reaffirmation of the value of subjective—imaginative and spiritual—adventures. As a programmatic assertion, it has been described as an expression "not so much of art as of vision" and as reflecting "consciously or unconsciously, efforts toward the rehabilitation of spiritual power."[20] The Decadent poetic moment was at the service of an attempt to revitalize a dead universe and to furnish spiritual sustenance to those who craved it in this particular form.

But we have been neglecting some important distinctions. Yeats's report that the doctrine of most of the Rhymers was "that lyric poetry should be personal," that "a man should express his life without fear or shame,"[21] warns us that the Decadent exploitation of temperament was carried on at a different level from Pound's. Symons himself, in his commitment to "moods," had added the proviso, "I claim, from my critics and my readers, the primary understanding, that a mood is after all but a mood, a ripple on the sea." This may be only a version of the defensive disclaimers of Pound's Fifine, but the metaphor speaks truly, for the self the Decadents exploited was closer to the surface than that which interested Pound. The form those poets' efforts to "rehabilitate the spiritual" actually took is crucial. Pound, too, could speak of ecstasy, and in a Decadent enough way, it would seem: "beyond a certain border, surely we come to this place where ecstasy is not a whirl or a madness of the senses, but a glow arising from the exact nature of the perception." But he goes on to say, "We find a similar thought in Spinoza where he says that 'the intellectual love of a thing consists in the understanding of its perfections'" ("Psychology and Troubadours," *SR* 91). And an important difference between Pound and his Decadent instructors lies in this distinction between *response* and *comprehension*. Symons' charge that the Decadents worshiped sensual experience for its own sake and that they remained "on the threshold of ecstasy" ("Choice," 290–291) was a blow at the characteristic strategy of Decadent poetry, his own included.

That strategy was, roughly, to construct a carefully isolated experience as laden as possible with devices to draw the reader emotionally into the poem. The younger Decadents "sought to 'spring imagination with a word or phrase'. . . the best writers aimed at intensity, suggestiveness . . . They strove to create what was called 'atmosphere,' leaving much to the intelligence of the reader."[22] The suggestive intensity—surely an anticipation of the allusiveness that demarcates Pound's poetic moments from Browning's—builds up until the speaker and (presumably) the reader ecstatically or hopefully conclude that the resultant emotional climax is in some way importantly "spiritual." Symons' "Hallucination: II" has this ritual manner—*Silhouettes*, what with "Maquillage," "Morbidezza," "Perfume," and a dozen others, abounds in this sort of poem.

If today we are apt to charge the poets of the nineties with a more indiscriminate appeal to fading opalescence than they indulged in, it is partly because the same pale lilies tend to show up in verse that presents really transcendent moments and verse that does not; often, that is, poets like Symons, Dowson, and Le Gallienne, in expressing their moments, expressed not spiritual release but merely a suggestive moment of sensual captivation. Such moments required keeping oneself exquisitely alive to sensual stimuli—delicate stimuli, no doubt, but sensual all the same; one became a fine machine for the registration of subtle external phenomena. In taking this course, the Decadents, consciously or not, were acting out the words of Pater, who had told them, "Not the fruit of experience, but experience itself, is the end." And he ironically foreshadowed the final limitations of Decadent poetry in his parting sentence: "For art comes to you proposing frankly to give nothing but the highest quality to your moments as they pass, and simply for those moments' sake." This sort of ideology may conduce to making "sharp and eager observation" the handmaid of a revitalized and cheered-up imagination, but it is apt to be imagination of a fairly uninteresting kind, and not the kind that informed Pound's work.

His remark about how Vorticism kindled his sense of form is preceded by sentences of crucial importance to the present context:

> One is more alive for having these swift-passing, departmentalised interests in the flow of life about one. It is by swift apperceptions of this sort that one differentiates oneself from the brute world. To be civilised is to

> have swift apperception of the complicated life of today;
> it is to have a subtle and instantaneous perception of it,
> such as savages and wild animals have of the necessities
> and dangers of the forest.

For Pound, in other words, the poetic moment is not merely enjoyable; it is informative as well, a moment of insight into or intuition of the meaning of the universe. We "love" a thing by *understanding* its perfections. The quotation is Decadent-oriented in its stress on perception and on the superior perceptivity of the artist, but it establishes a real distinction. Three years earlier Pound had written of the artist, in language even more similar to the language of the Decadent theorists: "An art is vital only so long as it is interpretative, so long, that is, as it manifests something which the artist perceives at greater intensity, and more intimately, than his public . . . The interpretive function is the highest honour of the arts, and because it is so we find that a sort of hyper-scientific precision is the touchstone and assay of the artist's power . . . Constantly he must distinguish between shades and degrees of the ineffable" ("Psychology and Troubadours," *SR* 87). All the proper Decadent concerns are here—intense perception, hyperscientific precision (to fix the last fine shade), the superior sensitivity of the artist. But his insistence upon "interpretative" sets him apart from his models. Pound's artist searches for an intelligibility the existence of which the Decadents denied.

The quality of the experience upon which Pound's moments tend to center is equally important in delineating the connection between him and the Decadents. His use of the term "ineffable" marks another significant distinction—especially if we consider him and the Decadents as disciples of Rossetti.

Decadent techniques stem ultimately from Rossetti, and they present at once a point of contact and a point of divergence between the Rhymers and Pound, who was by far the truer disciple. The Decadent hope that, given sufficient intensity, a sensual experience could be pushed to a spiritual adventure of sorts—

color, sound, and perfume might indeed minister to a more divine beauty—is exactly the notion that a misreading of Rossetti, and perhaps especially of *The House of Life*, would lead to. Lionel Johnson's assertion that Rossetti was gifted with "an etherealized apprehension of the physical" is symptomatic. Holbrook Jackson, again, speaks of the Decadent effort to find spiritual implications in physical circumstances as representing "nothing less than a demand for that unifying ecstasy which is the essence of human and every other phase of life."[23] Allowing for the grandeur of the language, we can see how some such concept might unite Rossetti, Pound, and the Decadents; the central issue is the reunion of levels of experience which modern thought has torn asunder and the rehabilitation of levels of experience which modern thought ignores. But there are vast areas—call them realms of experience or merely thematic choices—in Rossetti's work that the Decadents simply do not touch.

The Decadents had Rossetti's major thematic aims hindside to: he had a physicalized vision of the ethereal. Their confusion arose partly, no doubt, from the fact that for Rossetti, as in his "Heart's Hope," fleshly joys and spiritual joys seem to go so firmly hand in hand:

> Lady, I fain would tell how evermore
> Thy soul I know not from thy body, nor
> Thee from myself, neither our love from God.

And it seems a reasonable inference. The sonnet "Soul's Sphere" in *The House of Life* is not the work of a man who has "an etherealized apprehension of the physical":

> Who, sleepless, hath not anguished to appease
> Tragical shadow's realm of sound and sight
> Conjectured in the lamentable night? . . . .
> Lo! the soul's sphere of infinite images!

What sense shall count them? Whether it forecast
    The rose-winged hours that flutter in the van
    Of Love's unquestioning unrevealed span,—
    Visions of golden futures: or that last
    Wild pageant of the accumulated past
    That clangs and flashes for a drowning man.

On the contrary, the poem would seem to bespeak a sensibility
that for its major discoveries hardly needed the physical at all.
"The Blessed Damozel" is not about a girl leaning over a balcony
railing that we pass under in the street.

Symons had probably a better mind than Johnson but, let
him speak of spiritual existence as he might, not even he seemed
to subscribe to the role of art which Rossetti describes in "St.
Luke the Painter":

Give honour unto Luke Evangelist;
    For he it was (the aged legends say)
    Who first taught Art to fold her hands and pray.
Scarcely at once she dared to rend the mist
Of devious symbols: but soon having wist
    How sky-breadth and field-silence and this day
    Are symbols also in some deeper way,
She looked through these to God and was God's priest.

These lines first of all reveal an attitude toward symbols considerably different from the Decadents'. Theirs is a method
that does operate through "an etherealized apprehension of
the physical," which, when the quasi-mystical seizure fails to
occur, creates verse where "poppies and lilies are nothing but
gestures." [24] Rossetti tends to peer behind the veil; the Decadents
swoon at its beauty. For this very reason we shall see that the
Decadent contribution to the *verbal* techniques of Pound's

Imagist verse is greater than Rossetti's—but Rossetti's influence upon Pound's more mystical poetry exceeds theirs by far. So far I have spoken of Rossetti's short poems mainly in terms of emotionally charged occasions. But it is more accurate to see his work in terms of a continuum extending from moments of dramatic poise or balance—delicate sensory experiences, for example—to the mysticism or near-mysticism implied by this last sonnet and even beyond. "Dawn on the Night-Journey" presents such an emotionally charged moment, and "Silent Noon," the nineteenth sonnet in *The House of Life*, is another. If we take these moments as prototypes, we can list, say, Symons' "Perfume," Dowson's "Chansons sans Paroles," and Pound's "Erat Hora" as antitypes. But in those lines from "Heart's Hope" we move into a different kind of experience, and in the sestet of Rossetti's "Love's Testament" we have left the Decadents far behind:

> O what from thee the grace, to me the prize
> And what to Love the glory,—when the whole
> Of the deep stair thou tread'st to the dim shoal
> And weary water of the place of sighs,
> And there dost work deliverance, as thine eyes
> Draw up my prisoned spirit to thy soul!

—the Decadents, but not Pound, for this way of transforming a love experience into a mystical event (clearly an echo of the Tuscans) occurs in his work often, in "Sub Mare" and in the slightly earlier "Francesca":

> You came in out of the night
> And there were flowers in your hands,
> Now you will come out of a confusion of people,
> Out of a turmoil of speech about you.
>
> . . . . .

> I would that the cool waves might flow over my mind,
> And that the world should dry as a dead leaf,
> Or as a dandelion seed-pod and be swept away,
> So that I might find you again,
> Alone.

If we may copy out yet another poem, the sestet of Rossetti's "The Kiss" is exactly the sort of poetry the Decadents imitated and trivialized:

> I was a child beneath her touch,—a man
>   When breast to breast we clung, even I and she,—
>   A spirit when her spirit looked through me,—
> A god when all our life-breath met to fan
> Our life-blood, till love's emulous ardours ran,
>   Fire within fire, desire in deity.

In both action and theme this is strikingly similar, if inferior, to Pound's "Virginal" ("Slight are her arms, yet they have bound me straitly / And left me cloaked as with a gauze of aether / As with sweet leaves; as with subtle clearness. / Oh, I have picked up magic in her nearness")—the power of the lady's touch to sanctify the lover's body, the insistence upon the supernatural significance of the experience delineated, and the seriousness with which each poem presents its assertions of a spiritual change wrought by the lady's mysterious power. Now it may well be that some of the Decadents read this sonnet as Rossetti's spiritualized rendition of a trollop's rousing kiss—and it is of course perfectly possible to read Pound's poem in the same way, and to read "Francesca" as the etherealized apprehension of a perfectly physical lady at a cocktail party. To do so is to ignore implications that both poems insist upon, but this is essentially the extent of the Decadent appreciation of Rossetti. It indicates the extent of their "use" of his example and therefore the limitations of their usefulness to Pound.

"The Kiss" introduces another issue that points up Pound's distance from the Rhymers' Club and his proximity to Rossetti, and this is the mythic quality of the experience involved. The speaker himself likens his experience to Orpheus', and the whole poem presents the male equivalent of the dazed maiden seduced by a god. Pound, too, finds this connection of love and myth creditable, as a long list of his poems attests—"The Tree," "A Virginal," "Speech for Psyche," "The Flame," and so on—and there is a passage in "Psychology and Troubadours" where he relates the courtly love of Provence to pagan mythology: "That the spirit was, in Provence, Hellenic is seen readily enough by anyone who will compare the *Greek Anthology* with the work of the troubadours. They have, in some way, lost the names of the gods and remembered the names of lovers" (*SR* 90). And of course the whole essay is a provisional attempt to explain Provençal love poetry and a putative Provençal love cult as the re-emergence of impulses once recognized and celebrated in myth, but since lost or suppressed. That such a predisposition existed in Rossetti's work is obvious enough from his painting—in fact, from the whole Pre-Raphaelite pursuit of the *femme inspiratrice*—and in such a poem as "Astarte Syriaca," a sonnet describing one of his paintings:

> Mystery: lo! betwixt the sun and moon
>   Astarte of the Syrians: Venus Queen
>   Ere Aphrodite was. In silver sheen
> Her twofold girdle clasps the infinite boon
> Of bliss whereof the heaven and earth commune:
>   And from her neck's inclining flower-stem lean
>   Love-freighted lips and absolute eyes that wean
> The pulse of hearts to the spheres' dominant tune.

> Torch-bearing, her sweet ministers compel
> All thrones of light beyond the sky and sea
> The witnesses of Beauty's face to be:
> That face, of Love's all-penetrative spell
> Amulet, talisman, and oracle,—
> Betwixt the sun and moon a mystery.

None of the Decadents had a sustained interest in this kind of mythic vision or this kind of mythic subject matter.

Here, then, are two major areas of thought constituting an alignment between Pound and Rossetti and a disjunction between these two on the one hand and the Decadents on the other—the world "beyond" and the world of myth. Myth entails the idea of poetry as the benign act of renewing mankind's lost contact with the divine, and therefore opens into— or perhaps is a part of—a much larger one, that whole vast output of artistic and personal energy in the name of public betterment with which the Pre-Raphaelite movement was so busied and which occupied Pound almost from the beginning of his career. One thinks again of Yeats's summation of the Rhymers' poetic—"that lyric poetry should be personal"—and the particular meaning put upon that adjective by the Decadents. The possibility of their being preoccupied, like Pound and Rossetti, with the suprasensory impulses that unite all of mankind needs no protracted discrediting. It is hard to imagine a group of writers more urbanized and self-involved.

In the end, then, what the Decadents could offer to attract Pound's attention (aside from questions of style, which we shall survey in a later chapter) were a desperate kind of professionalism, an uncompromising insistence that art was important, a belief in its power to hypostasize important experiences and to allow the exercise of various human spiritual energies, and, from a more technical point of view, a cluster of models for handling moments of unusually intense emotional experience

—moments more limited in their implied content than Pound's, but nonetheless similar. Still from several important points of view—attitudes toward public life and the poet's role in the world, and the conception of what kind of experience is possible, to name just two—their usefulness for Pound had to be limited. Like Browning, they could offer him certain tentative orientations and certain useful techniques, but in the long run he had things to say which their mechanisms and orientations could not sustain. The subjectivity that informs Pound's work is of a vastly more far-reaching and complex sort than what the Rhymers were interested in. Their appeal to the heritage of Rossetti was in crucial ways incomplete.

iv

One Decadent poet did pursue and cultivate the tendencies we have been tracing in Rossetti and Pound, and that was Yeats. Clearly, much that Pound would have found congenial in Yeats's work also exists in other poetry of the nineties: commitment to a primarily subjective aesthetic, exploitation of unusual sensibilities, preoccupation with crucial nodes of experience in the form of "moods" or moments, and the loading of these moments with spiritual implications of varying intensity—all these are common to Yeats and the Rhymers. But in Yeats we find a thoroughgoing commitment to thematic concerns which the Decadents only played at and which even in Rossetti are not fully developed.

For one thing, there is the rationale of Yeats's poetic moments. He can sound like Symons: "What is literature but the expression of moods by the vehicle of symbol and incident? And are there not moods which need heaven, hell, purgatory, and faeryland for their expression, no less than this dilapidated earth?"[25] But Yeats's are not the self-pleasing moods of a man of delicate registrative abilities, and certainly not the poetic depiction of the piquant temperamental states of an "interesting" person;

the more a man lives in imagination and in a refined understanding, the more gods does he meet with and talk with, and the more does he come under the power of Roland . . . and of Hamlet . . . and of Faust . . . and under the power of all those countless divinities who have taken upon themselves spiritual bodies in the minds of the modern poets . . . for just as the magician or the artist could call [the moods] when he would, so they could call out of the mind of the magician or the artist . . . what shape they would, and through its voice and its gestures pour themselves out upon the world.

(*Mythologies*, 274, 285)

His poet-medium has the fluid identity of Pound's: "And just as the musician or the poet enchants and charms and binds with a spell his own mind when he would enchant the minds of others, so did the enchanter create or reveal for himself as well as for others the supernatural artist or genius, the seeming transitory mind made out of many minds, whose work I saw, or thought I saw [during a seance], in that suburban house."[28] So for the actor-speaker of "Histrion," the souls of great men "pass through us" and "some form projects itself" onto the receptive substance in the poet: the poet's ordinary self is invaded or taken over, melted, and the result is perhaps a "delightful psychic experience"—and a poem.

Later, in "Anima Hominis," Yeats wrote of finding "in an old diary" the words, "I think all happiness depends on the energy to assume the mask of some other life, on a re-birth as something not one's self, something created in a moment and perpetually renewed."[29] He had earlier spoken approvingly of Balzac's distinction between "the momentary self, which acts and lives in the world, and is subject to the judgment of the world," and "that which cannot be called before any mortal Judgment seat." Great literature, he wrote, is "written in a like spirit" ("At Stratford-on-Avon," *Essays and Introductions*, 102).

This is an adumbration of Yeats's theory of the mask or antiself; like Pound he is following a creative ideology that goes back to Browning and whose resemblance to Decadent ideas is only superficial. Instead of beautifying and then displaying one's personality and "making one's life into art," as Symons might advise or Wilde or some lesser figure might do, the poet as maker of poems must escape from personality, must abandon the identity around which his ordinary "life" revolves.

It is not much to the point to dismiss this fairly unusual attitude toward the self as a reaction against the more superficial self-celebration of the Decadents and the apparently similar self-exploitation of their Romantic predecessors, for all this apparatus is designed to solve a version of the very problem that bedeviled the Pre-Raphaelites (and perhaps all the post-Romantic poets of the nineteenth century): the doubtful validity of nonpractical, nonscientific thought, and the spiritual and emotional barrenness of a universe defined purely in post-Newtonian scientific terms. There being no room for meaningful poetic experience in Newton's abstract and lifeless universe, and precious little opportunity for it in the ugly and dirty world of modern industry, the poet must appeal not to the unique loveliness of his sensory apparatus, but to a different universe of discourse, to another level of reality. This elaborate manipulation of identity affords such a universe of discourse, one wherein poetry can deal with experiences not limited to strange dyes and curious odors.

The day-to-day personality is corrupt; it is designed to put up with a world narrowly delimited by positivism and centered on material things; and matter is lifeless, impermanent, and therefore "unreal." To a poet like Yeats, needless to say, an attempt to escape from such a world is not escapist in the least. To the extent that it is a flight to the imaginative and subjective, it is a flight to the living, the eternal—in short, to the real. The day-to-day mentality is actually cut off from this reality, this living universe, by the very sophistication that fits it for day-to-day life. The cure is the re-attainment of simplicity: "they are surely there, the divine people, for only we who have neither simplicity nor wisdom have denied them, and the simple of all times and the wise men of ancient times have seen them and even spoken to them . . . and we shall be among them when we die if we but keep our natures simple and passionate." [30] The world this simplicity opens up to one is not mere poetical musing. On the contrary, it is the meretricious worldliness of the "normal" self that deals in illusions and fantasy: "The other self, the anti-self or the antithetical self . . . comes but to those who are no longer deceived, whose passion is reality. The sentimentalists are practical men who believe in money, in position, in a marriage bell, and whose understanding of happiness is to be so busy whether at work or at play, that all is forgotten but the momentary aim" ("Anima Hominis," *Mythologies,* 331).

The reality that the liberated antiself is privileged to experience comes to it through "moods"—bursts of mysterious energy coming to the poet from that bedrock supernatural-seeming reality. In an essay called "The Moods" Yeats wrote: "It seems to me that these moods are the labourers and messengers of the Ruler of All, the gods of ancient days still dwelling on their secret Olympus, the angels of more modern days ascending and descending upon their shining ladder" (*Essays and Introductions,* 195). The mood is made intelligible by poetic structure. Yeats begins "The Moods" by saying that "Literature differs from explanatory and scientific writing in being wrought about a mood, or a community of moods, as the body is wrought about an invisible soul." Again, it is a substantial event, in the fullest sense of that adjective: "Sometimes the mystical student, bewildered by the different systems, forgets for a moment that the history of moods is the history of the universe." [31] From the point of view of the "normal," perhaps, the mood is an invasion of the quotidian "real" by the forces of either supernature or imagination; in slightly different terms, the poet in at least one of his roles "reports on moments of crisis when the tension between the ideal and the actual is greatest."[32]

The poetic impulse itself is part of the energy that wells up in a mood. At least in the days when the young Pound would have been reading him as a respected mentor, Yeats was perfectly definite about where creative energies come from. In "Magic" (1901), for example: "Our most elaborate thoughts, elaborate purposes, precise emotions, are often, as I think, not really ours, but have on a sudden come up, as it were, out of Hell or down out of Heaven" (*Essays and Introductions*, 40). Phrases like "on a sudden" and "moments of contemplation" point to matters we have seen before—the precious, brief poetic moment. Time and again in the early work of Pound, tangential references to ideas or even merely to terms like Yeats's open out to reveal important resemblances. The early Pound is like Yeats in conceiving of the universe as vitalized by kinds of energy which go far beyond what the prejudices of science and common sense can allow. These energies make themselves felt in the creative impulse, which in turn is received by those who are able to evade the limitations of self by casting off worldliness and adopting appropriate masks.

In *A Lume Spento* and the first *Personae* there is a note to "La Fraisne" which tries to explain the aim of the poem in terms of a Yeatsian mood. As a parallel text Pound gives a passage from Janus of Basel: "When the soul is exhausted of fire, then doth the spirit return unto its primal nature and there is upon it a peace great and of the woodland . . . Then becometh it kin to the faun and the dryad, a woodland dweller amid the rocks and streams." He goes on:

> Also has Mr. Yeats in his "Celtic Twilight" treated of such, and I because in such a mood, feeling myself divided between myself corporal and a self aetherial, "a dweller by streams and in woodland," eternal because

> simple in elements . . . Being freed of the weight of a soul
> "capable of salvation or damnation". . . leaving me thus
> *simplex naturae,* even so at peace and trans-sentient as
> a wood pool I made it.[33]

Pound's *simplex naturae* is essentially the simplicity Yeats
desiderates in *The Celtic Twilight.* Furthermore, the escape from
the normal self described here performs the same function it
did for Yeats. "La Fraisne" was part of that early group of poems
the writing of which Pound characterized as "casting off complete masks of the self" in his "search for the real," at the same
time a "search for oneself" and the "search for 'sincere self-
expression.'" Pound's casual and odd equating of *the real,
the self,* and *sincere self-expression* reflects a conviction that the
three are so closely related as to be aspects of a single thing.
The real, then, would seem to be the "true" contents of the soul.
As with Yeats, discovering whatever reality there is in oneself
requires breaking through the trivial surface personality that is
structured to deal with transience and trivia. Finding the
real in oneself is important because of the nature of the experience the poet deals with. Like Yeats, Pound (at least in his
youth) felt that "the 'Impulse' is with the gods . . . A man either
is or is not a great poet, that is not within his control, it is the
lightning from heaven, the 'fire of the gods'" ("How I Began,"
107). If he means this seriously, it would shed some light on his
strident insistence on the importance of technique. Pound's
stress on exactitude and on the duty of constantly distinguishing
between "the shades and degrees of the ineffable" gives the poet
a particular responsibility for the proper treatment of impulses
of which he is not necessarily the original instigator. The poet
owes allegiance to the forces that produce the psychic outburst
of energy which he is to make into a poem, and he must be faithful to that impulse. So true is this for the poet, so important
is the accurate rendering of the poetic experience, that no mat-

ter what *kind* of poet a man is, "Whether he be 'idealist' or 'realist' . . . bad technique is 'bearing false witness.'"[34] It is crucial, then, that the poet not distort the poetic impulse—that he refine and discipline himself as a recording instrument so as to bear true witness. This at once demarcates Pound from the Decadents; he will certainly appeal to their verbal techniques, for their preoccupation with style prefigures his own—his shades are to be even finer than theirs, considering where his come from—but our earlier distinctions obviously apply, and a poet like Pound would have to look, among the Decadents, to Yeats for a conception of art as a whole that paralleled his own.

It was Yeats, too, who could enunciate the corollary to this last problem. Speaking in "William Blake and His Illustrations to the *Divine Comedy*" of Blake's theory of artistic inspiration (which is in part his own as well), Yeats wrote: "If the 'world of imagination' was 'the world of eternity,' as this doctrine implied, it was of less importance to know men and nature than to distinguish the being and substance of imagination from those of a more perishable kind, created by the phantasy, in uninspired moments, out of memory and whim" (*Essays and Introductions,* 117). Talk of extrapersonal or quasi-divine impulses raises the question of distinguishing a genuinely poetic impulse from some trivial piece of self-deception or public-oriented pretense. In these terms, discovering the real in oneself still means finding out what one is truly capable of feeling, but as with Yeats, this real is closely related to—in fact continuous with—a permanent reality outside the poet. And the creative impulse itself is intimately related to the divine energy that animates the universe. In his explication of troubadour poetry, Pound said: "Our kinship with the ox we have constantly thrust upon us; but beneath this is our kinship to the vital universe, to the tree and the living rock [compare the note to "La Fraisne"], and, because this is less obvious—and possibly more interesting—we forget it." This distinction produces another, between two kinds of poet: the consciousness of some men, he continues, "seems to rest, or to have its center more properly, in what the Greek psychologists called the *phantastikon*. Their minds are . . . circumvolved about them like soap-bubbles reflecting sundry patches of the macrocosmos." [35] With others the mind is "germinal":

> Their thoughts are in them as the thought of the tree is in the seed, or in the grass, or the grain, or the blossom. And these minds are the more poetic, and they affect mind about them, and transmute it as the seed the earth. And this latter sort of mind is close on the vital universe; and the strength of the Greek beauty rests in this, that it is ever at the interpretation of this vital universe, by its signs of gods and godly attendants and oreads.

Some time later, in attempting to elucidate the poetic theory of Guido Cavalcanti, Pound linked this vital universe again with the exertion of poetic energy and also with the receptivity of a self liberated from protective, negative coverings. The poet deals with a supersensual "interactive force": "The senses at first seem to project for a few yards beyond the body. Effect of a decent climate where a man leaves his nerve-set open, or allows it to tune in to its ambience" (*LE* 152). As for actually making use of mysticism and a realm of special experiences (specific cases of vital energy), we have already seen a number of poems in which Pound does just that. He wrote to William Carlos Williams in 1908 that "men think and feel certain things and see certain things not with the bodily vision. About that time I begin to get interested" (*L* 5). He said the same thing in a notebook of poems written about 1908 but only recently brought to public view:

> In such a mood have I such strange sooth seen
> And shapes of wonder and of beauty's realm

Such habitants, that times uncertainty
Upwells within me and doth nigh o'erwhelm
My body's life, until Truth dawns to me
That where the treasure is the heart hath been.
   ("Sonnet of the August Calm," *ALSO* 118)

The general parallels, then, between Pound and Yeats are obvious enough—the poet escapes from his normal self and wins moments of insight into a special, supernatural realm. Yeats gave this realm the form now of a world of dreams, now of a world of myth, and finally the form of his own kind of spiritualism; it is easier to speak of a whole "other world" for him, for he himself did not hesitate to speak of it—Faeryland, for example. But for Pound's early work we need a more general term—"other levels of experience" or some such: he dealt not with an organized universe of myth, but with discrete mythic moments not necessarily related.

Although his treatment of myth does not take the same form as Yeats's, however, his conception of its significance in the human scheme of things is not dissimilar. Writing in *A Vision* of the importance of myth, Yeats said,

> A book of modern philosophy may prove to our logical capacity that there is a transcendental portion of our being that is timeless and spaceless . . . and yet our imagination remains subjected to nature as before . . . it was not [so] with ancient philosophy because the ancient philosopher had something to reinforce his thought,— the Gods, the Sacred Dead, Egyptian Theurgy, the Priestess Diotime . . . *I would restore to the philosopher his mythology.*[36]

There is no attempt here to unseat the more logical and accepted methods of science. Yeats's appeal seeks to complete the knowledge that humans have; it offers a means of structuring or embodying some "truths" not otherwise expressible even to oneself. Pound's attitude toward mythology was much like this. In *Guide to Kulchur* he refers to Q. Mucius Scaevola's distinction among three orders of theology: "the poet's anthropomorphic and false, the philosopher's rational and true but not for use, the statesman's built on tradition and custom." "A wisdom built of the first and third theologies," Pound observes—"It has taken two thousand years to get around again to meditating on mythology." Why should meditating on mythology be valuable? Because mythological exposition "permits an expression of intuition without denting the edges or shaving off the nose and ears of a verity" (*GK* 124–125, 127). As with Yeats, myth permits tentative affirmation of experiences too delicate, too complicated, or too arcane to be expressed in any other way. For both Yeats and Pound myth is "explication of mood" ("Psychology and Troubadours," *SR* 92)—hence Yeats's question, "are there not moods which need heaven, hell, purgatory and faeryland for their expression?" And when a given experience has no expressive analogue in established mythology, for both Yeats and Pound the poet must, as Pound says, "make a myth—a work of art that is—an impersonal . . . story woven out of his own emotion, as the nearest equation that he was capable of putting into words" ("Arnold Dolmetsch," *LE* 431).

But behind these general similarities there stand striking differences. For one thing, Yeats does not much deal in the structured precariousness of Pound's moments. For Pound, according to "Histrion," the moments are instantaneous, whereas Yeats prefers sustained experiences. Then, too, the early Yeats writes in a fairly homogeneous style; the speaking voice tends always to be the same. Pound changes style radically from poem to poem, and these stylistic shifts create a less constant relationship between the dramatic figure and the creating poet. Variations in theory lie behind these differences, of course. Yeats for some time found sufficient poetic fire and sufficient creative exercise in the tension and conflict between *a* self and its mask or antiself; in a still characteristic Rossettian fashion, he meets himself coming and going in "Shepherd and Goatherd." Pound from the beginning seeks poetic illumination in controlled attempts to assume a number of other selves.

Moreover, though I have spoken of Yeats's attempt to people the empty universe of modern thought as similar to Pound's, the term "vital universe" is Pound's only. Yeats's assertion is, "They are surely there, the divine people . . . and we shall be among them when we die." Pound's vital universe would be a most abstract notion by Yeats's lights, surely, just as Yeats's later spiritualism would seem to Pound unpoetically mechanical. Pound is more at home with modern science; his early critical writing is full of analogies drawn from the laboratory and from theoretical science. As we shall see, he comes very early to talk of poetry as a "confluence of forces," and he compares the poet's sensibility to a magnet held beneath a plate of iron filings and producing "pattern." He also has a more mathematical mind than Yeats had—there is, for example, his idea that a myth is an equation for a mood or experience, and in one early essay he compares a poem to the geometrical formula for the circle ("Vorticism," *GB* 105). And yet what all this finally means is that his poetic universe is less rationalized, more fluid and suggestive, than Yeats's. Pound's unseen world is energized not by ghosts, but by "fluid force"; it is "a world of moving energies," he says, "magnetisms that take form, that are seen, or that border the visible" ("Cavalcanti," *LE* 154).

For us this means a new form of discussion; we shall have to turn from viewing Pound's early work and theories through their resemblance to others'. We have seen Pound take up the dramatic lyric as a distancing, exploratory, defensive, and objectifying device from Browning. He carries the use of this form into a poetic realm like that explored by Rossetti, and his dramatic monologues are enactments of visionary poetic moments. He finds in the Decadents a congenial theory of the poetic personality, and among them writers who can turn everyday experiences into visionary loveliness. In Yeats he finds an obviously gifted poet whose ideology gives greater meaning to the finally superficial poetic experience of the Decadents and gives to his own developing theories, perhaps, the support of a respectable example. But Pound's work is more than the sum of its antecedents, and we must now look at the thing itself.

II

Thematic
Geography

There is a god within us; at his instigation we are fired;
in this impulse inhere the seeds of the divine mind.

—Ovid, *Fasti,* VI.5

EARLY AND LATE, Pound's work is pervaded by a concern with the
whole poetic process—some nineteen of the poems in *A Lume
Spento* and perhaps half a dozen of those added in *Personae* deal
with that theme.[1] His first five collections, in fact, can be divided
into those—*A Lume Spento, Quinzaine for This Yule,* and *Personae*
—that deal with the creative problem as such (what the poet is,
what he does, and why it matters) and the two—*Exultations* and
Canzoni—that center on modes of operation. As a youth Pound
wanted to become a poet in the way small boys want to be
firemen, and it is impossible to read certain of his early poems
without being struck by his naive candor in trying to deal with
this longing, a longing so incredibly intense that no pose is
too awkward if it will somehow shadow forth at least some of
the magic and wonder of the poet's calling.[2] A good number of
the early poems make much of this wonder at finding oneself
a poet and, taken together, they amount to a delineation of the
poet's nature, position, and job.

i

To begin with outer considerations, the artist is isolated from
ordinary men. There are Wordsworthian edges to the solitude of
the speaker in the very early "Over the Ognisanti":

High-dwelling 'bove the people here,
Being alone with beauty most the while,
Lonely?

63

> How can I be,
> Having mine own great thoughts for paladins
> Against all gloom and woe and bitterness?
> ("Quinzaine for This Yule," *ALSO* 89)

But this is not typical; Pound's early artist-speakers tend to be isolated and outcast rather than merely solitary, and their speeches convey a tone of aggressive satisfaction with this isolation. It is symptomatic that nearly all the influences and admirations figured in his earliest work can be seen as outcasts in one way or another—the Decadents certainly, Swinburne, Villon, the exiled Dante, and the heretical troubadours. In *A Lume Spento* "Anima Sola" is a very uncompromising poem along these lines:

> Exquisite loneliness
> Bound of mine own caprice
> I fly on the wings of an unknown chord
>> That ye hear not,
>> Can not discern
> My music is weird and untamèd
> Barbarous, wild, extreme,
> I fly on the note that ye hear not
> On the chord that ye can not dream.
>
> . . . . .
>
> I pendant sit in the vale of fate
>> I twine the Maenad strands
> And lo, the three Eumenides
>> Take justice at my hands.
> For I fly in the gale of an unknown chord.
> The blood of might is God's delight
> And I am the life blood's ward.
>
> . . . . .

And lo! I refuse your bidding.
I will not bow to the expectation that ye have.
Lo! I am gone as a red flame into the mist.
My chord is unresolved by your counter-harmonies.

Here is the Yeatsian self beyond any mortal judgment, the artist beyond salvation or damnation, who can only express or fail to express his being and who refuses to trim his cosmic sails to "normal" winds. His fellows include the down-at-heels scholar of "Famam Librosque Cano" and the dancer Fifine.

But though the status of outcast is useful in furnishing some of the poses in several early poems, it is not of itself the central issue for very long. In fact, the idea of the outcast is often only a piece of stage machinery which suggests merely the fate, not the nature, of the true poet. It is important in Pound's verse because it merges into the more significant posture of Poet as Seer.[3] We have already seen this process at work in "Fifine Answers." Fifine's criminality is not the issue: the poem is concerned with the opposition between her social and her spiritual conditions, not with her legal position. She shares the "exile" of Christ and, judging by the first seven lines of the poem, shares as well his bitter knowledge—she and her fellows are sharers in his drink; they *know* what it is like. The poet in "Famam Librosque Cano" and his hypothetical discoverer suffer a fate similar to Fifine's: the seedy-looking scholar's superior judgment and his commitment to things of lasting importance make him a slightly ludicrous, slightly unwholesome figure in the public eye. The early poem, "Masks," which we passed over near the beginning of Chapter One as exemplifying a relatively mechanical and trivial kind of defensive device, is a more outspoken example of how the posture of outcast can herald that of the seer in treating the artist as a visitor from some earlier time. So far is this poem from being "merely" a metaphor for the significance of poetry that Pound's formulation of the origin of myth is but a prose paraphrase, covering nearly every idea in the poem—this, some ten years after the publication of *A Lume Spento.*

Finally, the longish (for Pound) and very early "In Durance" is a more elaborate working out of the principle that the line between the outcast and the seer is faint:

> I am homesick after mine own kind,
>
> . . . . .
>
> "These sell our pictures"! Oh well,
> They reach me not, touch me some edge or that,
> But reach me not and all my life's become
> One flame, that reaches not beyond
> My heart's own hearth,
> Or hides among the ashes there for thee.
> "Thee"? Oh, "Thee" is who cometh first
> Out of mine own soul-kin,
>
> . . . . .
>
> Aye, I am wistful for my kin of the spirit
> And have none about me save in the shadows
> When come *they*, surging of power, "DAEMON,"
> "Quasi KALOUN." S. T. says Beauty is most that, a
>   "calling to the soul."
> Well then, so call they, the swirlers out of the mist
>   of my soul,
> They that come mewards, bearing old magic.

The poem goes on to reiterate the speaker's yearning for fellow initiates—for that is how it presents the people who "have some breath for beauty and the arts," these men "Flesh-shrouded bearing the secret," who "know the glory / Of th' unbounded ones." The poem reverses the implications of exile. Here, though the poet may be a social outsider, he becomes a kind of epistemological insider by gaining insights into orders of experience denied to ordinary mortals.

This is an eminently *fin de siècle* position, of course, particularly as expressed in the closing lines of another *A Lume Spento* poem, "Plotinus." The language, as usual at this period, is archaic and mannered, but the poem represents a reaction to a world bereft of any capacity for engaging the sympathies of the fully sentient man:

> But I was lonely as a lonely child,
> I cried amid the void and heard no cry.
> And then for utter loneliness, made I
> New thoughts as crescent images of *me*.
> And with them was my essence reconciled
> While fear went forth from mine eternity.

But Pound's poet is not merely the victim of a Philistine and ugly world. To the degree that he is a victim, he is a sacrificial victim of a very special sort, like the poets of "Prometheus" from *A Lume Spento*:

> For we be the beaten wands
> And the bearers of the flame.
> Ourselves have died lang syne, and we
> Go ever upward as the sparks of light
> Enkindling all
> 'Gainst whom our shadows fall.
>
> Weary to sink, yet ever upward borne,
> Flame, flame that riseth ever
>
> . . . . .
>
> For the way is one
> That beareth upward
> To the flame within the sun.

That these poets bring light and fire to others as they themselves are spent suggests that what is perpetrated against the poet in his life in the nonpoetic world is only a parody of what he perhaps does to himself in the service of art. Pound once drew an analogy between the power of Christian meditation to "draw back upon our minds some vestige of the unrememberable beauties of paradise" and a similar power exerted by poetry.[4] There is no need to call anything back unless it has been lost, and the self-sacrifice asserted in "Prometheus" is closely connected with what T. S. Eliot describes in "Tradition and the Individual Talent" as the artist's "continual surrender of himself as he is at the moment to something which is more valuable." Fifine as artist and Fifine as prostitute obliterates her self, in the one case as a person, in the other as a social being, in serving a life need not satisfactorily met by respectable society, and in this she is like the poet who would reconnect man with an equally natural dimension of life that is also ignored or derided by society at large. "Poet as Christ" is the obvious analogue, and indeed Pound does approach that posture in the immolation of self of which the persona is the emblem and device—a self-immolation strangely like a religious discipline, on behalf of art and of mankind.

The splendors of the Paradise reside, so far as the poet is concerned, in that realm of "fluid force" and "moving energies," the map of which is also the exposition of Pound's theory of poetry. What that is is suggested by his "hemichaunt" to Swinburne, "Salve O Pontifex!"—an early poem that touches upon enough of the issues involved in Pound's conception of the art to constitute a small-scale poetics.

It is also a large-scale literary allusion, to Swinburne's eulogy of Baudelaire, "Ave Atque Vale," and to his "Hymn to Proserpine," and it is in general a thoroughly literary poem. It begins with exactly the kind of gesture Pound soon came to abhor, "poetical treatment" of simple fact, in its ponderous literary chronicle: "One after one do they leave thee, / High Priest of

Iacchus"—an allusion to Swinburne's advancing years and to
such recent or untimely deaths as Morris' (1896), Lionel Johnson's (1901), and Dowson's (1900). The opening line reflects the
solitude of the poet, which later in the poem becomes isolation.
The "co-novices" of the Pontifex have "bent to the scythe" of
death,

> Leaving thee solitary, master of the initiating
> Maenads that come through the
> Vine-entangled ways of the forest.

This is the isolation of the magian poet who is

> Wreathed with the glory of years of creating
> Entangled music that men may not
> Over-readily understand.

The note of disdain for Philistine ignorance here is approxi-
mately characteristic of the Decadents and parallels a similarly
Decadent note some lines earlier. "High Priest of Iacchus,"
Pound writes, "the lines of life lie under thy fingers,"

> And above the vari-colored strands
> Thine eyes look out unto the infinitude
> Of the blue waves of heaven,
>
>   · · · · ·
>
> Thou fingerest the threads knowing neither
> Cause nor the ending.[5]
>   High Priest of Iacchus!
> Draw'st forth a multiplicity
> Of strands and beholding
> The color thereof, raisest thy voice
> Toward the sunset.

Here Pound carries Decadent "perception" and fine-shade-hunting into realms of ultimate metaphysical reality. Similarly with the matter of entangled music that men may not over-readily understand: the lines in part reflect what was at this time a stylistic ideal for Pound (note this very poem's emulation of Swinburne's hard style), and they have a surly-sounding counterpart in Pound's reply to William Carlos Williams' letter about *A Lume Spento*: "As for the 'eyes of too ruthless public': damn their eyes. No art ever yet grew by looking into the eyes of the public . . . You can obliterate yourself and mirror God, Nature, or Humanity but if you try to mirror yourself in the eyes of the public, woe be unto your art" (*L* 4). But the art is not great because of its obscurity, nor the music meaningful because entangled. The point is that the poet is *socially* a man apart because he is *absolutely*—by powers and function—a man apart. Hence the title, and hence the central image, which joins the imagery of entanglement in the middle of the poem:

> Breathe upon us that low-bowed and exultant
> Drink wine of Iacchus
> That since the conquering*
> Hath been chiefly contained in the numbers
> Of them that even as thou, have woven
> Wicker baskets for grape clusters
> Wherein is concealed the source of the vintage.
> *Vicisti, Nazarenus!

In figuring poetry as the wine of Iacchus and Swinburne as the High Priest, Pound is merely extending his expression of the ideas in "In Durance," with its reference to "mine own kind" who are "Flesh-shrouded, bearing the secret." Iacchus is an Eleusinian god, and the High Priest and his compeers are elucidators of the mysteries (at Bacchic festivals the performers, servants of Dionysus, were mediators between the worshiping audience and the divine power). The Bacchic or Iacchic wine with which the poem rather insistently identifies poetry has a twofold power—it confers divinity upon the initiate and it affords knowledge of the secret universe: "out of the secrets of the inmost mysteries / Thou chantest strange far-sourced canticles," and "All the manifold mystery / Thou makest wine of song of." In these terms poetry is worship, an acknowledgment of the existence of the gods and the soul. Its public function is to put its audience in touch with the vital universe and its representative deities—or, to put it less mythically, to render the vital universe more intelligible.

Of course, only the true master-poet has the secret of the divine drink, and the novice-speaker of "Salve O Pontifex!" pleads to be infused with the master's magic, a reasonably accurate image of Pound's relationship with earlier poets. What this plea posits, moreover, is connected with one of the main threads in Pound's poetic development—the present use of past energies and the persistence of these energies through time. The poetic priesthood has a special significance for the poet; it is a "thrice encinctured mystery,"

> Whereby thou being full of years art young
> Loving even this lithe Prosephone
> That is free for the seasons of plenty;
>
> Whereby thou being young art old
> And shalt stand before this Prosephone
>   Whom thou lovest
>
>   . . . . .
>
> Whereby thou being neither old nor young,
> Standing on the verge of the sea
> Shalt pass from being sand.

Besides placing the poet in contact with the vital universe, that is, poetry frees him from the constrictions of time by conferring upon it a kind of collapsibility. The significant moments of one century, for example, can be substantially juxtaposed with significant moments of our own or an earlier day; in literature "the real time is independent of the apparent, and [there] many dead men are our grandchildren's contemporaries, while many of our contemporaries have been already gathered into Abraham's bosom, or some more fitting receptacle" (*SR* 8).

The relevance of this kind of remark to the *Cantos*—which dart in and out of time, snatching an important burst of energy from the Trecento and placing it next to a contrasting burst from the twentieth century or the fourth century B.C.—needs no emphasis here. The idea remains curiously dormant during Pound's early years. It receives brief, Bergsonian notice in *The Spirit of Romance,* and it is one of the cornerstones of the Vorticist movement and Pound's immediately post-Imagist work, part of a program to free the imagination from the constrictions of time; yet even in Vorticist propaganda Pound makes little use of it. In his criticism it begins to emerge with recognized importance in *Guide to Kulchur* (1938). But it is very much present, if only implicitly, throughout the early work—as, for example, elsewhere in "Salve O Pontifex!" The Maenads come to the Pontifex

> Seeking, out of all the world
> Madness of Iacchus,
> That being skilled in the secrets of the double cup
> They might turn the dead of the world
> Into beauteous paeans.

Pound's note to his "Sestina: Altaforte" reads, "Loquitur: *En* Bertran de Born. Dante Alighieri put this man in hell . . . Judge ye! Have I dug him up again?" The lines from the poem to Swinburne show that, if Pound's question here is meant only metaphorically, his metaphors are at least systematic—and that these particular metaphors are the pegs on which he tends to hang his poetic theory. At any rate, we see here part of the logic of the dramatic lyric; a persona can be a means of literally rescuing certain energies from the passage of time, that great unrelenting flux from which the poet snatches the valuable experiences he fixes in his depictions of poetic moments. We are back in the realm of "Histrion," a vital universe where nothing ever really dies, where energies form, dissolve, and—by a perhaps lucky contact with some poet's magian sensibility—reform, their imprints entering the day-to-day world as works of art.

If we take "Salve O Pontifex!" at face value, it is plain that this universe is specifically religious—informed by a "religiosity" to which, characteristically, Pound brings the same thoroughgoing subjectivity we have seen in his pronouncements about the origins of art and myth. Religion is no less subjective than myths (which are "explication of mood" and "only intelligible in a vivid and glittering sense to those people to whom they occur"—"Psychology and Troubadours," *SR* 92), and its truths, like those of myth, are subjective truths. In fact, religion at its most significant is but communal myth, its history that of shared subjectivity, of shared mythology:

> Christianity and all other forms of ecstatic religion [as opposed to "the Mosaic or Roman or British Empire type," which are dogmatic and doctrinal] . . . *seem* little concerned with ethics; their general object appears to be to stimulate a sort of confidence in the life-force. [Compare the function of literature, which is to "incite humanity to continue living."] Their teaching is . . . a sort of working hypothesis acceptable to people of a certain range of temperament—a "regola" which suits a particular constitution of nerves and intellect, and in accord with which the people of this temperament can live at greatest peace with "the order," with man and nature. (*SR* 95)

According to Pound's essay on Arnold Dolmetsch, religion begins with myth (based, we recall, on some individual's "delightful psychic experience"); around it arises "a cult, a company of people who . . . understand each other's nonsense about the gods." The decline of the cult begins when the core of subjective experience congeals into dogma, which the cultists (now presumably of the British Empire type) attempt to impose on others. The psychic experience depicted in the myth Pound regards, according to "Psychology and Troubadours," as "a sort of permanent basis in humanity," and the same essay reinforces his assertion that the myths are true for people who believe in them. "For our basis in nature," he says, "we rest on the indisputable and very scientific fact that there are in the 'normal course of things' certain times, a certain moment more than another, when a man feels his immortality upon him." These moments, the basis of religious experience and therefore the basis of art, are moments of participation in the vital universe; they are an extension of man's potential beyond his "kinship with the ox," an extension and a participation which, if we need a representational metaphor, we may conceive of as "the gods." And we have Pound's word for it that "the gods exist" (*GK* 125):

> What is a god?
> A god is an eternal state of mind.
>
>   . . . . .
>
> When is a god manifest?
> When the states of mind take form.
> When does a man become a god?
> When he enters one of these states of mind.
>
>   . . . . .
>
> By what characteristic may we know the divine forms?
> By beauty.

And if the presented forms are unbeautiful?
They are demons.

("Religio, or The Child's Guide to Knowledge,"
PD 23–24; now in *PD* 2)

The line about demons may cast some light upon such phenomena as Cantos XIV and XV, but for now it is enough to note that these opinions, stated in print at various times between 1912 and 1938, are active in much of Pound's early poetry. In "The Tree," for example, the speaker means exactly what he says: "'Twas not until the gods had been / Kindly entreated, and been brought within / Unto the hearth of their heart's home" that they might help him become "a tree amid the wood."

All of this explains much of what happens in the course of Pound's general development and, for that matter, more minute issues. It explains, for example, why a sequence of lines in "Salve O Pontifex!" which "depict" poetry's pre-Swinburnian status as "ox-cart and post-chaise" for transmitting socially admired ideas in terms of a wasteland deserted by its god should find an echo eight or ten years later in the title of *Lustra*.[6]

These considerations surrounding Pound's poetic-religious universe are but extensions of that total subjectivization of reality implicit in his identification of "the real" with the self; it can lead to a remark like "a man's message is precisely his *façon de voir*, his modality of apperception" ("Remy de Gourmont, a Distinction," *LE* 340). This *façon de voir* constitutes the poet's only operative and "sincere" conception of reality.

Here is where Pound's subjectivism shades over into the religious, for it is in the service of this Bergsonian-looking epistemology that Pound bends the slogans and minor traditions of Christian meditation to which his work has repeatedly referred. In a note to his early poem "A Vision of Italy" (an excessively Dantesque allegorical account of his impressions of the cities of Italy), he refers to Richard St. Victor's definitions of cogitation, meditation, and contemplation.[7] Paraphrasing, "as

I have not the Benjamin Minor by me," Pound says that according to St. Victor the thought in contemplation "radiates from a
centre, that is, as light from the sun it reaches out in an infinite
number of ways to things that are related or dependent on it."
He adds, "Following St. Victor's figure of radiation: Poetry in
its acme is expression from contemplation" (*P 1* 58). Almost
thirty years later—and well into the *Cantos*—he still found this
interesting and put it in more candid terms: "Richard St. Victor
had hold of something: sic: There are three modes of thought,
cogitation, meditation and contemplation . . . in the third
[the mind] is unified with the object" (*GK* 77). This is why a
poem can be "stated" in no terms but its own: its rhythm, its
terminology, its images, and the emotional qualities implicit
in all these literally embody the experience that is the poem's
subject matter. By Pound's own standards, the poem is a failure
to the extent that it needs, or is vulnerable to, any kind of
paraphrase.

The second version of the statement on contemplation is a
major part of the rationale behind Pound's work, early and
late: these early poems are detached pieces of contemplative
intelligence—fusions, from a categorizing point of view, of
religious and subjective experience just as the *Cantos* consist of
related pieces of such intelligence under maturer technical
command. As for particular poems, the contemplative unity of
mind with object is both theme and substance of "The Flame,"
"Apparuit," and "The Return"—and it is also the procedural
rationale of all the poems using a persona, since in these poems
Pound is not imitating other men's manners but plunging into
history or imagination to rescue the real energies of the char-
acters he constructs or reconstructs. "Sestina: Altaforte" does not
imitate De Born, but "digs him up again."

Poetry, then, is the expression of unique subjective perceptions of reality; its humane function is to serve that part of man
which seeks some connection with the vital universe, with a life
force. It is not as "important" as religion—it is religion in a
purer, truer form, allowing the exercise of certain "enduring

constants" in human nature which have been customarily symbolized as "the gods." These gods and what they represent *must* be served, for they are valid manifestations of the life force; they are our means of access to the vital universe, and to cut off this access would be to pen up or kill that part of man which raises him above his kinship with the ox. "Without gods, no culture. Without gods, something is lacking" (*GK* 126).

ii

The Christian meditative tradition that Pound rather overeasily assimilates to his own conceptions is intimately related to another mode of thought crucially important to his work: neo-Platonism. When the poetic universe adumbrated here is set into action, it assumes a neo-Platonic shape. The glimpses of or into the vital universe I have been describing are tantamount to glimpses both *into* a more or less neo-Platonic *nous* and *of nous* in its sensible manifestations. That Pound was interested in the subject as such seems fairly clear: *Guide to Kulchur* is full of references to Renaissance writers who were deeply immersed in neo-Platonic thought, and the whole tradition seems to have been important to him in his early years. In July 1911 he mentions to his mother his abandoned plan for a book "which was to have been about philosophy from Richard St. Victor to Pico Della Mirandola, or more or less so" (*YL* 215). In an article in *The New Age* he speaks approvingly of the neo-Platonically oriented mysticism of the Italian writers:

> [Ficino] set to work translating a Greek that was in spirit anything but "classic." That is to say, you had ultimately a "Platonic" academy messing up Christian and Pagan mysticism, allegory, occultism, demonology, Trismegistus, Psellus, Porphyry, into a most eloquent and exciting and exhilarating hotch-potch, which "did for" the medieval fear of the *dies irae* and for human abasement generally.[8]

Now it is clear from the merest glance at his poetry that Pound is no more interested in the hierarchical details of neo-Platonism or its universe than he is in the precise rigors of Christian meditation. He has simply adapted two clusters of ideas, doing with neo-Platonism and meditation what he attributed to Dante: "he dips into a multitude of traditions & unifies them by their connection with himself" (*YL* 130, Autumn 1909).

The gods that most concern Pound are minor ones who have potentially tangible contact with men, not the unreachable One of neo-Platonic metaphysics; *nous* is as high up the neo-Platonic scale of being as he has cared to go. He seems to have seized principally upon the expressive possibilities of neo-Platonic imagery, and his use of it begins very early in his work. The description of contemplation he gives in the note to "A Vision of Italy" is a historical descendant of the image by which Plotinus accounts for the occurrence of the universe: *nous* emanates from the contemplating One, and from *nous* emanates Soul. In both cases the higher state of being is likened to a point of light from which emanation proceeds in all directions: "How did *Nous* come to be then? . . . It must be a radiation from It while It remains unchanged, just like the bright light which surrounds the sun, which remains unchanged though the light springs from it continually."[9] The poetic mind similarly seems to "radiate from a center" and reach out "in an infinite number of ways to things that are related or dependent on it"—bestowing being upon the objects it contemplates, as the divine mind does.

Plotinus' *nous*, moreover, can be described in terms that fit perfectly to Pound's vital universe. For Plotinus, *nous* is "no longer a structure, logically or mathematically conceived, of static universal norms, but an organic living community of interpenetrating beings which are at once Forms and intelligences, all 'awake and alive.'"[10] In *Guide to Kulchur* Pound speaks, in the very language of the *Cantos*, of the possibility of attaining *nous*: the Platonists, he says, "have caused man after man to be suddenly aware of the reality of *nous*, of mind, apart from any man's individual mind, of the sea crystalline and enduring, of the bright as it were molten glass that envelops us, full of light" (44). It is the poet's business to transmit the fruits of this awareness to his audience: "The worship of the supreme intelligence of the universe is neither an inhuman nor bigoted action. Art is, religiously, an emphasis, a segregation of some component of that intelligence for the sake of making it more perceptible." A work of art, he adds, "is a door or a lift permitting a man to enter, or hoisting him mentally into, a zone of activity, and out of fugg and inertia" (189–190). These statements were composed in 1938, but they are little more than clarifications of suggestions that Pound was putting forth at the beginning of his career, suggestions even then pointing toward the *Cantos* and whose similarity to neo-Platonic principles is obviously more than casual.

The elucidation of *nous* supplies another parallel. From the point of view of human experience, "*Nous* is the level of intuitive thought, a thought which grasps its object immediately and is always perfectly united with it, and does not have to seek it outside itself by discursive reasoning; and we at our highest are *Nous,* or Soul perfectly formed to the likeness of *Nous.*"[11] This is exactly the "level" at which Pound's mythopoeic poet operates. "Paracelsus in Excelsis," for example, shows that the ostensibly soulless rocks and trees with which the poet becomes one in that early note to "La Fraisne" are actually part of a neo-Platonic vital universe:

> Being no longer human, why should I
> Pretend humanity or don the frail attire?
> Men have I known and men, but never one
> Was grown so free an essence, or become
> So simply element as what I am.
> The mist goes from the mirror and I see.
> Behold! the world of forms is swept beneath—

> Turmoil grown visible beneath our peace,
> And we that are grown formless, rise above—
> Fluids intangible that have been men.

Here, as in the note to "La Fraisne," to become "simply element" means not at all to become rocklike from *loss* of soul; both speakers have withdrawn so far within themselves as to become "essence," so far as to reach that level of self which is "perfectly formed to the likeness of *Nous*." Had Pound not included this poem (from *Canzoni*) in the current *Personae* we might be inclined to regard the since-excised "Canzon: Of Angels" as only toying with similar ideas:

> He that is Lord of all the realms of light
> Hath unto me from His magnificence
> Granted such vision as hath wrought my joy.
> Moving my spirit past the last defence
> That shieldeth mortal things from mightier sight,
> Where freedom of the soul knows no alloy,
> I saw what forms the lordly powers employ;
> Three splendours saw I, of high holiness,
> From clarity to clarity ascending.

(Both of these poems, incidentally, are mythic in terms of Pound's contention that any myth is one man's attempt to convey to an audience a vivid subjective experience. "Paracelsus," in fact, is a myth upon a myth: the poet undergoes a mythic experience in "becoming Paracelsus" while he recreates the mythic experience of Paracelsus *in excelsis*. Whenever Pound speaks of the truth of myth, he is referring to this direct and nonreasoned knowledge of "the ineffable.")

The mechanism by which a work of art functions as a door "permitting a man to enter . . . a zone of activity" is strikingly similar to the circumstances by which art operates according to Plotinus. Art does not merely imitate what it sees; the arts go

back to the *logoi* from which nature derives; and also . . .
they do a great deal by themselves; since they possess
beauty they make up what is defective in things. Phidias
did not make his Zeus from any model perceived
by the senses; he understood what Zeus would look like
if he wanted to make himself visible. (*Enneads* V.8.1)

"The things of this world," in other words, "are beautiful
by participating in Form . . . So then the beautiful body comes
into being by sharing in a *logos* which comes from the divine
Forms" (*Enneads* I.6.2). This includes the work of art, which is
beautiful only because of the form that art has conferred upon it.
More important for the present argument, this form "was in the
man who thought it before it came into the stone," and it was in
him "because he had some art in him" (*Enneads* V.8.1). *Logos*,
then, is implanted in the artist. In his art he passes on to us an
impulse directly from *nous*. This is a very close parallel to the
operation of Pound's "germinal consciousness," which, when
acted upon by soul (the higher principle of which, according to
Plotinus, remains with *nous*), produces form:

> And I, "I have no song,"
> Till my soul sent a woman as the sun:
> Yea as the sun calleth to the seed,
> As the spring upon the bough
> So is she that cometh, mother of songs,
> She that holdeth the wonder words with her eyes
> The words, little elf words
>   that call ever unto me,
>   "Song, a song."
>
>   ("Praise of Ysolt")

The similarity to Pound lies in the fact that what we have seen
him refer to as *virtù* is actually *logos*: though "the soul of each

man is compounded of all the elements of the cosmos," there is in each soul "some one element which predominates, which is in some peculiar and intense way the quality or *virtù* of the individual; in no two souls is this the same." *Virtù* is "not a 'point of view,' nor an 'attitude toward life;' nor is it the mental caliber or 'a way of thinking,' but something more substantial which influences all these" ("Osiris—VI, on Virtue," *NA*). These remarks amount to little more than paraphrase of Plotinus: though each soul is a compendium of all the *logoi* in the universe, different individuals "are not related to their Form as portraits of Socrates are to their original; their different structures must result from different *logoi*" (*Enneads* V.7.1). A poet's *virtù* is not just a penchant for close observation, moreover, but rather, as Pound explains apropos Cavalcanti, a real force: "The Tuscan . . . declines to limit his aesthetic to the impact of light on the eye [or of sound on the ear] . . . There is the residue of perception, perception of something which requires a human being to produce it. Which may even require a certain individual to produce it. This really complicates the aesthetic. You deal with an interactive force: the *virtù* in short" ("Cavalcanti," *LE* 151–152).

In a way, this brings us full circle to the idea that the function of the poet is to draw back upon our minds the lost splendors of Paradise. Pound rests firmly within the tradition not only of Romance, but of romanticism. He is not "antiscientific," but with the great English romantics, as with Browning, Rossetti, the Decadents, and Yeats, he would insist on the inadequacy of any strictly scientific conception of life and the universe— inadequate to the full needs of human beings and inadequate to account for the facts as we know them. The gods are *"eternal states of mind."* They exist, and we can and should know them. In inferring from Pound's scattered remarks something of a formal cosmology, the insistence upon a detailed construct is mine and not his. The fact remains, however, that in his critical writings he has again and again called for a vital interaction between human beings and the universe around them, a universe suffused with energy—life force, *nous*, the Supreme Intelligence —whose presence we may neglect only at the risk of crippling valuable human capacities. He is a religious poet in a curious sense, whose religion is a strangely occult kind of humanism. Being fully human means being fully and intensely sentient. The poet, in his ecstatic or revelatory moments, is pre-eminently such a sentient man, suddenly aware—spiritually, emotionally, viscerally—of the life force emerging into form. "Poetry," Pound wrote at a very early date, "is about as much a 'criticism of life' as red-hot iron is a criticism of fire" (*SR* 222).

For Pound, then, the center of interest in these issues is not cosmology but human psychology. Although poetic mysticism is indeed a means of entry into another world, the most important thing about that other world is its answering to the needs of various human energies. The "zone of activity" into which one is lifted by art is as much a mental state (rather than some cosmo-geographical location) as the "fugg and inertia" one is lifted out of. The title of the essay on Provençal mysticism—"Psychology and Troubadours"—asserts in itself that the mysticism of the troubadours reflected genuine facts of human psychology. In *Guide to Kulchur* Pound asks whether Eleusis might in our day be "possible in the wilds of a man's mind only" (294).

Again, though it is easy to understand why Yeats's general ideological position should have attracted Pound as it did, it is not surprising that he had little sympathy with the older poet's interest in spirit rappings and his spook chasing in general. Yeats's belief in a rationally explicable spirit world—Uncle Ned's ghost pops in of an evening because Uncle Ned, like everybody else who is dead, *has* a ghost and it *wants* to pop in— must have struck Pound as far more intellectualized than the more poetically indefinite spiritual world of which he conceived. The *virtù* of the ineffable is its ineffability. The Image, originally conceived as a means of expressing ineffable intuitive experiences, was defined fairly early by Pound as "the word beyond formulated language" (*GB* 102). The difference is a matter of emphasis. The "other world" or other level appeals to Pound not so much because it has interesting things in it as because alert human beings can find interesting things in it. This produces a highly subjective theology; its end point, in fact, is the "interpretation of the cosmos by feeling" which Pound tentatively ascribes to the troubadours in "Psychology and Troubadours." He has always held that only a subjective theology can be valid—and, because poetry deals primarily in personal "religious" discoveries, this is what underlies his denigration of didactic and moralistic poetry. "Our only measure of truth," he writes, in the Dolmetsch essay, is "our own perception of truth." In these terms, his early abhorrence of didacticism is seen to be not a repetition, but an important extension, of the art-for-art's-sake position of the nineties. It was unhealthy that before Swinburne poetry should have been "merely the vehicle . . . the ox-cart and post-chaise for transmitting thoughts poetic or otherwise" ("A Retrospect," *LE* 11), primarily because it meant using the power in poetry to foist thoughts, opinions, and judgments upon people they did not fit, because it meant using the tools of insight and emotional truth in the service of dogma, and finally because it usually meant reducing an intensely experienced particular to an inexact and vaguely conceived generality. Over and over, in "Arnold Dolmetsch," in "Psychology and Troubadours," and pre-eminently in *Guide to Kulchur*, he has insisted that each man must define his own microcosm and that erecting subjective validities into putatively universal dogmata does violence to human needs and to truth.[12] For Pound, poetry begins in an interest not in the nature of the ruling deity, but in human experiences. This is one reason why his peculiar sort of neo-Platonism *had* to issue in a polytheistic religion, and why his mysticism did not emerge as specifically Christian—or even as religious, as one expects to think of that word. The more fortunate among us participate in the energy of the Supreme Intelligence, and since each individual is unique (owing to his own *logos* or *virtù*), each man's participation will be objectified in a unique way; yet the "gods" representing these objectifications will all be genuine.

Pound's religious concern, therefore—or, better, his moral philosophy—points inward, to one's true self and to the ordered exercise of one's natural energies—ordered and restricted sufficiently to avoid injuring or interfering with other people, but not limited by arbitrary (dogmatic) exclusions and repressions. These observations suggest again that the most important characteristic of Pound's cosmology is what we may call its metaphorical possibilities and that it is primarily a mechanism for the expression of purely subjective concerns. This is partly true, but like all basically neo-Platonic schemata Pound's is conveniently susceptible of translation into "mental" terms without having to give up its claim to objective reality. This very intangibility is poetically advantageous.

On the other hand, I have suggested that to speak of "this other level" as a useful source of metaphors for the operation of certain human impulses does not allow us to conclude that the impulses are completely private or that, cosmologically speaking, they represent benign delusions. The neo-Platonic drama may be internal, but its substantive arena is not confined to the head of the contemplator. "The gods exist." In an early essay on "The Serious Artist," Pound made this distinction:

> The prose author has shown the triumph of his intellect . . . but by the verses one is brought upon the passionate moment. This moment has brought with it nothing that violates the prose simplicities. The intellect has not found it but the intellect has been moved . . . In the verse something has come upon the intelligence. In the prose the intelligence has found a subject for its observations. The poetic fact pre-exists.   (*LE* 53–54)

The poet, that is, does not spin pretty fancies out of thin air or out of his dreams; he discovers things. Hugh Kenner refers to Pound's conviction that "the things the poet sees in the sea of events are really there . . . the values registered in the [*Cantos*] are not imported and affirmed by the poet, but discerned by him in the record of human experience."[13] This is an important perception, and Clark Emery's similar claim that there is a significant "Permanent" in the Poundian scheme of things is supported by many of Pound's utterances. That the gods are states of mind accounts for their presence in individuals; but since "mind" is "all about us" and since these are *eternal* states of mind, they are also transcendent realities.

This twofold reality of the force of the gods and of the substantial phenomena they embody is certainly not a late development, limited in relevance to the *Cantos* alone. Pound approximates some of the issues in *The Spirit of Romance*: "Thus the *Commedia* . . . in a further sense is the journey of Dante's intelligence through the states of mind wherein dwell all sorts and conditions of men before death . . . In a fourth sense, the *Commedia* is an expression of the laws of eternal justice; 'il contrapasso,' the counterpass, as Bertran calls it [*Inferno* XXVIII.142] or the law of Karma, if we are to use an Oriental term" (127). And on the following page:

> There is little doubt that Dante conceived the real Hell, Purgatory, and Paradise as states, and not places. Richard St. Victor had, somewhile before, voiced this belief, and it is, moreover, a part of the esoteric and mystic dogma. For the purposes of art and popular religion it is more convenient to deal with such matters objectively . . . It is therefore expedient in reading the *Commedia* to regard Dante's descriptions of the actions and conditions of the shades as descriptions of men's mental states of life, in which they are, after death, compelled to continue: that is to say, men's inner selves stand visibly before the eyes of Dante's intellect, which is guided by a personification of classic learning, mystic theology, and the beneficent powers.

In "The Tree" we are told of the subjective reward of proper ministration to the gods. On the other hand, we find in Canto II an example of what happens to those who fail to do honor to them. Some sailors have had the singularly unlucky notion to kidnap a young hitchhiker, who turns out to be Bacchus:

> God-sleight, then, god-sleight:
> > Ship stock fast in sea-swirl,
> Ivy upon the oars, King Pentheus,
>
> . . . . .
>
> Black snout of a porpoise
> > where Lycabs had been,
> Fish-scales on the oarsmen.

What are we to make of the sailors' misadventure? If we take the metamorphosis of the wicked sailors as a metaphor for the inevitable divine punishment which follows evildoing, the incident expresses a "law of eternal justice"—but at the same time it expresses the inner nature of the sailors.

Whatever one's conception of Bacchus' significance as a congeries of deified human impulses, one thing he does not represent is cupidity, and the attempted kidnaping images a particularly mean subversion of an eternal state of mind. Bacchus being the god of ecstasy and fertility, the subversion is also a particularly terrible one, involving as it does the perversion of nature's very life force in hope of gold. The ordered soul (in this poem, the pilot Acoetes) sees forthwith what the pretty youth is; the sailors, in their moral brutishness, are not even interested. The simultaneous public and individual applicability of the symbol is apparent: the misuse of nature's gifts and the use of art as an item of commerce are two referents of public concern, while the kind of *inner* self that countenances mayhem and personal violence and cupidity is made to "stand visibly before the eyes" of Pound's and his reader's intellect.

The passage figures the spiritual status of those who fail to accord such eternal states of mind their due respect—for to do so is also failure to greet a manifestation of *nous*, of which our nobler selves are a part.

Since man thus has within himself "all the elements of the cosmos," an ordered exercise of his natural energies is tantamount to an acknowledgment of these energies in *nous*, in the Permanent. The best general statement of the relevance of these issues to Pound's verse is Emery's:

> The creation of an art-object glorifying the gods is an act of faith on the part of the producer producing a revitalized faith . . . in the observer; it is an act of affirmation without taint . . . of pejorative tabu. To have found in the stone a god represents for the creator an active participation in the gods' most characteristic function—that of making quick the dead: for the observer, the art-object is a testament verifying his faith emotionally and intellectually. Here he has before him clear evidence of the substantiality of the gods. (p. 6)

But rich as Pound's cosmology may be in expressive possibilities, it results in a strangely inarticulable poetics. My own abstraction of it, such as it is, has drawn on documents scattered over thirty years' time. At its worst this cosmology issues in what may seem to outsiders metaphorical assertions of hopelessly private experience. When a man gives us "I stood still and was a tree amid the wood" as the nearest available equation for some feeling, we understand the words, nominally, but the experience remains opaque.

The conviction that mystical experiences are normal phenomena might by itself lead only to effusions or to ringing the changes on "The Flame" or to a long string of poems like "Night Litany." It is surely no accident, then, that Pound's interest in the Tuscan and Provençal poets goes at least as far back in his life as his neo-Platonist mysticism, for these poets, with Dante, offer a mode of operation admirably suited to express the concerns and insights of a Plotinian view of reality.

iii

It is roughly true that, starting with the Provençal poets, we find a love poetry in which the love becomes more and more rarefied until, in Dante, the Lady becomes almost completely a religious (and perhaps a psychological) symbol. Even in the troubadour period, the poetry (in the words of the commentator from whose book Pound probably first studied the troubadours) "in due course shows an increasing refinement and delicacy of sentiment," and the later troubadours "gradually dissociated their love from the object which . . . aroused it; among them, love is no longer a sexual passion; it is rather the motive to great works, to self-surrender."[14] This seems to be the stage at which the Tuscan poets began, and by the time of Cavalcanti we can say with Remy de Gourmont that "a study of his poems forces one to conclude that the poet is not addressing a woman, but the ideal"—a Platonic ideal of Feminine.[15] But the starting point of this development—for Pound as for medieval Europe— was Provence.

Now what Pound discovered in the troubadours may or may not correspond to anything "really" there. It is another of those traditions he dips into and unifies by their connection with himself. He sees that tradition as first and foremost "pagan." He says of the Provencals in "Psychology and Troubadours" that "if paganism survived anywhere it would have been, unofficially, in the Langue d'Oc. That the spirit was, in Provence, Hellenic is seen readily enough by anyone who will compare the *Greek Anthology* with the work of the troubadours. They have, in some way, lost the names of the gods and remembered the names of lovers" (*SR* 90). "Pagan" here means reverent toward divine energies, in a suitably unstructured and subjective way; it is an almost purely emotional religiosity which sees lovers and gods as somehow expressive of the same thing. His theory of Provençal art on the whole begins with the misleadingly simple notion that strong emotions produce poetry. But in "Psychology and Troubadours" Pound leaves more conservative commentators behind—and incidentally reveals more about his own conception of poetry than the troubadours'—in suggesting that the Provençal poets put their art to mystical uses and that in doing so they were perfectly right. He repeatedly proceeds from tentative formulations, such as "Did this 'close ring,' this aristocracy of emotion, evolve, out of its half memories of Hellenistic mysteries, a cult . . . for the purgation of the soul by a refinement of, and lordship over, the senses?" to definite claims of possibility: "we come to this place where ecstasy is not a whirl or madness of the senses, but a glow arising from the exact nature of the perception." He describes *trobar clus* as a ritual with purposes and effects "different from those of simple song. They are perhaps subtler. They make their revelations to those who are already expert." Perceiving a parallel between, as he would have it, the cult of courtly love and Christian mysticism, Pound suggests that the rigors of that love produced effects similar to those of devotional exercises, involving an "unofficial mysticism" based on experiences we would define as, to say the least, wholly secular. He mingles several different orders of occult experience, but focuses for the most part upon the possibility that the emotional intensity of courtly love took on "forms interpretative of the divine order," leading to an "exteriorization of the sensibility" and "interpretation of the cosmos by feeling."

But these are terms we have seen to be applicable to the work of Pound himself—the idea of poetry as a means of "interpretation of the cosmos by feeling" especially applies to him. He repeats in this essay the remarks of Richard of St. Victor about naming the most beautiful things we know in order to draw back upon our minds the splendors of Paradise, but here it leads to a theory more particularly related to his own poetry: "I suggest that the troubadour, either more indolent or more logical, progresses from correlating all these details for purpose of comparison, and lumps the matter. The Lady contains the catalogue, is more complete. She serves as a sort of *mantram*." He is here arguing, as in his accounts of the origin of myth, for a poetry that reconnects man with the energies of the vital universe, and at the same time he is suggesting in the Provençal Lady one important source for particularizing metaphors (and surely adumbrating the rationale of such poems as "Apparuit" and "The House of Splendour"). If the Lady, that is, is a *mantram* for conjuring the splendors of Paradise, then in the line from Piere Vidal that Pound quotes in support of his argument, "God" becomes synechdochic: "Good Lady, I think I see God when I gaze upon your delicate body."

From the Middle Ages at least to the Renaissance, the languages of love and religious devotion played back and forth upon each other, and an implicit assumption of "Psychology and Troubadours" is that the feelings behind them are very similar. Pound suggests that, by the time of the English Renaissance, "man is concerned with man" in literature "and forgets the whole and the flowing," and that "when we do get into contemplation of the flowing we find sex, or some correspondence to it." In a paragraph touching the very center of his early poetic rationale, Pound says:

> It is an ancient hypothesis that the little cosmos "corresponds" to the greater, that man has in him both "sun" and "moon." From this I should say that there are at least two paths . . . the one ascetic, the other for want of a better term "chivalric." In the first the monk or whoever he may be, develops, at infinite trouble and expense, the secondary pole within himself, produces his charged surface which registers the beauties, celestial or otherwise, by "contemplation." In the second, which I

must say seems more in accord with "mens sana in corpore sano" the charged surface is produced between the predominant natural poles of two human mechanisms.

The curious language of the last few sentences refers to an analogy that Pound had set up just previously: "In the telegraph we have a charged surface . . . attracting to it, or registering movements in the invisible aether." The phraseology is misleading (inclining the reader's expectation toward extrasensory communication), but Pound's meaning is clear: intensely concentrated emotion produces a "charged surface" which serves to register visions of the macrocosmos. And the emotion need not be, in the Christian sense, devout: "Sex is, that is to say, of a double function and purpose, reproductive and educational; or, as we see in the realm of fluid force, one sort of vibration produces at different intensities, heat and light." It is the farther reaches of this realm of fluid force—in its religious aspect a version of the *nous*—to which the Provençal Lady is the key. According to "Psychology and Troubadours," the intensity of his love laid the Provençal "cultist" open to "the exalted moment": "The electric current gives light where it meets resistance. I suggest that the living conditions of Provence gave the necessary restraint, produced a tension sufficient for the results, a tension unattainable under, let us say, the living conditions of imperial Rome." The tension is necessary, but the fostering impulse is emotion, and the troubadours were helpful to Pound partly because their poetry can be read as a reflection of their commonplace that "without love there can be no song." Four times in the *Literary Essays* alone Pound refers to Propertius' line, *Ingenium nobis ipsa puella fecit*.

This whole conception of troubadour poetry seems to share in the tradition represented by books like Eugene Aroux's *Dante, pasteur de l'église albigeoise de Florence* (1856) and *Les Mystères de la Chevalerie* (1858), and Josephin Péladin's *Le Secret des*

Troubadours (1906), all of which either assume or seek to prove that Provençal poetry was the secret language of Manichaeanism. But Pound was by no means sympathetic to such readings. On the contrary, on the one occasion in his work when someone else's "mystical" reading of important poetry came up (Luigi Valli's theories about "Donna mi prega"—see "Cavalcanti," *LE* 173ff), Pound was at some pains to confute it. The downright mystical interpretation of troubadour poetry has never been very respectable in romance scholarship, even in Pound's terms, and he seems to have been quite untouched by it. Judging by the books he has actually mentioned, his knowledge of romance literature came to him through the standard compilations and commentaries—Gaston Paris, Jeanroy, Mackail, Chaytor, Fitzmaurice-Kelly, and the like—and his own extensive scrutiny of the primary texts. Certainly none of these commentaries entertains for a moment any notion of mystical troubadours as such.

It seems, instead, that Pound's conception of this poetry was the result of an interaction between the obvious suggestive possibilities of the poetry itself and his own predispositions, aided no doubt by his acquaintance with G. R. S. Mead, the editor of the occultist journal, *The Quest*, in which "Psychology and Troubadours" first appeared. In short, we have another case of his grandly subjective assimilation of traditions. If he was moved to read the troubadours in the manner of "Psychology and Troubadours" by any external force at all, it was his own neo-Platonic leanings and the general bent of his thought— for his "mystical" reading of Provençal poetry was but part of a larger, evolving whole.

A helpful extension of that evolution, linking Pound's idea of the spirit of romance to his neo-Platonism, occurs in the Cavalcanti essay. Provence made its break with the classical world, he says, with "the dogma that there is some proportion between the fine thing held in the mind, and the inferior thing ready for instant consumption." The troubadours were better Platonists, that is, than the Greeks themselves. The phenomena of the physical world become spiritual stimuli to the exercise of *virtù*: "And dealing with it is not anti-life. It is not maiming, it is not curtailment. The senses at first seem to project for a few yards beyond the body. Effect of a decent climate where a man leaves his nerve-set open, or allows it to tune in to its ambience . . . The conception of the body as perfect instrument of the increasing intelligence pervades" ("Medievalism," *LE* 152). A few pages later Pound characterizes the world adumbrated in Provençal poetry and exploited by Tuscany as "the radiant world where one thought cuts through another with clean edge, a world of moving energies . . . magnetisms that take form . . . [a] harmony *of* the sentient, where the thought has its demarcation, the substance its *virtu*." This world is created by a state of mind which can completely transform the significance of what at first glance seems an unmistakably fleshly experience: "Consider in such passages in Arnaut as, 'E quel remir contral lums de la lampa,' whether a sheer love of beauty and a delight in the perception of it have not replaced all heavier emotion, whether or no the thing has not become a function of the intellect."[16]

One reason for Arnaut Daniel's general importance to Pound is that he marks a point in the development of Provençal art where largely emotional impulses do begin to extend into the more intellectualized poetic atmosphere later filled out by the Tuscans. The end point of this extension is the careful distinction, in the essay on Remy de Gourmont, between "aesthetic receptivity of tactile and magnetic values, of the perception of beauty in these relationships [,] and the conception of love, passion, emotion as intellectual instigation" (*LE* 343). Pound distinguishes between the achievements of Provence and Tuscany largely on this basis. "The cult of Provence," he says, "had been a cult of the emotions," and "with it there had been some, hardly conscious, study of emotional psychology"; in Tuscany "the cult is a cult of the harmonies of the mind" (*SR* 116). The distinction lies in the phrase *hardly conscious*.

Pound conceives of the troubadours as primarily interested in the expression of unanalyzed private experiences, whereas the Tuscans were concerned with the deliberate exploration, at once poetic and philosophical, of the psychological ramifications of experiences: "The art of the troubadours meets with philosophy at Bologna and a new era of lyric poetry is begun" (*SR* 101). These distinctions, and Pound's consequent tendency to emulate Tuscany, are precisely parallel to the distinctions that governed Pound's choice of Yeats over the Decadents as a creative model.

Emotion "instigates" poems that memorialize psychic adventures in the poetic cosmos mapped out above. The fruits of this instigation are first suggested in *The Spirit of Romance*, where Pound twice draws attention to what he considers Dante's exemplification of mystic ecstasy. Referring to *Paradiso* I.68–69, he says first, "Nowhere is the nature of the mystic ecstasy so well described [as] here: 'Gazing on her such I became within, as was Glaucus, tasting / of the grass that made him the sea-fellow of the other gods'" (p. 141). And later:

> The disciples of Whitman cry out concerning the "cosmic sense," but Whitman, with all his catalogues and flounderings, has never so perfectly expressed the perception of cosmic consciousness as does Dante in the canto just quoted:
>
> Qual si fe' Glauco nel gustar dell' erba
> Che il fe' consorto in mar degli altri dei.
>
> (p. 155)

An emotional experience of sufficient intensity is like an influx of force from the heavens or a channel of perception opened up between the microcosm and the macrocosm. For the poet, such moments constitute that "state when the feeling by its intensity surpasses our powers of bearing and we seem to stand aside and watch it surging across some thing or being with whom we are no longer identified" (*T* 18).

The energies unleashed in this process are eventually subsumed for Pound under the term *virtù*, defined in the introduction to his translations of Cavalcanti as "the potency, the efficient property of a substance or a person." According to alchemical philosophy, he says, "each thing or person was held to send forth magnetisms of certain effect":

> The heavens were, according to the Ptolemaic system, clear concentric spheres with the earth as their pivot . . . each one endowed with its *virtue*, its property for affecting man and destiny; in each its star, the sign visible to the wise and guiding them. A logical astrology, the star a sort of label of the spiritual force, an indicator of the position and movement of that spiritual current. Thus, 'her' presence, his Lady's, corresponds with the ascendancy of the star of that heaven which corresponds to her particular emanation or potency.

But a poem is built upon the poet's feelings about the Lady and clearly, in remarks like these, Pound is laying the groundwork for the expansion of personal feelings into a cosmos. That is, the Lady's particular emanation corresponds to a celestial emanation, but it comes to the poet as an emotion. This is the "interpretation of the cosmos by feeling" which Pound detects in Provençal poetry, and it means that the "moments" the poet deals with, again, represent a substantial connection with the divine.

So conceptual an analysis even of poetic theory may seem to conceal Pound's actual poetry in a cloud of abstraction. Quite the reverse, however: it enables us to see his early development as a single coherent process. Given what we have so far discussed, for example, it appears that the concerns of Pound's earliest work are abandoned in the poetry he wrote during what we may think of as his middle period (1913–1917) and that after this hiatus they reappear in the magnum opus: the references to particular poems in the earlier pages of this chapter suggest an arc from the early *Personae* to parallels in the *Cantos*. The urbane, hard-surfaced poetry of the middle years, satirical and aggressively modernistic, seems largely untouched by the concerns of the early work. Yet the basis of his poetry remains much the same, as his Vorticist theorizing clearly demonstrates. In 1914 he asserted a distinction that had been implicit in much of his earlier criticism: "There are two opposed ways of thinking of a man: firstly you may think of him as that toward which perception moves, as the toy of circumstance, as the plastic substance *receiving* impressions; secondly, you may think of him as directing a certain fluid force against circumstances, as *conceiving* instead of merely reflecting and observing" (*GB* 103). This is not a distinction between poetic and nonpoetic man, but between two kinds of poet. The first kind we have seen delineated in "Psychology and Troubadours"— the perceptive and relatively passive artist whose sensibility functions as a "charged surface." This conception of the poet is reflected in Pound's comment about his reluctance to claim credit for "Night Litany" and is best (or at any rate most obviously) exemplified in "Histrion," whose selfless narrator registers the appearance in himself of various alien personalities. Both of these suggest that the "conceptive poet" was for Pound a genuine and important development in his poetic theory, for his early work is indeed circumscribed by a notion of the poet as primarily receptive.

The two genres in which his earliest work was concentrated— the persona and the vision—both imply a receptive sensibility, and their workings are suggested in that earlier quotation having to do with the monkish and the chivalric paths toward the macrocosmos. The first mode, wherein the contemplative man develops a "secondary pole within himself, produces his charged surface which *registers* the beauties, celestial or otherwise, by 'contemplation,'" is essentially the process of the persona: the poet, contemplating a historical figure (as in "Piere Vidal Old") or a "mood" (as in "The Tree"), feels himself invaded by a flash of *nous*-like energy; this experience issues in a new form, a poem made by the poet, and the process of impersonation as a whole is the myth or the "nearest equation" for the poet's experience. The visionary poems are formed upon the same theoretical base, only taking the chivalric rather than the monkish path. The visions of which Pound writes center largely upon the idea of the Lady as source or cause, and instead of contemplating some idea of a hypothetical alien identity, the poet contemplates her charms—real or imagined—and again receives flashes of ethereal energy—in "Ballatetta," for example, "Lo, how the light doth melt us into song." At his most active, this receptive or perceptive poet merely keeps track of the delightful experiences which come to him under certain conditions.

These vision poems describe a continuum parallel to that on which Pound would place the Provençal and Tuscan poets. One vein of Provençal verse upon which Pound draws for themes is represented, in his own work, by poems like "Speech for Psyche" and parts of "Piere Vidal Old":

> Speech? Words? Faugh! Who talks of words and love?!
> Hot is such love and silent,
> Silent as fate is, and as strong until
> It faints in taking and in giving all.
>
> Stark, keen triumphant, till it plays at death.
> God! She was white then, splendid as some tomb
> High wrought of marble, and the panting breath
> Ceased utterly.

Both poems are concerned with the transcendent significance of intense physical pleasure—again, the theme of "A Virginal"—

and their most important model lies in the untranslated sections of the texts of Arnaut Daniel which Pound furnishes in *Translations*. This kind of poem is in a way the crudest manifestation of emotion as instigation; a more sophisticated version of the same kind of phenomena would be that line from Daniel about the lamplight.

Pound's more complex explorations of the exalting effects of love draw upon the Tuscans. The "refinements" that such a poet as Cavalcanti brought to the Provencal treatment of love and its effects are obvious enough in his "Chi è questa" and the ballata "Veggio ne gli occhi de la donna mia," part of which Pound translates as

> Light do I see within my Lady's eyes
> And loving spirits in its plenisphere
> Which bear in strange delight on my heart's care
> Till Joy's awakened from that sepulchre.
>
> . . . . .
>
> I seem to see a lady wonderful
> Forth issue from her lips, one whom no sense
> Can fully tell the mind of, and one whence
> Another fair, swift born, moves marvellous,
> From whom a star goes forth and speaketh thus:
> 'Lo, thy salvation is gone forth from thee!'[17]

In this kind of poem the imagery becomes a visual elucidation of a problem or experience in occult philosophy—the imagery of love poetry is fused with the imagery of religious mysticism. *Canzoni,* as we could perhaps guess from its title, is full of poems like this, in which Pound rehearses the fusion of troubadour love visions and Tuscan philosophizing—some bad, some good. "Ballatetta" is a preservation from this genre, Pound's own version of Cavalcanti's lady, it would seem:

> The light became her grace and dwelt among
> Blind eyes and shadows that are formed as men;
> Lo, how the light doth melt us into song:
>
> . . . . .
>
> In wild-wood never fawn nor fallow fareth
> So silent light; no gossamer is spun
> So delicate as she is, when the sun
> Drives the clear emeralds from the bended grasses
> Lest they should parch too swiftly, where she passes.

It seems, as I began by suggesting, that we must move from the e early poems to the *Cantos* in our pursuit of Pound's conceptual development, for the kind of event figured by the Lady does seem to disappear (except for brief appearances, as in "To Kalon" in *Lustra*) until those cantos where she reappears in the guise of Aphrodite, a symbol of captured beauty, the goddess (and "enduring constant") who moves the poet to such "perceptions" as

> there came new subtlety of eyes into my tent,
> whether of spirit or hypostasis,
>   but what the blindfold hides
> or at carneval
>   nor any pair showed anger
> Saw but the eyes and stance between the eyes,
> colour, diastasis,
>   careless or unaware it had not the
>   whole tent's room   (Canto LXXXI)

Granted the obvious tie with the early vision poems, what can all this have to do with poems like "Les Millwin"—a kind of imagistic satire on the audience at the Russian ballet—or "The

Game of Chess"—an imitation of an abstractionist painting of a chess board? The connection turns on Pound's distinction between the receptive and the conceptive poet. So long as the emotion that instigates the poet is restricted to love—in however many of its manifestations—the formal and thematic possibilities open to the poet are correspondingly limited. Pound's first step toward his idea of the conceptive poet was, as we have seen, to extend "love" into "emotion" as the moving force behind the poet's creation of forms—he was not far from this conception in his criticisms of Cavalcanti. Here as elsewhere in his development, his poetry outpaced his ability to formulate in critical terms what he was doing. For, whereas the abstract "The Return" appeared in 1912 (in *Ripostes*) and its decidedly nonamorous companion pieces began to appear shortly afterward, we do not find a coherent theoretical account until Pound's Vorticist propaganda of 1914 and 1915, much of which is a plea for a particular kind of nonrepresentational art and "plotless" poetry. In an important article in *The New Age*, he wrote:

> An organisation of forms expresses a confluence of forces. These forces may be the "love of God," the "life-force," emotions, passions, what you will. For example: if you clap a strong magnet beneath a plateful of iron filings, the energies of the magnet will proceed to organise form. It is only by applying a particular and suitable force that you can bring order and vitality and thence beauty into a plate of iron filings . . . The design in the magnetised iron filings expresses a confluence of energy. It is not "meaningless" or "inexpressive."
> ("Affirmations—II, Vorticism," *NA* XVI, 277)

The phrase "what you will" is important, because it reflects a competence for handling a much wider range of subject matter than Pound's earliest work encompassed. *Ingenium nobis ipsa puella fecit* is now only a specialized form of a far more general impulse: "energy creates pattern . . . I would say further that emotional force gives the image . . . Intense emotion causes pattern to arise in the mind—if the mind is strong enough."[18] One may seriously question whether Pound ever really believed that the instigating emotion was limited to love, but there are the companion questions of technical resources and the poet's conception of what is aesthetically possible. One fact we have: the contents of *Personae, Exultations, Canzoni,* and *Ripostes* are almost entirely comprised by the two genres of persona and love vision (a uniquely Poundian version of love vision). We cannot argue from what Pound did in practice to what he did not yet know about, of course. In fact we need infer no more from these collections than that, whether of necessity or by design, he oriented his early attempts toward the range of possibilities offered by a conception of love as the fostering impulse of poetry, toward the more tractable realm indicated by his reference to Ecclesiastes (in the letter to Williams)—his own inner experiences—before turning his attention to the more complicated issues presented by the world around him. Again, it is not a question of belief, but rather of the conceptions chosen as materials for poetry. The extension of love to emotion, then, may not represent a new thing learned.

The shift to the "conceptive poet" does. In *Gaudier-Brzeska* Pound explicitly separates "Heather" and "The Return" from the early personae as being different in kind, and as representing a new stage in his work. The change in terminology, from the "charged surface" that attracts energy from somewhere else and "registers" the envisioned beauty to the "strong magnet" that exerts energy of its own, is more than merely verbal. It is a change from the poet who receives "the vision unsought" to the poet who, like the nonrepresentational sculptor or painter, creates his own visions. One is tempted to read a conscious abandonment of the static electricity machine used as an analogy in "Psychology and Troubadours" into Pound's assertion in "As for Imagisme" that "the difference between man and a machine is that man can in some degree 'start his machinery going.' He can, within limits, not only record but create. At least he can move as a force; he can produce 'order-giving vibrations;' by which one may mean merely, he can departmentalise such part of the life-force as flowś through him" (*NA* XVI, 350). This is the poet who directs "a certain fluid force against circumstances," one who makes Images. He is still perhaps a receiver of, or a temporary receptacle for, the life force, but his role is much more active than the role of the receptive poet of the personae and visions. Between the inception of the poetry in *Ripostes* and the Vorticist essay in *Gaudier-Brzeska*, the conviction grew in Pound that the artist is actually the wielder of this ultimately celestial energy:

> The Image can be of two sorts. It can arise within the mind. It is then "subjective." External causes play upon the mind, perhaps; if so, they are drawn into the mind, fused, transmitted [transmuted?], and emerge in an Image unlike themselves. Secondly, the Image can be objective. Emotion seizing up some external scene or action carries it intact to the mind; and that vortex purges it of all save the essential or dominant or dramatic qualities, and it emerges like the external original.
>   In either case the Image is more than an idea. It is a vortex or cluster of fused ideas and is endowed with energy.   (*NA* XVI, 349)

Though Pound's first attempts at the kinds of poem suggested here can be detected in *Ripostes* (see "N.Y.," "Phasellus Ille," and "An Object"), the clearest examples appear in *Lustra*. We may follow Pound's hint and take as an image of the first kind "Heather," which "represents a state of consciousness, or 'implies,' or 'implicates' it":

> The black panther treads at my side,
> And above my fingers
> There float the petal-like flames.

> The milk-white girls
> Unbend from the holly-trees,
> And their snow-white leopard
> Watches to follow our trace.

Clearly the title is not descriptive—far from it: it establishes the fact that the speaker is not describing natural phenomena in a land where the leopards are white.[19] Whatever external causes played upon the mind to produce this image have indeed been "fused" to emerge in an image unlike themselves— again, the title is part of the poem's attempt *not* to refer to any objective event. The state of consciousness the poem implies is translatable only into the terms given (hence the value of this particular state of consciousness). Structurally the poem closely resembles "In a Station of the Metro," consisting as it does of a collocation of contrasting images and establishing a careful tension among its components: the deliberateness implicit in "treads," the floating flames, the almost formalistic deliberation of "The milk-white girls / Unbend from the holly-trees," and finally the ready poise implied in the watching leopard. The poem must be visualized; for one thing, the very slight difference between total suspension of activity and the near-suspension of action in the poem is crucial. Second, the poem attains a kind of resolution, moving from the blackness of the panther and the quivering flames, through the stately bending of the girls, whose whiteness contrasts with the holly trees but then parallels (quite arbitrarily, if one is looking for "plot") the "snow-white leopard," whose whiteness and static alertness complete the resolution.

Of the poem's objective source, again, we cannot speak; it has been transmuted into the images we see on the page, and our attention is directed to formal values only. The poem represents one kind of image. The other, the "objective" image, is exemplified by another poem from *Lustra*, "Les Millwin":

The little Millwins attend the Russian Ballet.
The mauve and greenish souls of the little Millwins
Were seen lying along the upper seats
Like so many unused boas.

The turbulent and undisciplined host of art students—
The rigorous deputation from "Slade"—
Was before them.

With arms exalted, with fore-arms
Crossed in great futuristic X's, the art students
Exulted, they beheld the splendours of *Cleopatra*.

And the little Millwins beheld these things;
With their large and anaemic eyes they looked out
    upon this configuration.

Let us therefore mention the fact,
For it seems to us worthy of record.

Kenner's excellent thumbnail elucidation of this poem is worth looking up. Claiming rightly that the poem is not a brickbat in a factional culture-quarrel, he adds, "The centre in relation to which the components of this poem are balanced . . . is to be looked for in the ironic impersonality that reduces the writer to a recorder of social contours more autonomously complex than any formulable attitude and locks into semi-comic relation scriptor, lector, Millwins, students, and ballerinas alike."[20] In other words, the poem is largely a comic picture, all the components of which contribute to the humor, and not a political cartoon with a victim to be laughed at by all right-minded readers. In it, an "external scene or action" is carried intact to the mind; "that vortex purges it of all save the essential or dominant or dramatic qualities, and it emerges like the external original."

Now there is a good deal of argument in these last two clauses and, indeed, an important fallacy in the wholehearted insistence on "objectivity" that Kenner's comment represents. The particular record we get of a given "social contour" depends entirely on who does the recording. The value judgments in the poem are too obvious to need comment here, and they are there precisely because the poem does fulfill Pound's definition of the objective image. The poem does not comment explicitly upon the various cultural phenomena to which it refers. It gains its impact from the juxtaposition of its components—but these are the residue of external scenes carried into the poet's mind and purged of all save what his sensibility interprets as the essential or dramatic qualities. It is wrong to assert that the poem is untainted by the attitudes of the poet—and Pound would be the first to complain that such an assertion deprives the poem of its importance. What gives the poem significance as an experience for its readers is the fact that it presents "circumstances" acted upon by the unique sensibility of a man with peculiar gifts of expression. In order to understand the kind of truth to which such poems aspire—it is rather more limited than what some of Pound's critics claim for him, as we see—we must adduce the principle of the *façon de voir*.

The poems we have been discussing, and the kinds they represent, constitute the "segregation of some component" of the Supreme Intelligence or, to use the earlier formulation, a "departmentalization" of the life force. We may take the very early poems as the extension of the poet's feelings into poetic statements about the divine order. The poems in *Lustra*—devoted to social commentary, humor, epigrammatic wit, the construction of nonrepresentational formal patterns—represent a similar extension of the poet's feelings into poetic statements about the physical and social world. The technique of juxtaposition displayed there precludes any rhetorical appeal to readers to accept the poet's interpretation as their own, but it does not, and is not intended to, conceal the fact that the defining center of the world of *Lustra* is the sensibility of Ezra Pound. This is a most important claim. The self-assertive voice of Pound is heard throughout every one of his collections. Each book of poems from *A Lume Spento* through *Lustra* presents a subjectively defined universe, an expansion of Pound's particular "real" into a cosmos.

The conceptual basis upon which "Heather" and "Les Millwin" are built is reflected, with some variation, throughout *Lustra*. Moreover, *Lustra* includes poems that date from early 1913 and poems that date almost from the eve of the first tentative gesture toward the *Cantos*. This implies that the great arc my earlier references described, from, say, *Canzoni* or *Ripostes* to the *Cantos*, was the creation of convenience and does not reflect any unaccountable shift, temporary and bizarre, during the years immediately prior to the *Cantos*. As for that magnificent climax of the development traced in this chapter, two remarks Pound made about Dante may suffice to indicate the significance of these conceptions. The first is the one in *The Spirit of Romance* where he describes the *Commedia* as "the journey of Dante's intelligence through the states of mind wherein dwell all sorts and conditions of men before death." Certainly this is as applicable to the *Cantos*—Pound's great subjective adventure through history—as it is to the *Divine Comedy*. More to the point, perhaps, is his description of Dante's dipping into a multitude of traditions and unifying them "by their connection with himself," a description eminently consonant with nearly everything described here. Three years after this letter, he was able to extend this perception concerning Dante into a principle of poetic theory: "Having discovered his own virtue the artist will be more likely to discern and allow for a peculiar *virtù* in others. The erection of the microcosmos consists in discriminating these other powers and in holding them in orderly arrangement about one's own" ("Osiris—VI, On Virtue," *NA*). The governing imagery of the *Cantos* suggests a similar conceptual basis: the radiant point of light, symbolic of the poet's divinely founded intelligence, now shedding "the light of a single ray upon innumerable objects," now "diffusing itself in every direction" in such a way that it produces "a sphere of light"[21]—a universe interpreted, made intelligible, by the governing intelligence of the poet. Complicated as they are, the *Cantos* are the culmination of forty years of thought and experiment whose coherence need not be questioned.

iv

The subjective religiosity and the Platonic orientation of Pound's aesthetics point to some ancillary discriminations. Many of the concepts we have just inspected have a striking Bergsonian coloration, and this fact has played no little part in raising the critical dust around the question of Pound and T. E. Hulme. That much of the discussion *is* dust seems true for a number of reasons. First, though Hulme was doubtless very useful to Pound in the articulation of certain tendencies, it should be clear that Pound was not a clean slate for anyone to write upon. Second, much of the literary thought credited to either Pound or Hulme (or, for that matter, Eliot or Ford Madox Ford) was the result of a corporate and communal endeavor (Hulme, after all, was but one of a group of very strong personalities). Third, there is Pound's own denial of Hulme's exclusive pre-eminence, in *The Townsman* of January 1939: if Pound is not telling the truth in those remarks, it would be the first time he ever *denied* a once-felt influence—few men have been more candid, not to say fanatic, about their admirations.

As Pound writes of him in *The Townsman*, Hulme was what we would expect him to have been—one of the things that was going on in London at the time—and his ideas are indeed clearly similar to Pound's. Pound's description of the artist as engaged in discrimination and demarcation finds its companion in Hulme's notes on "Bergson's Theory of Art," and so does the assertion that art lifts man into a zone of activity.[22] Pound's idea that our perceptions become habituated and require the new eyes of the artist to liberate them is like Hulme's assertion that "human perception gets crystallized out along certain lines . . . it has certain fixed habits, certain fixed ways of seeing things, and is so unable to see things as they are" (*Speculations* 146), but one must remember that this was a leading idea of Vorticism, in which Hulme was not involved and of which Pound was certainly not sole proprietor. It was also a leading idea among the Pre-Raphaelites (recall Hunt, for example), which must surely make it public domain.

So it is with other of Hulme's ideas, which on the basis of mere resemblance might well look like sources for Pound. In "A Lecture on Modern Poetry" Hulme says that modern poetry "has become definitely and finally introspective and deals with expression and communication of momentary phases in the poet's mind," and, in "Notes on Language and Style," that in the making of a poem "a transitory artificial impression is deliberately cultivated into an emotion and written about."[23] But with Rossetti, Yeats, Pater, and the Decadents in Pound's background, these statements cannot be in themselves the oracular utterance that opened Pound's eyes to modernism in literature. These ideas of Hulme's in part grow out of the same literary tradition as Pound's. Whatever Hulme's role in developing the slogans and the theoretical vocabulary of the new poetry, probably the most reliable assessment we can make of his effect on Pound would be to say that Pound found in him a sympathetic general outlook and the source of a critical dialectic in which he himself could participate.

We find a similar situation when we turn to the "Bergsonian coloration" in Pound's thought, of which Hulme was probably the supplier. Certainly all we have said about the poet's stance with respect to the flux of day-to-day experience is Bergsonian enough. Bergson's emphasis on mobility as the essence of the real parallels Pound's talk of the vital universe and his reading of troubadour poetry as an attempt to express a concern with "the whole and the flowing." The role of intuition for Bergson in dealing cognitively with this flux seems closely akin to the ideology of the persona—the poet meditating himself into an identity with some temporarily assumed consciousness and aiming at a contemplative unification of mind with object.[24] Furthermore Bergson defends intuitionism against the charge that it would reduce philosophy to the mere scrutiny of subjective trivialities by replying that "to talk this way . . . is to misconceive . . . the essentially active, I might almost say violent character of metaphysical intuition."[25] This is to say that intuition is deeply involved in the *energy* which is life—the "world of moving energies," no doubt, which Pound's kind of poetic cognition explores.

It is also possible to see Pound's feelings about the salient differences between poetic and nonpoetic cognition as Bergsonian. In his view of dogma as congealed experience and his hatred of it in poetry, Pound is defending immediate experience (intuitive, subjectively alive and sensuously real) against the abstract no-longer-alive, defending vision as against revision, a distinction much like Bergson's differentiation between intuition and concept. For Bergson, the concept is only a "symbol"—actually a sign—which generalizes and distorts the reality it seeks to express. It can deal only with the immobile, the fixed, the discontinuous. The concept is cut off from the living reality it seeks to embody; lifeless itself, it is akin to lifeless matter. Intuition, on the other hand, is "capable of following reality in all its sinuosities and of adopting the very movement of the inward life of things." This living flexibility, moreover, makes intuition the *only* mode of cognition which permits us "to affirm the existence of objects inferior and superior (though in a certain sense interior) to us, to make them co-exist together without difficulty, and to dissipate gradually the obscurities that analysis accumulates around these great problems" of knowledge[26]—the only mode of cognition, that is, which leads to the kind of departmentalization that the proper Poundian poet strives for.

For Pound the metaphor of congealing is apt. The prime duty of his poet is to catch experience on the wing, and the mythopoetic mentality is true to the evanescence of real experience. "The undeniable tradition of metamorphosis teaches us," he says in the essay on Dolmetsch, "that things do not remain always the same. They become other things by swift and unanalysable process" (*LE* 431). Dogma attempts to lie about this, to pretend that what was real at one unrepeatable moment can be real forever. In short, the immediate experience congeals into a concept.

Behind this parallel lie two others. To *impose* dogma is to do violence to human uniqueness, for not all people are constructed alike. This fact extends, for Pound, even into cognitive realms; the shape of an idea depends on the modality of the mind receiving it. This is so for Bergson, for whom each thing and each organism changes from moment to moment because each moment of existence includes all preceding moments, so that even when two people agree on some conclusion, they do so for different reasons: "Each must solve problems from within, on his own account."[27] And finally, because of these apparently crucial differences between individual cognitions, there is the problem of communication, of shared experience. Our best hope is not conceptual discourse, for obvious reasons, but (for Bergson the best of a bad lot, for Pound and Hulme the precisely adequate sign) the *image*. Images are only approximative for Bergson, but the image has "at least this advantage, that it keeps us in the concrete," and besides, "many diverse images, borrowed from very different orders of things, may . . . direct consciousness to the precise point where there is a certain intuition to be seized."[28] Both ideas obviously harmonize with the modality of Pound's mind—the last clause is reminiscent of his remarks about suggestiveness and his use of allusion in the poems discussed earlier. Much later, in the first chapter of *ABC of Reading*, there is a remarkable parallel to these remarks of Bergson's. Explaining the superiority of the cognitive mode of the Chinese ideogram over the abstracting tendency of Western thought, Pound says, "In Europe, if you ask a man to define anything, his definition always moves away from the simple things that he knows perfectly well, it recedes into an unknown region, that is a region of remoter and progressively remoter abstraction . . . if you ask him what red is, he says it is a 'colour.' If you ask him what a colour is, he tells you it is a vibration or a refraction of light."[29] The Chinese ideogram, on the other hand, "is based on something everyone KNOWS." The concept *red* is embodied in an ideogram that brings together "the abbreviated pictures" of "rose," "cherry," "iron rust," and "flamingo"—a cluster of images that interact to bring the mind to a recognition of the concept to be grasped.

These interesting similarities could be more comfortably accounted for if Pound had not, in that *Townsman* article, described Hulme's London "evenings" as being so "diluted with crap like Bergson" that "it became necessary to use another evening a week if one wanted to discuss our own experiments or other current minor events in verse writing."[30] Similarly, in "Cavalcanti" he describes Hulme as "trying to be a philosopher" and "fussing about Sorel and Bergson." In an attempt to account for "influence," these remarks are hard to come to terms with—especially when we find Pound writing to his mother in 1911 that "Hulme is giving rather good lectures on Bergson" (*YL* 232). Pound owns up to any number of unfashionable once-influential forces in his poetic history, and in his well-known letter to René Taupin (*L* 216) he gives Hulme himself all the credit one could wish; it would be inexplicable if he should falsely deny Bergson.

The possibility of a solution lies in the fact that many of the similarities between Pound and Bergson are points of contact between Pound and other writers as well, particularly Pater and that whole strain of nineteenth-century thought in which Pound shares. Of reality as flux, Pater (not to mention Heraclitus) wrote long before Bergson (in an essay on Coleridge in 1866):

> Modern thought is distinguished from ancient by its cultivation of the "relative spirit" in place of the "abso-

lute" [Compare Hulme: "Philosophers no longer believe in absolute truth. We no longer believe in perfection . . . we frankly acknowledge the relative"—*Further Specula-tions*, 71] . . . Those sciences of observation reveal types of life evanescing into each other by inexpressible refinements of change . . . The faculty for truth is recognised as a power of distinguishing and fixing delicate and fugitive detail.[31]

So with the subjectivism that sees a fact as shaped by the mind which entertains it: Pater writes in the "Essay on Style" that literary art "like all art which is any way imitative or reproductive of fact—form, or colour, or incident—is the representation of such fact as connected with soul, of a specific personality, in its preferences, its volition and power," and "Such is the matter of imaginative . . . literature—this transcript, not of mere fact, but of fact in its infinite variety, as modified by human preference in all its infinitely varied forms."

In dealing with these aspects of Pound's thought, in fine, we may be dealing with a constellation, not necessarily of influences in any simple sense, but of congenial pre-existent crystallizations of his own thought, and of support for approaches basically his own. That Pater and the Decadents on the one hand and Bergson and Hulme on the other should overlap is no real surprise, for the two basic figures, Pater and Bergson, are both deeply indebted to common areas of nineteenth-century theory—specifically to German romanticism, especially Schelling and Novalis.[32] These basic "forces" come together when Pater, in the conclusion to his *Renaissance*, makes that earlier-quoted remark about the revivifying power of art and precedes it with a plainly Bergsonian quotation from Novalis: *Philosophiren ist dephlegmatisiren, vivificiren.* For Pater, as for Bergson and Novalis, the alert and attuned thinker is in touch with the revivifying life force—and so is Pound's artist.

Again, the dynamism of the metaphysics of both men is Schelling-like in its conception of the ultimately real as Becoming. Lovejoy points out that Schelling "repeatedly insists, in phrases sometimes almost identical with Bergson's, that we must cease to think of reality as made up of *things*, must understand that it in essence consists of *doings*."[33] He goes on to depict, accurately, the "characteristic God" of the German romantics as "the *ewiges, lebendiges Tun* which Goethe so often glorifies." A similar conception of the ultimately real as a power that realizes itself in the constant unfolding of its activities is behind both Pater's and Bergson's notions of what kind of real world men confront—the main difference being between Pater's melancholy about its mutability and Bergson's militant celebration of its dynamism. More important, both conceptions are congenial to Pound—and he himself has more than temperamental affinities with the German romantics. In the long essay on Cavalcanti, for example, he makes a distinction between the idealizing tendency in Cavalcanti (a descendant of the same tendency in the troubadours) and the "Greek aesthetic," which "would seem to consist wholly in plastic, or in plastic moving toward coitus" (*LE* 150), just as he also centers the "whole break of Provence" with the Hellenic world on the distinction between "the fine thing held in the mind" and the "inferior thing ready for instant consumption." In "Psychology and Troubadours" he makes a similar distinction with respect to Rome: "I suggest that the living conditions of Provence gave the necessary restraint, produced the tension sufficient for the results [the mystical experiences he ascribes to Provençal poetry], a tension unattainable under, let us say, the living conditions of imperial Rome" (*SR* 97). These very sentiments are described by Lovejoy as a platitude of German romanticism, and the dualistic turn of mind they reveal is equally central to German romantic thought: "Upon one characteristic of [the romantic spirit] there was . . . general agreement among the German Romanticists: the habit of mind introduced by Christianity was distinguished by a certain insatiability; it aimed at infinite objectives and was incapable of lasting satisfaction with any goods actually reached."[34]

All of these remarks—especially the references to dualism—point to the thought of Plotinus as the probable middle term holding this constellation of values together for Pound. Plotinus' *nous* is like Bergson's Reality—"an organic living community of interpenetrating beings"—and both are like Pater's fluid universe of fleeting combinations and dissolutions, even if Pater does come to his by way of the dismal discoveries of science. Bergson's intuition is like Plotinus' mystical unions (see *Enneads* VI.9.10–11), just as the strong dualistic current in his treatment of the *élan vital* and his whole idea of the Real as a kind of striving-to-perfect are fundamentally neo-Platonic. That is, those aspects of both these writers' work (and of German romanticism) which are most relevant to Pound go back to Plotinus. Pater, of course, has no system, only a series of more or less useful observations; Bergson had a system, but Pound quite definitely did not like it. Plotinus, on the other hand, presents a system embodying the useful aspects of Pater and Bergson—a system, furthermore, which has found an attractive and significant expressive outlet in genuine works of art.

It is certainly true that some of Bergson's ideas formed part of the ambiance of Pound's formative years—but it is as stubbornly true that Pound did not like Bergson's thought as a whole, if we are to judge by Pound's own words. On the other hand, to say that Pater, or something one might wish vaguely to term the Decadent precedent, was more important is an exaggeration (though Pater's *Greek Studies* makes very interesting reading with respect to Pound's ideas on myth). Whatever confirmation Pound may or may not have found in Bergson, the temperamental set that could have made Bergson's presence acceptable to him was probably founded in Pound's reading in the neo-Platonic philosophers of Renaissance Italy. This is made fairly clear by the whole approach to "Donna mi prega" in Pound's Cavalcanti essay in *Literary Essays,* and close to indubitable by the introduction to the Cavalcanti section of the *Translations.* No doubt this same cluster of Renaissance writers is behind his peculiar handling of Provençal poetry in "Psychology and Troubadours." We know he liked this sort of thought (his prose works are peppered with the writers' names—Gemisto, Iamblichus, Ficino, and the like), and that he even thought of writing a book about it. The tone of his remark in *The New Age* about the "exhilarating hotch-potch" of Renaissance mysticism suggests the presence of a genuinely exciting pantheon of neo-Platonists, compared with whom Bergson might well seem tiresome and marginal.

III

A Language To Use
and a Language
To Think In

"It's fang-de-seeaycle *that does it my dear, and education, and reading French."*

—John Davidson, *Earl Lavender*

WE HAVE LOOKED at Pound's early attempt to articulate for himself what poetry is all about, or at any rate what his own poetry would be all about. There remains the concomitant process of working out a language with which to express these discoveries and convictions. Pound himself, in retrospect, was aware of it as a process, and a necessary one. Of his 1910 translations of Cavalcanti, he wrote that "I did *not* see Guido at all . . . What obfuscated me was not the Italian but the crust of dead English, the sediment present in my own available vocabulary." He goes on:

> You can't go round this sort of thing. It takes six or eight years to get educated in one's art, and another ten to get rid of that education.
>
> Neither can anyone learn English, one can only learn a series of Englishes. Rossetti made his own language. I hadn't in 1910 made a language, I don't mean a language to use, but even a language to think in.
>
> ("Cavalcanti," *LE* 193–194)

He became aware very early just what form this process had taken for him. "The artist's inheritance from other artists," he observed ruefully in 1913, "can be little more than certain enthusiasms, which usually spoil his first work." There is an uncomfortable degree of truth in that remark, and Pound knew it. But this inheritance also yields "a definite knowledge of the modes of expression, which knowledge contributes to perfecting his more mature performance" ("Troubadours—Their

119

Sorts and Conditions," *LE* 102). A survey of his earliest books reveals a fairly natural swinging of the pendulum between spoiling and education.

i

There is certainly no doubt that the language Pound had at his disposal at the outset of his career was not his own—was even less so, in fact, than when he was working on the Cavalcanti translations only four or five years later. The apparently undiscourageable experimentalism of his first collections assumes in *A Lume Spento* a nineteenth-century English orientation. And judging by this first book, Pound's problem with style was the same as his problem with "identity": just as in his earlier work he could deal with experiences in a satisfactory manner mainly by assuming the mask of an identity other than his own, so in his first collection he can speak in a satisfactory voice only by the wholesale adoption of someone else's verbal manner. This, at any rate, seems to be what happens in *A Lume Spento*. This diffuse and baldly experimental volume moves between two poles—on the one hand, style and the problem of sound (the construction, more or less, of a viable poetic diction); on the other, style and the problem of meaning. The first problem doubtless accounts for the wholesale borrowings that mark *A Lume Spento*.

We have already glanced at Pound's stylistic emulation of Browning and have remarked upon the closeness of what can only be described as imitations in poems like "Cino" and "Marvoil." Parts of "Fifine Answers" and "Famam Librosque Cano" resemble Browning's work even more closely. Here Pound's long, tortuous sentences, issuing in a series of floating clauses connected only obscurely with any grammatical subject, are characteristic of Browning, and so are the semantic exigencies that apparently necessitate this obscurity of syntax: most often the detached and interjected clauses and phrases are modifications of the main clause, imitative of a speaker's groping for a difficult but important shade of meaning: "That, spite your carping, still the thing is done / With some deep sanction, that, we know not how, / Sans thought gives us this feeling" ("Fifine Answers"), or

> Such an one as the world feels
> A sort of curse against its guzzling
> And its age-lasting wallow for red greed
> And yet, full speed
> Though it should run for its own getting,
> Will turn aside to sneer at
> 'Cause he hath
> No coin . . .
> Such an one . . .   ("Famam Librosque Cano")

The effect of such syntax is to hold what is to be the full meaning of the sentence in suspension, so that—and this is characteristic of Browning's sentences—the particular relevance of each part to the whole does not become apparent until the end. The lines from "Famam Librosque Cano" do just that. The initial adjectives and the adjective clauses beginning "Such an one" open a series of preliminary descriptions that lead to no main clause until, some seventeen lines later, we arrive at "Loquitur."

Again, when the lady loves in "Cino" are trying to seem detached ("'Cino?' 'Oh, eh, Cino Polnesi / The singer is't you mean?'"), they echo any one of a dozen of Browning's dramatic monologues—close enough to genuine colloquialism to be called "realistic" and yet mannered to fit both the metrical needs and the temporal setting of the poem.

There is little point in amassing textual parallels, for what is involved is the adoption of the entire manner of another poet. Clearly the pull of Browning on Pound was very great—there is the title of "Mesmerism," for example, and Pound's description of Browning's attraction in the remark "At least *I've* caught the disease." There is also the opening of Canto III, half uneasy, half impatient, like a declaration of independence:

> Hang it all, Robert Browning,
>   there can be but one "Sordello."
> But Sordello, and my Sordello?
> Lo Sordels si fo di Mantovana.

It may have cost Pound considerable effort, as these things imply, to get out from under the thumb of Browning but, as we have seen, Pound's own poetics made the escape inevitable. The very closeness of his Browningesque poems to their models bespeaks a kind of influence which no poet can find profitable save as a starting point, an admired and for a while closely studied set of instructions for new creation. In following Browning, the young Pound learned mainly that voice as such—and the voice as a whole remained part of his verbal equipment—but beyond that, its contribution to Pound's own language has been largely confined to the controlled, often ironic, prosiness of the verse of the *Lustra* period—where, of course, it is thoroughly diluted by the influence of Walt Whitman:

> How many will come after me
>   singing as well as I sing, none better;
>   Telling the heart of their truth
>   as I have taught them to tell it;
> Fruit of my seed,
>   O my unnameable children.
>
> ("Dum Capitolium Scandet")

But if the influence of Browning cannot importantly account for the form of a "dramatic monologue" like "Plotinus," it can account even less for the language of a poem like "Anima Sola." There are many such poems in Pound's early work, poems that have nothing to do, linguistically or thematically, with anything in Browning. These are the overdressed poems like "Anima Sola," and "In Morte De" in *A Lume Spento*:

> O wine-sweet ghost, how are we borne apart
> Of winds that restless blow we know not where
> As little shadows smoke-wraith-sudden start
> If music break the freighted dream of air;
> So fragile curledst thou in my dream-wracked heart,
> So, sudden summoned dost thou leave it bare.

Far more than they are marked by dependence on Browning, these poems are marked by a kind of naive aestheticism: a tendency to depend on the bizarrerie of the opalescent word, precious aural patterns, quasi-Symbolist images of vague import, and the atmospheric effects of images of flame, "saphirs," and symbolical winds. We can see in Pound's use of this kind of style a search for delicacy and subtle suggestiveness—for a language whose discriminations are suitable to the delicate thematic discriminations with which Pound's early work was to be concerned. This need for the suggestive and the mildly gorgeous was a strong guard against any total captivation by Browning and, as an aid to its attainment, Pound turned to Swinburne—who, of all the poets alluded to in *A Lume Spento*, wins the most extensive praise—sometimes in the same extreme way in which he appealed to Browning:

> Lord God of heaven that with mercy dight
> Th' alternate prayer-wheel of the night and light
> Eternal hath to thee, and in whose sight
> Our days as rain drops in the sea surge fall,
>
> As bright white drops upon a leaden sea
> Grant so my songs to this grey folk may be:

> As drops that dream and gleam and falling catch the sun,
>
> . . . . .
>
> So, bold My Songs, seek ye such death as this.
>
> ("Grace before Song," *ALS*)

The "bright white drops" that dream and gleam are aural kin to Swinburne's days and hours "That sleep not neither weep they as they go" and to the vowel play in such phrases as "long leaves cover me" and "That sleep were sealed upon me with a seal," in "Laus Veneris." There is, in fact, a close parallel to Pound's poem—Swinburne's "Envoi":

> Fly white butterflies, out to sea
> Frail pale wings for the winds to try,
> Small white wings that we scarce can see,
>   Fly.

One can pick parallel passages almost at random. Swinburne's "Threnody," for example, uses "vowel music" and rhythmic patterns similar to some of the acoustical effects in *A Lume Spento*:

> Suns that sink on the wan sea's brink, and moons
>   that kindle and flame and fade,
> Leave more clear for the darkness here the stars that
>   set not and see not shade
> Rise and rise on the lowlier skies by rule of sunlight
>   and moonlight swayed.

Compare, from "Anima Sola":

> The blood of light is God's delight
> And I am the life blood's ward.

O Loneliness, O Loneliness
Thou boon of the fire blown . . .

and the same poem's "viol-strings that out-sing kings." Reminiscent of Swinburne's "hard" style—"Though all things feast in the spring's guest-chamber, / How hast thou heart to be glad thereof yet?" ("Itylus")—the jaw-testing sounds in "For E. McC.":

Thou trusted'st in thyself and met the blade
'Thout mask or gauntlet, and art laid
As memorable broken blades that be
Kept as bold trophies of old pageantry.

But such imitations do not constitute the only way in which Swinburne was useful to the building of Pound's own language. *A Lume Spento* is burdened with a good deal of factitious archaism, much of which results from Pound's way of constructing similes, his tendency to introduce them with "as" and his apparently deliberate clogging of their rhythm:

But came fate murmuring as undersong

. . . . .

And died as faint wind melody
Beneath our gates.   ("Li Bel Chasteus")

Blown of the winds whose goal is "No-man-knows"
As feathered seeds upon the wind are borne
To kiss as winds kiss and to melt as snows.
                    ("The False Dawn and the True")

Swinburne's "Ballad of Death"—which Pound singled out for special praise in his review of the Gosse *Life* of Swinburne—

abounds in such things:

> Even she between whose lips the kiss became
> As fire and frankincense;
> Whose hair was as gold raiment on a king,
> Whose eyes were as the morning purged with flame.
> Whose eyelids as sweet savor issuing thence.

The archaic (but also usefully compact) adverbs like the *whereby*'s of "Salve O Pontifex!" and in phrases like "Though sight of hell and heaven were price thereof" (in "Scriptor Ignotus") and "the wind thereof is my body" (in "De Aegypto") stem from the same research. They all find counterparts not only in "A Ballad of Death" but in "Laus Veneris," "Phaedra," and any number of Swinburne's poems.

In some of the lines I have quoted from Pound's early poetry, the phrasing seems curiously arbitrary—in "the wandering of many roads," for example, from "Praise of Ysolt," and the line "Of such his splendour as their compass is" from "Grace before Song." Occasionally this odd phrasing is a means of subduing a recalcitrant thought or sentence to the iambic swing. But most often it seems merely to reflect a young poet's idea of properly poetic discourse: "and fast / My pulses run, knowing thy thought hath passed / That beareth thee as doth the wind a rose." What the practice amounts to is manipulating word order in the service of aural effects—even at the expense of clear expression—and as such it seems a direct enough reflection of what Pound admired in Swinburne: an emphasis upon the surface musical qualities of language. Certainly there is no scarcity of such manipulations of phrasing in Swinburne's verse ("If any glad thing be or any good," for example, from "Ballad of Death").

The metrics of *A Lume Spento*—for that matter, of all of Pound's work to date—evince a fourth characteristic which seems to stem from his emulation of Swinburne, a characteristic more definite and more important, a specific and permanent acquisition. Pound displays, in his later work especially but in the early verse too, a striking muscularity of line; he is a subtle metrist, but in his maturer verse the reader is never in doubt as to the tempo of a given line, and this is particularly true of his slower lines. When he wants a verse read slowly and pondered, he sees to it that the reader will read slowly and ponder. This involves principally an implication of emotional weight by rhythmic means—primarily the adept manipulation of spondees or, in the absence of genuine spondees, the immediate juxtaposition of two or more primary stresses—in Canto XLV, for example: "With usura hath nó mán a house of góod stóne." The technique is foreshadowed in some of the poems written at the time of *Ripostes*: "As you move among the bright trees . . . Make a clear sound," and "ah, see the tentative / Movements, and the slow feet." In *A Lume Spento* we find it in "La Fraisne," in "Vana," and in the chantlike "Threnos." As for its historical model, the device is characteristic of Swinburne's verse. We find it again and again in "A Ballad of Death":

> With the fair kiss, and lips much lovelier
> Than lips of amorous roses in late spring
>
> . . . . .
>
> Sweet still, but now not red,
> Was the shut mouth, whereby men lived and died.
> And sweet, but emptied of the blood's blue shade.

Pound's final assessment of Swinburne was that his major importance lay in his insistence on the autonomy of poetry at a time when, according to Pound, the art was regarded chiefly as a vehicle for pretty thoughts. He came eventually—soon, judging by how early Swinburne drops out of sight as an influence on Pound's style—to recognize Swinburne's more strictly aesthetic strengths and weaknesses, and his remarks about him in the review of the Gosse *Life* are apt criticism of those poems of his own where Swinburne's influence is most strongly felt: "Swinburne recognized poetry as an art, and as an art of verbal music . . . There is a lack of intellect in his work . . . He neglected the value of words as words, and was intent on their value as sound . . . Unusual and gorgeous words attracted him." The same review helps to explain his attractiveness for Pound:

> Moderns more awake to the value of language will read him with increasing annoyance, but I think few men who read him before their faculty for literary criticism is awakened—the faculty for purely literary discrimination as contrasted with melopoeic discrimination—will escape the enthusiasm of his emotions, some of which were indubitably real.
>
> ("Swinburne vs. His Biographers," *LE* 292–294)

Pound sounds worst when most Swinburnian, but Swinburne was still an important force in Pound's development, no matter how temporary. The extravagances of phraseology and diction, and Pound's naive tendency to imitate Swinburne as he imitated Browning, are faults, but they spring from the same impulse that later led to "absolute rhythm" and the use of foreign tags in the *Cantos*—the impulse toward ever more precise delineation of emotional perceptions. For Pound the lesson of Swinburne was that there is a tangible beauty in controlled linguistic arrangements per se: "the conception of poetry as a 'pure art,'" he said in "A Retrospect," revived with Swinburne. And if Swinburne neglected the significance of words as units of meaning, neglected the "Technique of Content," his very vagueness made him in some ways more useful to Pound's stylistic education than Browning. Browning, committed so much to narrative values (Pound remarked in his review of

Prufrock and Other Observations that Browning's intensity was sometimes diluted by "ratiocination" and "purely intellectual comment"), is forced to write in an apparently less flexible style, a style imitated by Swinburne with damaging ease in *Seven Against Sense;* whereas Swinburne's language, devoted not to facts but to feeling and emotion, could be correspondingly suggestive and necessarily approximate instead of discursive and definite. What remained for Pound was to learn how to connect pleasing sounds with felt emotions, to use them in their proper place in a total expressive medium rather than to depend on their isolated magic. And here again the work of Yeats came to his aid.

ii

Confronted by a poem like "Laudantes Decem Pulchritudinis Johannae Templi" in *Exultations,* with its naked appeal to the language of Yeats ("The unappeasable loveliness is calling to me out of the wind"), one tends to conclude that in his development of a language Pound made the same wholesale use of Yeats that he made of Browning. But "Laudantes Decem" is fortunately one of only a small group of poems in which he does this. Yeats was, in fact, a treasury of very particularized stylistic tools for Pound, more particularized than his Swinburnisms, and more significant. Though "Laudantes Decem" and its fellows make a somewhat abstracted use of a single stylistic effect—do, in fact, closely imitate Yeats—the poems in which Pound appeals to Yeats's work generally take us closer to the matter of style and meaning.

For better or worse, Pound was not destined to reproduce the stylistic qualities of Yeats any more than he was to duplicate Browning. One reason for this is apparent in *A Lume Spento:* even at this early date he strives to create a particular rhythm and sometimes a particular diction for each occasion. We have seen examples of this already: the choked intensity of the speaker in "La Fraisne"—

> By the still pool of Mar-non-otha
> Have I found me a bride
> That was a dog-wood tree some syne.
> She hath called me from mine old ways
> She hath hushed my rancour of council,
> Bidding me praise
> Naught but the wind that flutters in the leaves

the raucous bounce of "Mesmerism"—

> Aye you're a man that! ye old mesmerizer
> Tyin' your meanin' in seventy swadelin's,
> One must be a hang'd early riser
> To catch you at worm turning. Holy Odd's bodykins!

the ballad rhythms from Villon in the two "Villonauds"—

> Drink ye a skoal for the gallows tree!
> François and Margot and thee and me,
> Drink we the comrade merrily
> That said us, "Till then" for the gallows tree!

Yeats's metrical effects about this time are designedly less spectacular; he is not without variety, but his rhythms are deliberately muffled and more nearly uniform in their effect. In "The Symbolism of Poetry," written about 1900, he speaks of how "we would cast out of serious poetry those energetic rhythms, as of a man running," in favor of "those wavering, meditative, organic rhythms, which are the embodiment of the imagination, which . . . only wishes to gaze upon some reality, some beauty." He writes as a man expressing the perceptions and inventions of a moody, "Celtic" imagination, writing evocative poetry, the language of which must be also evocative, subtle, suggestive; Pound explores the emotional possibilities of concrete sensibilities different from his own. Without implying that he was by any means the better poet, an approximation to the sensibility implied by, say, *The Wind among the Reeds* or *In the Seven Woods* is but one of several personae he explored in *A Lume Spento;* it is, however, an important dimension of the collection, one that grows considerably in scope in Pound's next two books, and we can see him striving for Yeatsian effects in several of the poems in this first volume.

"La Fraisne," for example, almost openly avows its connection with Yeats:

> For I was a gaunt, grave councillor
> Being in all things wise, and very old,
> But I have put aside this folly and the cold
> That old age weareth for a cloak
>
> . . . . .
>
> For I know that the wailing and bitterness are a folly.
> And I? I have put aside all folly and all grief.

Yeats's "In the Seven Woods" has:

> I have heard the pigeons of the Seven Woods
> Make their faint thunder, and the garden bees
> Hum in the lime-tree flowers; and put away
> The unavailing outcries and the old bitterness
> That empty the heart.

The thematic parallel is fairly obvious. Yeats's poem involves a tentative identification with a certain kind of nature, in flight from "new commonness / Upon the throne and crying about the streets / And hanging its paper flowers from post to post"— what Pound refers to in "La Fraisne" as "the old barren ways of men." As currently printed (in the 1926 and 1949 *Personae*), Pound's poem seems simply to delineate the madness of an old man who has fled to wild nature to escape the pangs of a cruelly thwarted love—it is this as much as Yeats's poem is about a man who finds relief from the world in the hum of bees. For the moment let us leave it at that. Granted this superficial thematic parallel, there are other lines in "La Fraisne" where we can see Pound trying on the style of Yeats—in imagery, in verbal effects, and in particular actions described:

> I have curled mid the boles of the ash wood,
> I have hidden my face where the oak
> Spread his leaves over me, and the yoke
> Of the old ways of men have I cast aside.

There are at least two lines that an unwary reader might take for Yeats and not Pound at all: "I wrapped my tears in an ellum leaf / And left them under a stone."

The ambiguity in the movement of Yeats's verse is partly caused by his characteristic manipulation of run-on lines so as to produce simultaneously a feeling of enjambment and of pause. The uses of the device are at least two. The end of a line is a natural position of emphasis, and Yeats sometimes compromises syntax and line structure in order to use that emphasis without having to interrupt the movement of his phrases by end stopping. In those lines from "In the Seven Woods," for example, we have

> I have heard the pigeons of the Seven Woods
> Make their faint thunder, and the garden bees
> Hum in the lime-tree flowers.

A less skillful poet—the Pound of *A Lume Spento*, perhaps—might have more pointedly qualified *bees* so as to stress their participation in a private mythical world with the pigeons. But to have "garden bees" hum lends concreteness and immediacy to the speaker's experience (keeping him out, say, of the smoky world of Pound's "Anima Sola"), while the line structure sufficiently establishes the connection between the bees and the pigeons as elements of the Seven Woods. The device is a subtle one, but real. Enjambment usually overrides and therefore temporarily subordinates line endings in favor of other interests; but Yeats's enjambments, almost everywhere in his verse, seem to call attention to the line endings. In unrhymed poems, such as "In the Seven Woods," the technique furnishes the emphasis usually caused by the kind of rhyme that indicates connections between the rhymed words.

Pound uses the device in "La Fraisne" (where the peculiarity of line structure is more obviously self-imposed than in the example from Yeats—there is no metrical or syntactical necessity for the lines' ending where they do):

> Being in all things wise, and very old,
> But I have put aside this folly and the cold
> That old age weareth for a cloak.

The rhyme here places additional emphasis upon the already ambiguous nature of an ostensible run-on line ending. The first connection of *cold* is accomplished by means of rhyme. The other connection is established of course by the syntax, but also by the placement of *cold* and *cloak* in successive line-ending positions; this serves to underscore the relationship between the two words and stresses the mild paradox of the statement.

An important variant of this combined manipulation of syntax and run-on line endings is the momentary suspension of syntactic implication at the ends of lines, which creates within a sentence a meaning different from or supplementary to that of the whole statement. In "No Second Troy" Yeats asks,

> Why should I blame her that she filled my days
> With misery or that she should of late
> Have taught to ignorant men most violent ways [?]

The first line states a certain thought, but after *days* the tenor of the utterance is quite reversed. In spite of the reversal, both implications of *she filled my days* make themselves felt, the pleasanter meaning by means of the structure of the line, the other through the "real" syntax of the complete statement. Again, this is a technique and not an accident: consider the semantic effect of altering the word order of these lines to something like "Why should I blame her for the misery that filled my days?"

The same device is responsible for the impudent humor beneath the surface of "He Remembers Forgotten Beauty":

> When my arms wrap you round I press
> My heart upon the loveliness
> That has long faded from the world:
>
> . . . . .
>
> The roses that of old time were
> Woven by ladies in their hair . . .

The interruption of syntactical functioning implied by the structure of the first line, subtle as it is, sets the tone of the whole poem. One is led to expect the object of *press* to be the lady, or at least some attribute of hers. Such, alas, is not the case; the rather aesthetical and very subjective egotism of the narrator (which is to exclude, for the next seventeen lines, any reference whatsoever to the lady being embraced and presumably praised) directs all attention to the part of him that is being pressed. The effect of the next line is more obvious: he presses his heart upon the loveliness not of the present lady but upon that "long faded from the world," the loveliness, dim and poetical, of ladies of the distant past, of whom the poet thinks while embracing the lady of the poem.

The other two lines of the quotation function similarly to those from "In the Seven Woods" in producing a meaning supplementary to that of the entire syntactical unit. Here the rhyme-enforced suspension at *were* draws attention to the line as a statement in itself: "The roses that of old time were" emphasizes the present (and romantic) nonexistence of the roses and to some extent remind us of what the speaker should, but does not, have his mind on.

Pound, too, uses this kind of verbal peripeteia. In "Na Audiart" the speaker warns the lady that she may be reincarnated

> in a form
> That hath no perfect limning, when the warm
> Youth dew is cold
> Upon thy hands.

The exceedingly arbitrary line ending at *warm* marks the point of reversal. The effect, of course, is to note the present warmth of Lady Audiart's touch and to emphasize the distasteful change to *cold*; and this term is itself emphasized by the interruption of the sentence at the end of the second line. A similar emphasis is gained by this means a few lines later, as the speaker continues his description of how it will be when the lady's soul "Finds the earth as bitter / As now seems it sweet."

Its very obviousness makes this example perhaps less telling than the last passage we shall examine from this poem. The poet offers

> Just a word in thy praise, girl,
> Just for the swirl
> Thy satins make upon the stair . . .

What happens at *swirl* is quite literally a moment of suspension. Syntactically and metrically the second and third lines form an enjambment, yet *swirl* almost demands, if not a pause, then some measure of elongation. One effect is a rhythmic imitation of the implied emotion: the rhythm hovers over *swirl* as if the speaker's emotion hovered there also. This in turn causes the meaning of the word to play backward upon *girl* as well as ahead (in keeping with the real syntax) to *satins*, an effect intensified first by the rhyme and then by the fact that there is no immediate indication that the word is to be attached to anything but *girl*.

Not all instances of Pound's emphasizing the key words of an ostensible enjambment perform so meaningful a function. In "La Fraisne," the device is mainly a gesture toward a kind of realism; he breaks up his sentences to represent the barely coherent outbursts of a man driven mad. And though the rhythmic "image" created in *swirl* in "Na Audiart" is eminently successful, some attempts at similar effects seem naive. Occasionally this habit creates the wrong kind of ambiguity, as in "Aux Belles de Londres":

> I am aweary with your smiles and your laughter,
> And the sun and the winds again
> Reclaim their booty and the heart o' me.

On the other hand, given Pound's soon-to-develop interest in *vers libre* and absolute rhythm, we are not amiss in taking his use of this device as groundwork for those later techniques. The iambic orientation of the early collections is not completely concealed by the abundance of experiment, and for a poet trying to escape the iambic straitjacket—Pound promptly made attempts—the making of such things as line structure operatively relevant to subject matter, the emulation of Yeats's more flexible rhythms in general, and this device of syntactic suspension in particular would seem to offer good starting points.

Earlier I suggested a contrast between the meaningful rhythms of "Na Audiart" and the druidic snake dance of "Anima Sola." The same preoccupation with surface verbal effects for their own sake which underlies Pound's early emulation of Swinburne seems to have led to early experiments with Yeats's "hieratic chant."[1] "Anima Sola" is one of the most blatantly—and unsuccessfully—incantatory poems in *A Lume Spento*. Its reflection of Yeats lies not so much in its rhythms as in its general strategy:

> My music is weird and untamèd
> Barbarous, wild, extreme
> I fly on the note that ye hear not
> On the chord that ye can not dream.

The preponderantly short rhythmic units (the intervals between strong primary stresses) and the short lines give a certain ritual monotony to the movement, and the shifts from short to longer rhythmic sweeps are Yeatsian enough. These effects buttress—maybe too much—the gorgeous otherworldly imagery with which the poem is laden. The whole poem is "overwrought"; a druidic tone is intended, but the effect could be gained with a little less incense.

> My music is your disharmony
>
> . . . . .
>
> For the clang of a thousand cymbals
> Where the Sphinx smiles o'er the sand,
>   And viol strains that out-sing kings
> Are the least of my command.
> Exquisite, alone, untrammeled
> I kiss the nameless sign
> And the laws of my inmost being
>   Chant to the nameless shrine

Yeats did similar things, but generally with more interesting rhythms (and with far less suggestion of the boy poet disdaining the world), notably in "He Bids His Beloved Be at Peace":

> I hear the Shadowy Horses, their long manes a-shake,
> Their hoofs heavy with tumult, their eyes glimmering
>   white;
> The North unfolds above them clinging, creeping night,
> The East her hidden joy before the morning break,
> The West weeps in pale dew and sighs passing away,
> The South is pouring down roses of crimson fire.

It is, perhaps, a technique in which "disaster on disaster follows thick," but it is one way to lend concreteness to preternatural visions. "Into the Twilight" centers upon the same impulse as Pound's poem—with stronger rhythms than "He Bids His Beloved" and less clotted imagery:

> Out-worn heart, in a time out-worn,
> Come clear of the nets of wrong and right;
> Laugh, heart, again in the grey twilight,
> Sigh, heart, again in the dew of the morn.
>
>   . . . . .
>
> Come, heart, where hill is heaped upon hill:
> For there the mystical brotherhood
> Of sun and moon and hollow and wood
> And river and stream work out their will;
>
> And God stands winding His lonely horn,
> And time and the world are ever in flight;
> And love is less kind than the grey twilight,
> And hope is less dear than the dew of the morn.

There is a closer relationship between this poem and "Anima Sola" than their mere sharing in the use of "out-worn," as Yeats's (originally Blake's) "nets of wrong and right" become in Pound's poem "your out-worn harmonies" that are "behind me." As in Yeats's poem, anything connected with the daylight world is inferior to the poet's special world, and the poet's concrete realities are superior to the world's nets of conventional abstraction:

> I die in the tears of the morning,
>   I kiss the wail of the dead.
> My joy is the wind of heaven,
>   My drink is the gall of night,
> My love is the light of meteors;
>   The autumn leaves in flight.
>
> . . . . .
>
> For I am a weird untamèd
> That eat of no man's meat
> My house is the rain that ye wail against
> My drink is the wine of sleet.

There is a difference in stance, of course, and this may be partly responsible for the superiority of Yeats's poem. Yeats pursues a method of presentation such as Pound was soon to desiderate in his critical writing, while Pound, in this one case at any rate, falls back upon "this embroidery of language, this talk about the matter, rather than presentation" ("How to Read," *LE* 29), which he criticized in Elizabethan poetry. Yeats assumes his mask and allows the reader to witness his dance; Pound constructs his mask before the reader's eyes and bullyrags him about its spiritual profundity as he does it. Though to pile effect on effect makes for a kind of intensity, it is a factitious intensity when, as here, the technician is unskillful. Interestingly enough, it is an eminently Pre-Raphaelite technique, with its two aspects of exoticism and suggestiveness. The first has been described in a comment which, with only slight alteration, could be applied to the early work of both Pound and Yeats: "With Rossetti's group, and still more with its disciples, we find from time to time a reliance on exotic, antique, mystical accessories, which are used with an unjustified confidence that their mere presence in the picture or poem will give it high artistic value." What T. E. Welby here complains of is merely a gesture toward the symbolism that Yeats was to develop more rigorously, traces of which Pound also employs in these early poems.

The same critic adumbrates the second aspect of the technique when he describes Rossetti's work as "a poetry without relief," a characteristic arising "from his refusal to admit into his House of Life anything which has not an intimate association. He will not allow himself or the reader the relief of indifferent things in that House which is a reliquary."[2] "Intimate association" is akin to "the continuous indefinable symbolism" that Yeats designated in "The Symbolism of Poetry" as "the substance of all style." As for "the relief of indifferent things," we may question whether any artist allows it; the quality the phrase is intended to fix is the sustained suggestiveness of Rossetti's manner of presentation. He is rarely content to "make his picture" without some implication that more is there than could possibly meet the eye. The exotic accessories comprise not only images of romantic things, but imagery generally dim and ghostly, druidic rhythms, exotic or archaic diction, and often the sudden, arcanic focusing of emotional importance at seemingly arbitrary points. A similar technique invaded the Rhymers' Club: the compeers of Yeats's youth wrote poems with imagery delicate and fleeting if not dim and ghostly, rhythms subtle and suggestive, a tone of somnolent pathos, around themes concerning "this poor hour of ease" or the "Love that in life was not to be our part." Pound does it also in "Salve O Pontifex!" and, with a different purpose, in the "flame and wane" and "saphir sea" of "The Decadence":

> Tarnished we! Tarnished! Wastrels all!
> And yet the art goes on, goes on.
> Broken our strength, yea as crushed reeds we fall,
> And yet the art, the *art* goes on.
>
> Bearers of beauty flame and wane,
> The sunset shadow and the rose's bloom.
> The saphir seas grow dull to shine again
> As new day glistens in the old day's room.

The very aim of such techniques, of course, is exactly "absence of relief," and its rationale is easily comprehended. Yeats's early interest in a poetry of evocation—"The Symbolism of Poetry" is entirely a plea for just this—is shared by Pound. In *The Spirit of Romance* Pound several times approaches a position at least similar to Yeats's, though somewhat less systematically committed. We have seen his suggestion that "most moving poetry" calls upon the reader for "a completion of the detail, a fulfillment or crystallization of beauty implied." Again, praising Guinicelli's "preciseness of definition," he remarks, "In more sophisticated poetry an epithet would suffice, the picture would be suggested." *The Spirit of Romance* is the work of a poet not wholly formed, and we should not be surprised when we find in it sometimes divergent directions. The two sentences just quoted do not seem to harmonize with the assertion in the same book that "No poem can have as much force as the simplest narration of the events themselves." Nor does the conglomeration of many "devices" for the sake of suggestiveness seem to conform to the spartan conception of poetry as "a sort of inspired mathematics, which gives us equations . . . for the human emotions" (*SR* 105, 218, 14). But, in the first place, "If one have a mind which inclines to magic rather than to science, one will prefer to speak of these equations as spells or incantations."

Second, though "The true poet is most easily distinguished from the false, when he trusts himself to the simplest expression, and when he writes without adjectives" (*SR* 208), "simplest expression" has to be taken as relative to what is expressed. Cavalcanti and Petrarch both use metaphor, but only Guido uses the simplest expression: "In Guido the 'figure,' the strong metaphoric or 'picturesque' expression is there . . . to convey or to interpret a definite meaning. In Petrarch it is ornament, the prettiest ornament he could find, but not an irreplaceable ornament" ("Cavalcanti," *LE* 154).

"Ornament," in Pound's judgment, is any device, any component of a poem, which does not pull its weight in terms of expression and which seems to be inserted merely for the sake of, or at the excuse of, poetical prettiness—"embroidery of language, this talk about the matter, rather than presentation" ("How To Read," *LE* 29). It leads to Pope's Buskin style:

> Apply thine engine to the spongy door,
> Set *Bacchus* from his glassy prison free,
> And strip white *Ceres* of her nut-brown coat.

None of this is intended to excuse a handful of not very good poems but to suggest that, if Pound had not yet learned to bring the sun's lance to "rest on the precise spot verbally,"[3] the impulse was nonetheless there. The incantatory poems I have mentioned do not, in fact, suffer from ornament in the sense defined; on the contrary, their various components function only too well, and the poems lose their effect by having too much effect—by being too "rhetorical" and attempting to persuade the reader that the mask of the moment is both real and wondrous. The result, in "Anima Sola" and kindred poems, often borders on the absurd.

All the merely suasive poems—"Anima Sola," "Salve O Pontifex!", "Plotinus," "Prometheus," and "Redivivus"—were excised from Pound's collections after 1910. The issue these poems raise is clearly enunciated in Pound's propaganda for Imagism and in his assertion, in the memoir "Harold Monro," that "a presented image" is "the perfectly adequate expression or exposition of *any* urge, whatsoever its nature" (*PE* 13). He wrote to Iris Barry in 1916 that "the whole art is divided into"

 a. concision, or style . . .
 b. the actual necessity for creating or constructing something; of presenting an image, or enough images of concrete things arranged to stir the reader.

He adds that the poet can also "make simple emotional statements of fact, such as 'I am tired,'" but that "there must be more, predominantly more, objects than statements and conclusions, which latter are purely optional, not essential, often superfluous and therefore bad" (*L* 90–91). It is not the business of the poet to inform readers of his state of internal health, nor for that matter to bore them with overdressed statements of how it is to be a poet.

 Pound is most apt to fall into the cymbal-clashing style when he writes of the Poet—as distinct from the occasions when he writes *as* a poet and simply communicates his visions without editorializing. The hopefully magian poems in *A Lume Spento* have companion pieces in *Personae* and *Exultations*—it is as if during this time (1905–1909) Pound could not approach the subject without donning his pointy hat and his mystical plaques. One exception among the very early poems is "To the Dawn: Defiance" in *A Lume Spento*; it expresses its rather shaky confidence (which has to be reinforced by italics in the last line) not quite in terms of a vision, but in terms of wholly visual metaphors. The images are definite and concrete, and even though they border on preciosity they are precise enough to convey a real meaning:

> Ye blood-red spears-men of the dawn's array
> That drive my dusk-clad knights of dream away.
> Hold! For I will not yield.
>
> My moated soul shall dream in your despite
> A refuge for the vanquished hosts of night
> That *can* not yield.

But until 1910 nearly all these poems about the poet violate one of Pound's—originally Yeats's—prime rules: the priority of the particular and concrete over the general and abstract. The poems are "yatter about," not presentation of, the poet's nature. Pound's most efficacious approximations to Yeats's tone almost always occur in poems involving visions, or particular visitations conveyed with at least something of the definiteness he found in the Tuscan poets, and one of the principal advances of the poems immediately after *A Lume Spento* lies in their greater tangibility of presentation.

Despite the crudity of its early manifestations, vestiges of this Rossettian-Yeatsian-magian manner recur in Pound's later work, though he comes to depend less upon outré imagery, more and more upon rhythm and upon a much more adroit appeal to strange diction and word order. One of the first things to go, in fact, when Pound accomplished his first important change in style (between 1910 and 1912), was the excessive and false archaism that gives "Anima Sola" and related poems so much of their quasi-mystic tone.

Even before that change, Pound had refined the incantatory style into something more restrained and less mawkish than its earlier forms. But this merely means that the final result, even of the developments after 1910, was a refinement and not an elimination: the early poems are false starts, not early irrelevancies or wrong orientations. *Ripostes*—the very volume that announced the Imagists—preserves in some of its poems both the magian and archaic strains which get so out of hand in *A Lume Spento*, but uses them with much greater control. "The Alchemist," a "Chant for the Transmutation of Metals," is thoroughly hieratic with none of the awkwardness of "Anima Sola":

> Elain, Tireis, Alcmena
> 'Mid the silver rustling of wheat,
> Agradiva, Anhes, Ardenca,
> From the plum-coloured lake, in stillness,
> From the molten dyes of the water
> Bring the burnished nature of fire;
> Briseis, Lianor, Loica,
>
> . . . . .
>
> By the bright flame of the fishing torch
> Remember this fire.
> Midonz, with the gold of the sun, the leaf of the
> poplar, by the light of the amber,

"Phasellus Ille" is knowingly mannered. Flatness of tone is played off against inflated sentence structure, which in turn is played off against Pound's particular style of insult:

> This *papier-mâché*, which you see, my friends,
> Saith 'twas the worthiest of editors.
> Its mind was made up in "the seventies,"
> Nor hath it ever since changed that concoction.
> It works to represent that school of thought
> Which brought the hair-cloth chair to such perfection,
> Nor will the horrid threats of Bernard Shaw
> Shake up the stagnant pool of its convictions.

But "A Virginal" uses this archaic-magian style straightforwardly—and again successfully—to invoke an atmosphere in
which its own emotions can have some human meaning:

> No, no! Go from me. I have left her lately.
> I will not spoil my sheath with lesser brightness,
> For my surrounding air hath a new lightness;
> Slight are her arms, yet they have bound me straitly
> And left me cloaked as with a gauze of aether;
> As with sweet leaves; as with subtle clearness.
> Oh, I have picked up magic in her nearness
> To sheathe me half in half the things that sheathe her.

The most impressive example of how the apparently naive
style of "Plotinus," "De Aegypto," and even "Anima Sola"
developed surprisingly soon into a beautifully controlled expressive language is "The Flame," in *Canzoni* (1911), which
succeeds almost exactly where the others fail, in the manipulation of tone. It must be quoted in full:

> 'Tis not a game that plays at mates and mating,
> Provence knew;
> 'Tis not a game of barter, lands and houses,
> Provence knew.
> We who are wise beyond your dream of wisdom,
> Drink our immortal moments; we "pass through."
> We have gone forth beyond your bonds and borders,
> Provence knew;
> And all the tales of Oisin say but this:
> That man doth pass the net of days and hours.
> Where time is shrivelled down to time's seed corn
> We of the Ever-living, in that light
> Meet through our veils and whisper, and of love.

O smoke and shadow of a darkling world,
These, and the rest, and all the rest we knew.

'Tis not a game that plays at mates and mating,
'Tis not a game of barter, lands and houses,
'Tis not "of days and nights" and troubling years,
Of cheeks grown sunken and glad hair gone gray;
There *is* the subtler music, the clear light
Where time burns back about th' eternal embers.
We are not shut from all the thousand heavens:
Lo, there are many gods whom we have seen,
Folk of unearthly fashion, places splendid,
Bulwarks of beryl and of chrysophrase.

Sapphire Benacus, in thy mists and thee
Nature herself's turned metaphysical,
Who can look on that blue and not believe?

Thou hooded opal, thou eternal pearl,
O thou dark secret with a shimmering floor,
Through all thy various mood I know thee mine;

If I have merged my soul, or utterly
Am solved and bound in, through aught here on earth,
There canst thou find me, O thou anxious thou,
Who call'st about my gates for some lost me;
I say my soul flowed back, became translucent.
Search not my lips, O Love, let go my hands,
This thing that moves as man is no more mortal.
If thou hast seen my shade sans character,
If thou hast seen that mirror of all moments,
That glass to all things that o'ershadow it,
Call not that mirror me, for I have slipped
Your grasp, I have eluded.

The poem offers interesting evidence of the improvement Pound's technique had undergone by 1910 or 1911. The theme is like that of "Anima Sola," but, first of all, the tone is much less bluntly hortatory—partly because the metaphors of "The Flame" are both less exotic and more concrete than those in "Anima Sola." The "net of days and hours" is the precise metaphor of which Pound wrote in "Cavalcanti," not an affective bizarrerie like "the blood of light." The "subtler music" and the "clear light" depart from metaphor altogether in being but designations of things perceived—compare, from "Anima Sola," the "gale of an unknown chord" and the spectacular but ineffective "My love is the light of meteors." The "places splendid" and "bulwarks of beryl and of chrysophrase" are concrete visions; they have no correspondingly definite counterpart in either "Anima Sola" or "Salve O Pontifex!" And whereas the net of days and hours *means* something, we would be hard put to describe in just what respect the love of "Anima Sola" is to be identified with the light of meteors. The speaker in "The Flame," of course, has a more definite conception of what he is talking about than the persona of "Anima Sola" has. Like the earlier poem, "The Flame" has its suasive section. But the poet does not stop with the claim that "We are not shut from all the thousand heavens": he demonstrates his claim by entering into one of them, and the images leading up to the end of the poem do so exactly and meaningfully—in "I say my soul flowed back, became translucent," "my shade sans character," and the iterative crescendo of the image of the mirror—so that when we reach the lines "for I have slipped / Your grasp, I have eluded," the question of any affront to credibility never arises.

As for rhythmic superiority, the greater congruence with its subject matter of "Thou hooded opal, thou eternal pearl," as compared to the dogtrot of "Thou cup of the God-man's own," is suggestive. Where "Anima Sola" whisks us off on a rhythmically homogeneous witch's ride, "The Flame" unfolds before us, in its metrical subtleties, a process. The poem begins in an unexcited, meditative rhythm, and as the speaker counts the blessings of his calling he is finally caught up in a kind of contemplative ecstasy, a spiritual union with the object of contemplation which is foreshadowed in the two lines in which the poet first addresses that object: "O smoke and shadow of a darkling world, / These, and the rest, and all the rest we knew." And when the speaker is caught up, when his nominal personality becomes one with the flame, the rhythm—and the tone—of the first part of the poem completely disappear: "O thou dark secret with a shimmering floor, / Through all thy various mood I know thee mine." The rhythm changes again in the last eight lines, so as to present, simultaneously with their descriptive function, a reinforcement of the change in tone, culminating with splendid effectiveness in the foreshortened final line. If a certain Yeatsian orientation makes itself felt in the poem, we need not carp: this is a feat of rhythmic definition of which Yeats himself could have been proud.

iii

We have seen that these early poems are the beginning of a fairly unified attempt to lay open to the imagination a world beyond everyday and that Pound was very close to Yeats in this endeavor. But if the impulse and some of the technique reflect an admiration of Yeats, why are the poems so much more cluttered than their models with "devices"? For the answer to this we must look again to Rossetti, for the intrusion of his name into a discussion of the aggressively magian poems is symptomatic. Completely aside from his feelings about the world beyond, Rossetti was the purveyor in English of a poetry that Pound felt was very definitely a matter of visions—Dante's *Vita Nuova* and the various poets translated in *The Early Italian Poets*. Rossetti's are the translations most often quoted in *The Spirit of Romance*, and it was Rossetti whom Pound described as "my father and my mother" in the matter of translating Cavalcanti and in his knowledge of Tuscan poetry (introduction to "Cavalcanti Poems," *T* 20). In "Guido's Relations," he admitted that "my early versions of Guido are bogged in Dante Gabriele and Algernon" (*LE* 194). As for Rossetti's work with Dante, Pound says in the same essay that when he began his own Italian translations he saw that Rossetti was "sent" to translate the *Vita Nuova*. What he found upon inspecting Rossetti's rendering of Cavalcanti were poems like this:

> O thou that often hast within thine eyes
>> A love who holds three shafts,—know thou from me
>> That this my sonnet would commend to thee
> (Come from afar) a soul heavy in sighs,
> Which even by Love's sharp arrows wounded lies.
>> Twice did the Syrian archer shoot, and he
>> Now bends his bow the third time, cunningly,
>
>>>>> . . . . .
>
>> The first gives pleasure, yet disquieteth;
> And with the second is the longing for
>> The mighty gladness by the third fulfill'd.[4]

And in *The Spirit of Romance* Pound quotes at length from the mannered prose and verse of Rossetti's version of the *Vita Nuova*:

> Then I, beholding them, said within myself: "These pilgrims seem to be come from very far; and I think they can not have heard speak of this lady, or known anything concerning her". . . . And when the last of them had gone by me, I bethought me to write a sonnet . . .

> Ye pilgrim folk, advancing pensively
>> As if in thought of distant things, I pray,
>> Is your own land indeed so far away—
> As by your aspect it would seem to be—

That this our heavy sorrow leaves you free
    Though passing through the mournful town mid-way;
    Like unto men that understand to-day
Nothing at all of her great misery?

. . . . .

It is her Beatrice that she hath lost;
Of whom the least word spoken holds such grace
    That men weep hearing it, and have no choice.

(II, 92–93)

Now with this one group let us juxtapose a nearly successful
poem from *A Lume Spento* and its Yeatsian model:

I stood still and was a tree amid the wood,
Knowing the truth of things unseen before;
Of Daphne and the laurel bow
And that god-feasting couple old
That grew elm-oak amid the wold.
'Twas not until the gods had been
Kindly entreated, and been brought within
Unto the hearth of their heart's home
That they might do this wonder thing;
Nathless I have been a tree amid the wood
And many a new thing understood
That was rank folly to my head before.

Pound's tree is a shoot from Yeats's "He Thinks of His Past
Greatness":

I have drunk ale from the Country of the Young
And weep because I know all things now:
I have been a hazel tree and they hung

> The Pilot Star and the Crooked Plough
> Among my leaves in times out of mind:
> I became a rush that horses tread:
> I became a man, a hater of the wind,
> Knowing one, out of all things, alone, that his head
> Would not lie on the breast or his lips on the hair
> Of the woman that he loves, until he dies;
> Although the rushes and the fowl of the air
> Cry of his love with their pitiful cries.[5]

We may note two things: Pound, in spite of his successful emulation of Yeats's liquid metric, has lost Yeats's concreteness and
particularity—of the two, only Yeats's tree has leaves. Pound's
poem is a general statement of an event, which claims (twice)
a phenomenon it does not demonstrate, a characteristic of a
number of his early poems. Second, though compared to "Anima
Sola" the language of "The Tree" approaches beatific simplicity,
its manneredness from the sixth line to the end closely parallels
the angularity of the English that Rossetti used to render the
"mannered Italian" (Pound's phrase) of the *Vita Nuova*. Here
as elsewhere we find Yeatsian pretensions diluted at least in
part by the language of Rossetti and Swinburne—"The Tree"
could almost have been written by Yeats trying to write like
someone else. The reflections of Yeats in "La Fraisne" are
similarly elbowed out of the way by the thicker archaisms and
obstructed rhythms of Rossetti's translation style. And if "Anima
Sola" and "Salve O Pontifex!" suggest a Yeatsian strategy
gone wrong, they go wrong in the direction of the Pre-Raphaelites. Similarly, "Praise of Ysolt" begins somewhat as a rework-
ing of Yeats's "The Everlasting Voices":

> In vain have I striven to teach my heart to bow;
> In vain have I said to him
> "There be many singers greater than thou."

But his answer cometh, as winds and as lutany,
As a vague crying upon the night
That leaveth me no rest, saying ever,
    "Song, a song."

But before long the voice of Rossetti breaks in again:

Lo, I am worn with travail
And the wandering of many roads hath made my eyes
As dark red circles filled with dust,
Yet there is a trembling upon me in the twilight.

The image of the reddened eyes is from the *Vita Nuova* by way of Rossetti: "Mine eyes . . . wept until they are circled now by Love / With a red circle in sign of Martyrdom" (Rossetti, II, 91).

Now it is certainly true that Rossetti is much present in Pound's versions of Cavalcanti:

And airs grown calm when white the dawn appeareth
And white snow falling where no wind is bent,
Brook-marge and mead where every flower flareth,
And gold and silver and azure and ornament:
                       ("Sonetto XVIII," *T* 61)

If these lines look toward the greater originality of "The Seafarer," they also look back to the Pre-Raphaelite manner. And much later, in "Dance Figure" from *Lustra* (1916), we can see vestiges of Pound's early admiration for Rossetti:

Gilt turquoise and silver are in the place of thy rest.
A brown robe, with threads of gold woven in
    patterns, hast thou gathered about thee,

The gesture presented by these three lines has been filtered through the nineties, but it is primarily Rossetti's. For that matter, in the same volume with the sturdily non-Rossettian, non-Yeatsian "Seafarer" we find "Apparuit," one of Pound's most successful attempts in Rossetti's manner:

> Golden rose the house, in the portal I saw
> thee, a marvel, carven in subtle stuff, a
> portent. Life died down in the lamp and flickered,
> caught at the wonder.
> . . . . .
>
> Swift at courage thou in the shell of gold, cast-
> ing a-loose the cloak of the body, camest
> straight, then shone thine oriel and the stunned light
> faded about thee.
>
> Half the graven shoulder, the throat aflash with
> strands of light inwoven about it, loveli-
> est of all things, frail alabaster, ah me!
> swift in departing.
>
> Clothed in goldish weft, delicately perfect,
> gone as wind! The cloth of the magical hands!
> Thou a slight thing, thou in access of cunning
> dar'dst to assume this?

The resemblance to Dante's confrontation with Beatrice in *Paradiso* XXX is of course not accidental. In the *Vita Nuova*, Dante's "animate spirit" says at the first meeting with Beatrice, *Apparuit jam beatitudo vestra* (Rossetti, II, 31), and touches of both scenes play round the edges of Pound's poem. The general form has little to do with Rossetti, and the language is Pound's, but certain aspects of the mode of presentation resemble Rossetti's work: the beginning *in medias res*, the emphasis on visual phenomena and color, and the fleeting but well-remembered detail:

> . . . the roses bend where
> thou afar, moving in the glamorous sun,
> drinkst in life of the earth, of the air, the tissue
> golden about thee.
>
> . . . . .
>
> Half the graven shoulder, the throat aflash with
> strands of light inwoven about it . . .

This poem, along with "The Tree," "La Fraisne," and the others we have been considering, suggests how Pound was seizing upon the possibilities offered by Rossetti and Yeats. In fact the fleeting but well-remembered detail is an important component in Pound's pursuit of suggestiveness and heightened awareness. In one remark of Pound's we can see him translating a technical device into an ideological concern: in an early essay on poetic theory he wrote that "The artist seeks out the luminous detail and presents it. He does not comment."[6] In the present context "luminous detail" is an image which assumes strong emotional weight for the paradoxical reason that its choice as an object of special attention seems arbitrary. Coleridge used the device for some good dramatic effects (the light of the setting sun, for example, shining through the stalks of flax in "Fears in Solitude"), but rarely if ever built whole poems around it. Rossetti did, and so, to an even greater extent, does Pound. Just as the scenes depicted in Rossetti's paintings and poems and in Pound's verse are striking momentary details from an implied sequence of actions, so these images are emotionalized details within the scene. We have seen one example in Rossetti's "Dawn on the Night-Journey," in the moth which quivers in silence. Here the detail is an intensely perceived particular that functions in the poem as a kind of minuscule

exemplum of what the speaker is feeling. In "The Lady's La-
ment" Rossetti simply juxtaposes an emotionally charged image
to a statement of mood:

> Never happy any more!
> Aye, turn the saying o'er and o'er,
> It says but what it said before,
> And heart and life are just as sore.
> The wet leaves blow aslant the floor
> In the rain through the open door.

Both of these examples are very close to the "superpository"
technique of Pound's later haiku poems, in which a definitive
image is superposed upon the described experience.

This definitive image occurs in Pound's "Apparuit" as a
cluster of emotionalized details imitative of the speaker's
feverish attempt to express the total beauty of his vision. Of
his lovely, mysterious Lady, he has seen "Half the graven shoul-
der, the throat aflash with / strands of light." Sometimes the
pregnant detail is an attempt to fix precisely some subtle or
complex emotion; in such cases its finickiness gives his poems
the mannered air he found in the Tuscans and Provençals.
Psyche, in "Speech for Psyche in the Golden Book of Apuleius,"
says of Cupid that "as the petals of flowers in falling / Waver
and seem not drawn to earth, so he / Seemed over me to hover,"
and in "Erat Hora" the woman departs "as the ray of sun on
hanging flowers / Fades when the wind hath lifted them aside."

A different use of the charged detail appears in Rossetti—
one which accounts to a large extent for the spectral (and often
melodramatic) suggestiveness of his work. In the paintings we
may point to the sword which thrusts dramatically athwart the
diagonal formed by Lancelot's arm in "Lancelot in the Queen's
Chamber," or, as we have remarked, Hamlet's arm in "Hamlet
and Ophelia," or again, the sword in the center of composition
in "How They Met Themselves." In the poem "The Bride's

Prelude," a description of Aloyse includes the observation that "Her arms were laid along her lap / With the hands open." In none of these is it the disguised or compressed narrative device it is in the preceding examples, but a purely sensory one whose emotional implication has no logical or paraphraseable signification. So in Pound's dramatic lyric "Cino," the emotionally charged details are distinctly Rossettian:

> I have sung women in three cities.
> But it is all one.
> I will sing of the sun.
> ... eh? ... they mostly had grey eyes,
>
> . . . . .
>
> I will sing of the white birds
> In the blue waters of heaven,
> The clouds that are spray to its sea.

Again, in the early version of "De Aegypto":

> I have beheld the Lady of Life,
>
> . . . . .
>
> Green and gray is her raiment,
> Trailing along the wind.

(Here not only the device but the particular image is traceable to Rossetti: the garb of the Lady of Life is taken from his story "Hand and Soul."[7]) "Camaraderie" is also a cluster of these charged details.

We are not to ask, of course, what the precise significance of green and gray raiment is, or why the color of the eyes of Cino's ladies should be important. The purpose of the device is to suggest an intense, nearly overpowering perception, less to define any clear-cut emotion than to imply (and stir in the reader) some strong but indefinite feeling, the very inarticulability of which is calculated to heighten its intensity. (This makes it very handy for, among other things, atmospherics, and the charged detail is most prominent in those of Rossetti's poems where atmosphere is most important—it is pervasive, for example, in "The Bride's Prelude.") In Pound's "Piere Vidal Old" we are told that on the night Piere first enjoyed the love of La Loba, "God! but the purple of the sky was deep!" And Piere recalls that "Green was her mantle, close, and wrought / Of some thin silk stuff that's scarce stuff at all." The speaker of "Francesca" similarly fixes upon a physical detail that seems to serve as a focal point for an otherwise inexpressible emotion: "You came in out of the night," he says, "And there were flowers in your hands." Again, the speaker of "The House of Splendour" finds it inexpressibly significant that when he saw his Lady in the sun, "Her hair was spread about, a sheaf of wings, / And red the sunlight was, behind it all." The implications here are similar to those in another poem of Rossetti's, "The Woodspurge," where in a moment of intense "perfect grief" there has been burned upon the speaker's memory the, at first glance, meaningless perception that "the woodspurge has a cup of three."

This last example may serve to remind us that Pound's impacted details are often of a more obvious relevance to the situation at hand than Rossetti's are, but there is a more important difference, suggested by Rossetti's "Sudden Light" on the one hand and Pound's "Satiemus" on the other. In "Sudden Light" the effect of the details upon the speaker is partly explained. They surprise him into remembrance:

> You have been mine before,—
> How long ago I may not know:
> But just when at that swallow's soar
> Your neck turned so,
> Some veil did fall,—I knew it all of yore.

The feeling thus triggered by the lady's neck leads into a reflection that banishes the concrete emotional starting point:

> Has this been thus before?
> And shall not thus time's eddying flight
> Still with our lives our love restore
> And day and night yield one delight once more?

Rossetti is not interested in the quality of the lady's neck, but in the *dejà vu* and what it may mean. The corresponding images in "Satiemus" are clearly part of, perhaps emblems of, the speaker's delight.

> What if I know thy speeches word by word?
>
> . . . . .
>
> And all the time thou sayest them o'er I said,
> "Lo, one there was who bent her fair bright head,
> Sighing as thou dost through the golden speech."
>
> . . . . .
>
> What if my thoughts were turned in their mid reach
> Whispering among them, "The fair dead
> Must know such moments, thinking on the grass;
> On how white dogwoods murmured overhead
> In the bright glad days!"

The latter part of the poem is not a conceptualization but an extension of the pleasure of the original scene. Rossetti, in a way familiar enough in English poetry, tends to use either the scene or the image to spring an emotional moment that overflows into reflection or reminiscence. Pound, on the other hand, tends to rest upon the emotional suggestiveness of the perception itself, or at most attempts to express the emotion purely in terms of the perception—as in the early "Ballatetta":

> The light became her grace and dwelt among
> Blind eyes and shadows that are formed as men;
> Lo, how the light doth melt us into song :

In general, if Pound's charged details are less often instigations to general statements than Rossetti's, they are also less symbolically nonarticulate. It is important to remember in this connection that the earliest of Pound's poems considered here were written only about six years before the "founding" of Imagism. More and more as his work develops, Pound comes to concentrate upon the visual perception, moving closer and closer to the formulation of that "presented image . . . the perfectly adequate expression of *any* urge, whatsoever its

---

Rossetti, "Paolo and Francesca"
The Tate Gallery, London

Blown of the winds whose goal is "No-man-knows"
As feathered seeds upon the wind are borne,
To kiss as winds kiss and to melt as snows
         . . . . .
An hour to each! We greet. The hour flows
         . . . . .
Weaving the Perfect Picture
("That Pass between the False Dawn and the True")

"The roots of the Image—'that which presents an intellectual and emotional complex in an instant of time'" (p. 162).

nature." With the charged detail as the repository of concentrated emotion, Pound was already close to the roots of the Image—"that which presents an intellectual and emotional complex in an instant of time" ("A Retrospect," *LE* 4).

In both his poetry and his visual art Rossetti's interests are directed toward these concentrations of significant energies, but again we have an important distinction embedded in an apparent similarity. In poems like "Camaraderie," "The Tree," "Donzella Beata," and "That Pass Between the False Dawn and the True," Pound is at the beginning of his development toward the ability both to fix brief moments of significant experience and to weave numbers of them into a coherent structure. Rossetti, using such a Dantescan technique often better than Pound uses it, is in an analogous position in such poems as "The Blessed Damozel" and "Three Shadows"—the technique and the position, however, are those not of the *Commedia* but of the *Vita Nuova*, where momentary but unusually striking thoughts or perceptions are put into verse. From this position Pound went on to the *Cantos*, where each perception, arcane or no, is related to every other perception and placed in a single unifying context. Rossetti, it may be, never felt the need to go on.

Moreover, it is no exaggeration to say that Pound brings, even to those very early Rossettian translations, an expressive ability far beyond the gifts of Rossetti. The question of native abilities aside, it certainly seems that Pound was operating with a more consciously worked-out theory of translation. His talk of objectivity and accuracy and his denigration of the "crust of dead English" that blurred his perception (of Cavalcanti in this case) postulate a kind of one-to-one relationship between particular experiences and particular forms for expression. Procedurally, this was apt to imply that single poems (if not "poetry") may consist of a content and a quite separate form of expression, which might not automatically convey the content, though ideally the two are inseparable. This approach gives rise to the striking mechanicality of Pound's experimentation. The eyes "as dark red circles filled with dust" we have already seen to be candidly lifted from Rossetti, as was the green and gray raiment of Pound's Lady of Life. Pound also lifted "items" out of his own poems, to try them elsewhere. An image in the "Canzon: Of Angels," where the Lady "takes motion from the lustrous sheath / Which, as the trace behind the swimmer, gleameth / Yet presseth back the aether where it streameth," is reused as the aura surrounding the lover in "A Virginal," just as the image of the parting of the aether is tried out again in "Apparuit."

With respect to translation—at least for Pound, who aims to reproduce in English the whole experience embodied in the original—this conception of poetic language entails certain consequences:

> The point of the archaic language in the Prov. trans. is that the Latin [on which *Homage to Sextus Propertius* is based] is really "modern." We are just getting back to a Roman state of civilization, or in reach of it; whereas the Provençal feeling is archaic, we are ages away from it. (Whether I have managed to convey this or not I can't say; but it is the reason for the archaic dialect.)
>
> (*L* 179)

Seeking to remain faithful, that is, to the kind of feeling embodied in the poems he was translating, he translated not into the going idiom, but into forms of expression as congruent as possible with the mode of feeling involved—when need be, into expressive forms concocted, patched together, invented, or what you will, for the specific occasion.

This notion applies even when the "theme" is nothing more than the very rhythms in which the poem presents itself: a given feeling might be expressible only in a certain kind of rhythm; the poet must find the one proper rhythm and need not embed the feeling in the kind of "plot" implied, for example, by "I wandered lonely as a cloud." "The term 'meaning' cannot be restricted to strictly intellectual . . . significance. The how much you mean it, the how you feel about meaning it [as in "the horrid threats of Bernard Shaw" in "Phasellus Ille" above], can all be 'put into language.'"[8] A botched expression can becloud our view of the experience. In other words—and the idea is neither arcane nor unique with Pound—one rhymes *girl* with *swirl* to reveal a connection between the two things, not to make a pretty noise—although, as Pound would say, there are at least a thousand exceptions to this. Rossetti's translations, fine as some are, clearly demonstrate this power of language to obfuscate one's view of the matter at hand. The surface of his translations of Cavalcanti consists precisely of a crust of dead— or at least dated—English. The same medium—a manner worked out by a translator and not related to the manners of the originals —is employed for Cavalcanti, Cino da Pistoia, Dante, and all the rest in *The Early Italian Poets.*

What Pound eventually did with this manner, after taking over so much of it from Rossetti, was to break up the crust by discarding the old stand-by's of Victorian archaism—the splendiferous mechanism of *ye* and *that* (for *who*), the syllabicizèd verb endings, and other poetical usages. Rossetti, for example, translates Cavalcanti's *anima dolente* as "a soul in heavy sighs" (II, 131), which is neither close to the Italian nor particularly precise English. Where Cavalcanti has simply "Una figura de la donna mia / S'adora, Guido, a San Michele in Orto" (Sonnet 35), Rossetti writes:

> Guido, an image of my lady dwells
> At San Michele in Orto, consecrate
> And duly worshiped.   (II, 121)

We note the excrescent *dwells* and the poetical pietism of the nineteenth-century "consecrate and duly worshiped." Pound is more direct and less dated: "My lady's face is it they worship there / At San Michele in Orto, Guido mine." Cavalcanti continues:

> Che di bella sembianza, onesta e pia,
> De' peccatori è refugio e conforto:
>
> E quale a lei divoto s'umilia
> Chi più languisce più n' ha di conforto:
> Gl'infermi sana, i demon caccia via,
> E gli occhi orbati fa vedere scorto.
>
> Sana in pubblico loco gran languori:
> Con reverenza la gente l'inchina;
> Due luminara l'adornan di fuori.
>
> La voce va per lontane cammina;
> Ma dicon, ch'è idolatra, i Fra' Minori,
> Per invidia, che non è lor vicina.[9]

Rossetti turns this into Victorian archaism:

> Fair in holy state
> She listens to the tale each sinner tells:
> And among them that come to her, who ails
> The most, on him the most doth blessing wait.

This may be closer to the Italian than Pound's version, but it transforms, in "who ails the most," a thirteenth-century impulse into the artificial language of a bad imitator of Milton. Naturally *i demon* must become "the fiend," and *luminara* "tapers":

> She bids the fiend man's bodies abdicate;
> Over the curse of blindness she prevails,
> And heals sick languors in the public squares.
> A multitude adores her reverently:

> Before her face two burning tapers are:
> Her voice is uttered upon paths afar.

Pound has:

> Whoso before her kneeleth reverently
> No longer wasteth but is comforted;
> The sick are healed and devils driven forth,
> And those with crooked eyes see straightway straight.
>
> Great ills she cureth in an open place,
> With reverence the folk all kneel unto her,
> And two lamps shed the glow about her form.

The vigor of Pound's conclusion is far beyond Rossetti's and, in addition, more faithful to the complaining tone of Cavalcanti's poem:

> 'Till brothers minor cry: 'Idolatry',
> For envy of her precious neighborhood.   (Pound)
>
> Yet through the Lesser Brethren's jealousy
> She is named idol; not being one of theirs.   (Rossetti)

"Sick languors" may be closer to the Italian than "great ills," but it is so only in terms of etymology, and it is unfortunately congruous with standard poetic diction. "Afar," "a multitude adores," and "over the curse of blindness she prevails" need no comment. Now there are perfectly good reasons for Rossetti's version being as it is—notably his commitment to an English sonnet form; Pound reproduces the rhythm of the original and is thus freed at least from the constrictions of the iambic heave. We need not contemn it as a poem. In a way Rossetti has paralleled Pope's achievement with Homer, translating a foreign work into the going idiom. But (completely aside from one's critical opinions of this particular going idiom) this immediately fixes the translation in time: this is not Cavalcanti, nor the expression of any other thirteenth-century sensibility; it is a thoroughly Victorian poem.

Pound's version, though no less mannered than Rossetti's, carries us back to an earlier date. It is, perhaps, as laden with devices as the earlier poems we have inspected, but with the important difference that the devices are not the automatic ones of poetic diction; they do not form a wall of prefabricated poeticisms between us and the original, whereas Rossetti literally buries Cavalcanti—excepting only the "plot"—beneath a layer of Victorian verbiage. Many of Pound's early translations likewise bury their original, but after 1912, when the Cavalcanti poems were published, he was no longer to take current or past poetic language as he found it. To paraphrase Schopenhauer's "Essay on Style" (which Pound recommends in *Guide to Kulchur*), he no longer shoves around memorized counters with ready-attached meanings and connotations, but chooses the terms he wants in full consciousness of how they will function once they are turned loose on paper.

iv

In these translations, as in the stylistic variousness that sets Pound off from Yeats even in his most Yeatsian endeavors, we can see the early stage of an ability that becomes more and more important as his career progresses—the ability to invent modes of expression *ad hoc*: for "The Seafarer," one kind of speech; for "The Return," another; for the satiric mode of "Ancora," still another. And this interest in the particular kind of verbal precision and delicacy (or preciosity) of effect which that ability presupposed sends us again to the Decadents, for "to fix the last fine shade, the quintessence, of things; to fix it fleetingly, to be a disembodied voice, and yet the voice of a human soul,"[10] which was their hope, means expending great care on style, and in this aim Pound is obviously at one with them.

It was indeed for their stylistic accomplishments that he admired the *fin de siècle* poets. He praises certain poets of the nineties for refinements of sound and manner: Symons "shows himself a master of cadence," and "The impression of Lionel Johnson's verse is that of small slabs of ivory, firmly combined and contrived. There is a constant feeling of neatness, a sense of inherited order."[11] For all Johnson's "hardness" and his inherited order, he was not, Pound admits, the most striking figure among the Decadents—at least not to the young; and when important approximations to Johnson's manner do begin to appear in Pound's work, they are in conjunction with the impressionism he abjures in this same essay. In the beginning it was the more sensational figures who attracted him most:

> In America ten or twelve years ago one read Fiona MacLeod, and Dowson, and Symons . . . One was drunk with "Celticism," and with Dowson's "Cynara," and with one or two poems of Symons' "Wanderers" and "I am the torch she saith":
>
> > "I am the flame of beauty
> > And I burn that all may see
> > Beauty."   (*LE* 367)

Pound refers approvingly to this same poem in his *Athenaeum* article five years later—as well he might, for it is a kind of image with which he frequently embodies the emotions that come to the poet in his more fortunate hours, as in "Praise of Ysolt," "Apparuit," or "The Flame."

Pound, of course, took up the *fin de siècle* care for style with a vengeance, and even at the very beginning of his career, though inferior to Symons and the rest as a stylist, he is (to use a comparison he himself makes somewhere) inferior to them somewhat as a year-old infant is intellectually inferior to a full-grown dog. Pound's scope in experience, stance, and style is far wider than the Decadents', and the experimentalism of *A Lume Spento* is so historically oriented that anything approaching enthusiasm for the nineties is pretty effectively suppressed. But the presence of the nineties would be more perceptible than it is were it not overshadowed by the considerable influence of Rossetti and Yeats. The Browning-oriented "Fifine Answers," for example, bears a striking resemblance in syntax, tone, meter, and ideology to Symons' "The Beggars":

> Wandering on eternal wanderings,
> They know the world; and, tasting but the bread
> Of charity, know man; and, strangely led
> By some vague, certain, and appointed hand,
> Know fate; and, being lonely, understand
> Some little of the thing without a name
> That sits by the roadside and talks with them.[12]

Pound's cross-rhythms are almost identical with Symons':

> Wherefore we wastrels that the grey road's call
> Doth master and make slaves and yet make free,
>
> . . . . .
>
> We claim no glory. If the tempest rolls
> About us we have fear, and then
> Having so small a stake grow bold again.

"That Pass Between the False Dawn and the True," for all its mannered diction, deals with what is primarily a nineties-like setting and appeals to the emotional attitudes and imagery of the period—"Blown of the winds whose goal is 'No-man-knows,' / As feathered seeds upon the wind are borne," and "An hour to each! We greet. The hour flows." The poem suggests

Paolo and Francesca, but it might better suggest Arthur Symons:

> We are blown together as fire is blown into fire,
> We return as the wandering tide returns to the sands.
>
> . . . . .
>
> Soul of my life, let us live! for the hours pass.
>
> ("The Bond," *Poems*, II, 216)

In Pound's "In Morte De," the archaic disguise is even less effective at concealing the real ancestry of the language. This poem is the work of a poet who has read his romantics—perhaps Shelley—with eyes of the 1890s. It is more heavy-handed than the Decadents usually were, but the emotional stance implied by the drifting, impermanent images, and its labored preciosity is much like theirs. Similarly "Grace before Song" is invaded by the coloristic preoccupation of the nineties which Pound was later to take into his verse more straightforwardly and to better purpose.

The most unfortunate of these Decadent invasions—none of them is particularly good—undercut the import of the poems in which they occur. For instance, though Pound made a deliberate attempt in "The Decadence" to construct an "expression of the decadent spirit as I conceive it," the implications of its style are quite opposite to what it pretends to express; the poem is very heavy-handed, and its occasionally accurate fragility is repeatedly shattered by the heave-ho language of things like "Broken our manhood for the wrack and strain"— the right idea, perhaps, but decidedly the wrong terms. On the other hand, "Prometheus" comes accidentally closer to the "decadent spirit" than it ought to:

> For we be the beaten wands
> And the bearers of the flame.

Ourselves have died lang syne, and we
Go ever upward as the sparks of light
Enkindling all
'Gainst whom our shadows fall.

Weary to sink, yet ever upward borne,
Flame, flame that riseth ever
To the flame within the sun

The strongest verb in the poem is the flat "Go," and the only
other active verb governed by *we* is the singularly inapt "have
died." Even if the job of fire bearer is an unwelcome one, we
should expect, given the title of the poem, some more robust
expression of the anguish involved than "Weary to sink," followed by a passive verb that wafts the bearers of the flame
helplessly toward the Empyrean. In terms of emotional attitude,
this is a thoroughly Decadent Prometheus and one, moreover,
whose means of expression are inferior to real Decadent technique.

In *A Lume Spento* we can see the *fin de siècle* delicacy of style
at work in those passages whose wording seems to have been
laid out with great care in order to attain maximum aural value.
This is especially true when Pound approximates the low-keyed
tones of Dowson, as in "Scriptor Ignotus":

Dear, an this dream come true,
Then shall all men say of thee
"She 'twas that played him power at life's morn,
And at the twilight Evensong,
And God's peace dwelt in the mingled chords
She drew from out the shadows of the past,
And old-world melodies that else
He had known only in his dreams
Of Iseult and Beatrice.

So, too, "Li Bel Chasteus," though it may take its mannerisms from Rossetti and Swinburne, proceeds with an almost obtrusive deliberation reminiscent of Lionel Johnson. The apparently arbitrary line division, for example, is designed to organize definite rhythmic clusters:

> That castle stands the highest in the land
> Far-seen and mighty. Of the great hewn stones
> What shall I say? And deep foss way
> That far beneath us bore of old
> A swelling turbid sea

Compare these lines from Johnson's "A Stranger":

> Her face was like sad things: was like the lights
> Of a great city, seen from far off fields,
> Or seen from sea: sad things, as are the fires
> Lit in a land of furnaces by night.

Pound, of course, is considerably more eclectic a stylist than his *fin de siècle* predecessors—more eclectic a stylist than anyone perhaps. Much of the aural nicety of the nineties poets comes by way of France—in Johnson's case, by way of Latin poetry—and tends to be homogeneous, narrow in range, delicate; it pretends at least to a certain kind of emotional precision. Pound, aiming at quite the same goal of precision, is apt to load his speech with, say, the flowing rhythm of Dowson, a dab of archaic diction to supply the proper degree of distance and an atmosphere, and possibly the mannered syntax of Rossetti's Italian translations. He does exactly this in "Cameraderie," partly to heighten the psychical implications of the experience described:

> Sometimes I feel thy cheek against my face
> Close-pressing, soft as is the South's first breath

That all the subtle earth-things summoneth
To spring in wood-land and in meadow space.

Despite the close parallel in both subject and form with Dowson's "Terre Promise" (see p. 29), Dowson's poem seems much less cluttered.

But Pound's extra freight is not merely clutter; Dowson's poem collapses into a reverie after the first stanza, for it centers upon a limp sort of *Sehnsucht*. Pound's carries out a mystical communion. Still, the screen of archaic diction and the Italian epigraph about which the poem is embroidered fail to disguise the strong family resemblances of Pound's imagery to the effects the nineties found so useful—some of which, in fact, are in "Terre Promise"—the lady's hair, the tremor in the rain drops, the quickened pulse, the gently wind-swept flower. What Pound has done is to take many of the stylistic elements with which Dowson works, and a similar setting, and then simply carry out the Rossettian communion that Dowson only wishes were true.

We have already looked at some of the differences between the Decadents and Pound. We have seen that the Decadent strategy more often than not involved an attempt to sweep the reader into the mood of the poem. This technique is really less poetic than it is psychological, a kind of linguistic trickery to which Pound hardly ever comes close, superficial resemblances notwithstanding. His "Speech for Psyche in the Golden Book of Apuleius," for example, contains several typical Decadent gestures employed in non-Decadent ways:

> as the petals of flowers in falling
> Waver and seem not drawn to earth, so he
> Seemed over me to hover light as leaves
> And closer me than air,
> And music flowing through me seemed to open
> My eyes upon new colours,
> O winds, what wind can match the weight of him!

Except for the fourth and seventh lines, the images here are standard nineties fare, and the speaker does indeed seem bent on fixing the last fine shade. But, as in "Cameraderie," the shade is Decadent and the substance is Rossettian. What is fixed is the speaker's experience, and it is fixed by her utterance— it is not our experience, instigated by the poet's utterance. Although the poem moves to a logical and emotional conclusion, it is not an emotional pyramid to whose apex we are swept.

This is what Hugh Kenner had in mind when he said that Pound "asks of us complex acts of discernment, not immolation," and it reflects an interesting split in Pound's aesthetic. In his pioneering study of Pound, Kenner went to some lengths to establish Pound's aesthetic as almost exclusively mimetic; if this is only half the story, it is yet a valid half. But we have seen in some detail that the *origins* of Pound's poems are subjectivist in the extreme. He is as romantic as anyone in his sponsorship of the visionary and in his indulgence in "self-expression," where he is very close to the Decadents. The split comes with the expressive ·act, which Pound will make as mimetic as possible— the poem a perfect imitation of the experience, not a recreation in which we may participate but a mimesis we observe. His use of language differs from Decadent practice accordingly.

The archaism and the general spookiness of language discussed earlier are in part atmospherics which help to set the poems apart from more mundane discourse. We have seen how in the Cavalcanti translations Pound aimed at a language that might preserve the medieval flavor of the originals. He similarly attempts to remove his own poems from the realm of the quotidian by means of a mannered archaism, so that style itself becomes in both cases a kind of metaphor—and a distancing device. In practice this means that the style of each poem presents a certain tone of voice and signals a certain mode of experience. And those of his poems which approximate the mood of Symons' "Hallucination: II" are carefully removed from the linguistic universe of less intense moods, whether the universe of "The Altar":

> Let us build here an exquisite friendship
> The flame, the autumn, and the green rose of love
> Fought out their strife here, 'tis a place of wonder;

or of the translations from Heine:

> In evening company he sets his face
> In most spiritu*el* positions,
> And declaims before the ladies
> My *god-like* compositions.

It is through this deliberate linguistic removal that "The Flame," "Speech for Psyche," and "The House of Splendour" avoid the trap set by Symons' more "contemporaneous" manner of presentation. By speaking too familiar a dialect, Symons captures—and skillfully—all the savor of sensuality, but correspondingly fewer of the ethereal implications. His language confirms what we have already seen: his ecstasy is fleshly. Pound's, by the implications of language as well as content, is beyond the flesh.

This is not necessarily to praise Pound at anyone's expense: it is one thing to employ a specially distanced language to attain dimensions that standard speech no longer affords, but quite another to retreat to such a dialect to evade responsibility for full control of one's expressive medium. If some of the early poems are evasive in this manner (and I am not sure that they can be said to be completely so), Pound did finally overcome the need for mechanical distancing. The speech of Psyche perhaps needs its archaism for purposes other than insulation; it is less certain that we can say the same of "The Flame" or "The House of Splendour." What is certain is that the *Cantos* and much of the poetry before them treat similar experiences in a language of considerably more integrity. In terms of freedom from artificial poetic insulation it is as superior to the language of "The Flame" as that poem is superior to "Anima Sola":

> This fruit has a fire within it,
> > Pomona, Pomona
> No glass is clearer than are the globes of this flame
> what sea is clearer than the pomegranate body
> > holding the flame?
> > > Pomona, Pomona,
>
> > Lynx, keep watch on this orchard
> > That is named Melagrana
> or the Pomegranate field
>
> > · · · · ·
>
> > Here are lynxes   Here are lynxes,
> > Is there a sound in the forest
> > > of pard or of bassarid
> > or crotale   or of leaves moving?
> > > > > (Canto LXXIX)

The substratum of Decadent imagery, emotional stance, and rhythmic effect in Pound's earliest work indicates the extent to which the poetic language of the nineties was his natural speech, and the strong Decadent influence on the "Speech of Psyche" is only one example of how the *fin de siècle* hangs on in his work even after the earliest books—in fact, its presence becomes decidedly stronger in *Personae* and *Exultations* than it is in *A Lume Spento*, and it even enters into his experiments with Provençal. But granted that Pound's voice was first attuned, like that of almost every young poet, to the active voices of his own time, there is further evidence that he was aware of what he was about and had an informed conviction that he was not about the same business as the men from whom he perhaps learned to write.

v

I have stated that many of the poems in *A Lume Spento* are experiments with or embroideries upon older literary sources and that a few make direct appeal to past works. "Mesmerism" comments on Browning, "Salve O Pontifex!" on Swinburne, and "Redivivus" on Dante. Two other poems are deliberate reworkings—critical commentaries—on works by Rossetti and Dowson. Some twenty-five years after *A Lume Spento*, Pound mentioned "criticism in new composition" as the most intense form of criticism: "For example the criticism of Seneca in Mr. Eliot's *Agon* is infinitely more alive, more vigorous than in his essay on Seneca" ("Date Line," *LE* 75). He exemplifies this kind of criticism—though we may question the intensity— in "Donzella Beata" and a correction of Dowson, "In Tempore Senectutis." Though they are among Pound's earliest poems, their deviations from Rossetti and Dowson point toward some of his most characteristic qualities: the linguistic energy and controlled irony of "The Return," the pugnacity of "Salutation" and "Salutation the Second," the grotesque abuse in Canto XV, and the general sally into public reform that was one of the salient features of Vorticism.

Rossetti's "Blessed Damozel" presents a vision of the beloved in heaven, yearning for the approach of her earth-bound lover. The vision impelling the speaker in "Donzella Beata"— an instance of metempsychosis—is no less celestial or mystical. But by Pound's lights, the Rossetti poem depicts an ideological failure of really serious proportions. The damozel longs for the time when she and her lover will bathe in the divine light, and she will teach him heavenly songs. She yearns for their eternal reunion:

> There will I ask of Christ the Lord
> Thus much for him and me:—
> Only to live as once on earth
>   With Love—only to be,
> As then awhile, for ever now
>   Together, I and he.

But an interesting split develops. Clearly the speaker, in seeing what he sees, is being granted a celestial vision, a glimpse of the ethereal. Just as clearly, his unstated attitude pulls the vision toward the flesh. The longings of the damozel are not sensual, though they may well be personal and idiosyncratic; neither is her appearance, so far as our knowledge of it depends on solid facts—she is full of religious emblems, with the three lilies in her hand and the seven stars in her hair and her robe which "no wrought flowers did adorn, / But a white rose of Mary's gift." But sensuality there is, and it all belongs to the narrator, who duly notes that "Her hair that lay along her back / Was yellow like ripe corn" and that "her bosom must have made / The bar she leaned on warm." This is Rossetti's "physicalized vision of the ethereal"; we catch him, or his narrator, in the very act of transmuting the celestial into the earthly ("now, and in this place, / Surely she leaned o'er me—her hair / Fell all about my face"). In a way this is a betrayal of the vision, the speaker's inability or refusal to be drawn upward and his tendency to draw the vision downward.

In "Donzella Beata," instead of perceiving the very carefully delineated physical form of his lady, Pound's speaker perceives, and says so, a soul "Caught in the rose-hued mesh / Of o'er fair earthly flesh." Pound pointedly reverses the scheme of values:

> Soul,
>
> . . . . .
>
> Stooped you this thing to bear

Again for me? And be
Rare light to me, gold-white
In the shadowy path I tread?

Pound's diction puts earthly attributes in their properly sub-ordinate place: the Soul's new manifestation is a "mesh" of "earthly flesh"; the new body and the life it is to lead are "this thing" that the loved one is to "bear . . . for me." The speaker's earthly life is "the shadowy path I tread." The second stanza achieves an additional anti-Rossettian corrective in its energetic rejection of the woebegone passivity of Rossetti's damozel:

Surely a bolder maid art thou
Than one in tearful, fearful longing
That should wait
Lily-cinctured at the gate
Of high heaven, Star-diademd,
Crying that I should come to thee.

Stylistically, too, the poem is "criticism in new composition." Pound uses the Rossettian devices of hyphenated adjectives (with which his early volumes are liberally sprinkled) for his own purposes in "rose-hued flesh," "gold-white in the shadowy path," "star-diademd," and in what amounts to a rhythmic if not typographical equivalent, "o'er fair." His substitution of "lily-cinctured" for Rossetti's "She had three lilies in her hand" is not only an allusion but also an exemplification of his later comment in *The Spirit of Romance* that in "more sophisti-cated poetry" a suggestive epithet might take the place of detailed description. The exaggerated lachrimosity of the second stanza ("one in tearful, fearful longing") underscores Pound's general criticism of the posture of Rossetti's damozel and the ideology she implies. Pound's spiritual visitors are energetic and descend readily from their celestial balconies.

The other instance of criticism in new composition in *A Lume Spento* is "In Tempore Senectutis." Its literary referents are Dowson's poem of the same name in *Verses* and Yeats's "Ephemera," with a side glance at "When You Are Old." The Dowson poem is one of his "languishing" opuscula:

> When I am old,
>   And sadly steal apart,
> Into the dark and cold,
>   Friend of my heart!
> Remember, if you can,
> Not him who lingers, but that other man,
> Who loved and sang, and had a beating heart,—
>   When I am old!
>
> When I am old,
>   And all Love's ancient fire
> Be tremulous and cold:
>   My soul's desire!
> Remember, if you may,
> Nothing of you and me but yesterday,
> When heart on heart we bid the years conspire
>   To make us old.
>
>   . . . . .
>
> Remember nought of us but long ago,
> And not at least, how love and pity strove
>   When I grew old![13]

As so often with the poets of the nineties, one reads this with a feeling that the poet is toying self-indulgently with a mood. We note, at any rate, that the speaker is not yet old; he is, depending on one's tastes or sympathies, tenderly or in a state of debility anticipating the days of decrepitude, and his request is that the loved one will banish what will then be the present and linger in memory over better days gone by, even as now (stanza 2) they would banish the passion-torn present in favor of calmer old age. With the departure of passion, nothing will be worthwhile—*pleasant* would seem a more accurate word, but perhaps in the ideology of the poem the two are equivalent.

One is reminded of Pound's statement that the poets of the nineties confined their improvements in poetic technique "chiefly to sound and to refinements of manner," for the poem answers to his complaint against poetry that rests upon "talk about the matter, rather than presentation." We are left with a general impression of a rather melancholy state of mind, but neither old age nor pleasurable love is other than vaguely presented.

Pound's poem, as we might expect, is closer to Yeats than to Dowson. His mode of presentation is a dramatic dialogue, placed literally *in tempore senectutis:*

> For we are old
> And the earth passion dieth;
> We have watched him die a thousand times,
> When he wanes an old wind crieth,
> For we are old
> And passion hath died for us a thousand times
> But we grew never weary.

This method has one obvious advantage over Dowson's—dramatic credibility. To ask why Dowson's narrator should raise such a subject as old age at all might be to reveal some degree of literal-mindedness, but Pound's poem forestalls the question altogether. Moreover, just as in our comparison of "Donzella Beata" with its Rossettian counterpart, Pound attains a closer harmony between theme and presentation. Dowson would presumably hypostasize the present; but with the same perversity of treatment that dislocates "The Blessed Damozel" from its conceptual base, he places a premium on a subordinate scene. So far as anything in his poem approaches vividness, it is his apprehension of old age: "When I . . . sadly steal, / Into the dark and cold . . . And all Love's ancient fire / Be tremulous and cold . . . And every star above / Be pitiless and cold." As for Pound, just as he avoids a split between what "Donzella Beata" purports to say and what its structure actually emphasizes, so here he begins from the theme that "what we have now is good," and by presenting a dramatic scene he is able to concentrate upon the *now*, the moment of utterance, and does not trick himself into bestowing his more impressive presentation upon lesser scenes.[14]

Pound, like Dowson, deals with an attitude, and again he differs from his predecessor. Dowson's speaker—no believer in *carpe diem*—turns from present bliss to the contemplation of future sadness, the repugnance of which is in turn rejected in favor of memory. Pound's speaker lets memory die—"Memory faileth"—but the idea is used to buttress the suggestion of long-lived, vigorous, and prized love. His couple "grow never weary / For we are old." The suggestion in the conjunction *for* is that something has replaced the exertions of passion, something that saves the couple from Dowsonian decrepitude. This repetition of the opening line reinforces the suggestion in the first stanza that the expenditure of passion is a source of strength, and that suggestion becomes explicit:

> The strange night-wonder of your eyes
> Dies not, though passion flieth
>   Along the star fields of Arcturus
> And is no more unto our hands;
>   My lips are cold
> And yet we twain are never weary,
> And the strange night-wonder is upon us,
>
>   . . . . .

The wind fills our mouths with strange words
For our wonder that grows not old.

In their acts of love they have participated in the life force of the universe, and in "the strange night-wonder" they are about to be gathered wholly and eternally into that force, each manifestation of which has in the past brought an accrual of wonder. These last remarks rather complicate the claims of the fourth stanza that the twilight of life ushers in the dawn of immortality, but the poem can nonetheless be taken as an illustration of what Pound advanced to William Carlos Williams as one of the thematic bases of *A Lume Spento*: "The soul, from god, returns to him" (L 6).

There is another difference between Pound's poem and Dowson's. If the earlier poem is vulnerable to Pound's implied conceptual attack—if, that is, it is too delicately one-sided in its insistence that *tempus senectutis* is wholly regrettable—these first four stanzas of Pound's might be open to similar attack. But Pound at least presents a view opposed to the speaker's in his penultimate stanza:

> He saith: "Red spears bore the warrior dawn
> Of old
> Strange! Love, hast thou forgotten
> The red spears of the dawn,
> The pennants of the morning?"

But the woman makes the final assertion of value:

> She saith: "Nay, I remember, but now
> Cometh the Dawn, and the Moth-Hour
> Together with him; softly
> For we are old."

Pound's poem is not altogether superior. The revelation of part of the theme through the gradual accumulation of capital letters, for one thing, seems a rather naive device—maybe evidence of a young poet's dawning awareness that identical words may bear divergent implications, but evidence, too, of a tendency to manage semantic metamorphosis by rather crude means. Moreover, the language of the poem is in its own way as pretentious as Dowson's. Finally—though this need not lower our assessment of either poem—Pound's is a close imitation of Yeats's "Ephemera," just as Dowson's is a loose one of "When You Are Old." The form of Pound's poem is almost the same as that of "Ephemera"—a dialogue between the man and woman with the speeches designated "He saith" and "She saith." The red spears and pennants of the morning are perhaps attempts to parallel the use of symbols in Yeats's poem, though they also attempt a vivid presentation of what the old man offers as cause for regret. The lines are not especially successful, but they offer another point of difference from Dowson's poem. In what seems a damaging lapse of originality Pound dips into "When You Are Old" for the image of passion's departure "along the star fields of Arcturus." Original or no, Pound's image is knit a good deal more closely into its context than Yeats's abrupt reference to "how Love fled / And paced upon the mountains overhead / And hid his face amid a crowd of stars." The star fields are perfectly consonant with the presence of night-wonder, and passion's being absorbed by the northern coldness and being no longer a source of sensual joy parallel the fact that "my lips are cold." Finally, of course, the chill star fields to which passion has flown are about to be dimmed even more—and permanently—by the approaching dawn.

Elsewhere it may well be that "In Tempore Senectutis" is ornamented and overdeliberate. Still, the poem bespeaks a conscious and wise limit to Pound's admiration of the Decadent posture. We may take the difference as a sign that, for all his admiration of the Decadents, Pound was not the man to spend his career collecting precious experiences or to limit his verse to the expression of a rare and delicate nervous system. "In Tempore Senectutis" suggests in particular that he would not join the Decadents either in collapsing in the face of a dead universe or in making the best of a bad lot; he would replace "clanging space" with the "vital universe." He repeats his criticism of Dowson and the others in the 1909 *Personae*, in "Revolt against the Crepuscular Spirit in Modern Poetry." Blustering and self-conscious in an almost adolescent way, it is not a good poem. But it is certainly explicit, as the last two stanzas show:

> Great God, if men are grown but pale sick phantoms
> That must live only in these mists and tempered lights
> And tremble for dim hours that knock o'er loud
> Or tread too violent in passing them;
>
> Great God, if these thy sons are grown such thin
>   ephemera,
> I bid thee grapple chaos and beget
> Some new titanic spawn to pile the hills and stir
> This earth again.

Pound did not live in these mists and tempered lights, though he continued to speak through them. Characteristically, the speaking was part of a vigorous program devoted to the strengthening of his own voice.

IV

Research and the
Uses of London

To write on [his] plan, it was at least necessary to read and think. No man could be born a . . . poet, nor assume the dignity of a writer, by descriptions copied from descriptions, by imitations borrowed from imitations, by traditional imagery, and hereditary similes, by readiness of rhyme, and volubility of syllables.

—Samuel Johnson, "Life of Cowley"

A LUME SPENTO, for the most part containing poems Pound had written before he went to Europe, was published privately in Venice in 1908. Shortly after arriving in London, he had *Quinzaine for This Yule* printed.[1] *Personae* came out in the spring of 1909 and *Exultations* in the fall of the same year. At the time *Exultations* went to press, Pound was working on the third chapter of *The Spirit of Romance*, and in 1910 Small, Maynard, and Company published his *Provença*, a selection from the earlier poems plus a few that were to appear in *Canzoni* the next year. Such a rapid succession of books should make us cautious about an over-ready use of the term "development," but the collections published after *A Lume Spento* reveal changes that look ahead to the features of Pound's more mature work.

From a biographical point of view, it is evident that London made a strong impression on him. We can see some sort of dawn breaking in a 1909 letter to his father in which Pound says that Elkin Mathews, the Vigo Street publisher, "has turned his shelves over to me to browse in and I find the contemporary people seem to be making as good stuff as the theoretical giants of the past" (*YL* 99). A few weeks after Mathews published *Personae*, Pound wrote to William Carlos Williams that "There is no town like London to make one feel the vanity of all art except the highest. To make one disbelieve in all but the most careful and conservative presentation of one's stuff." "I have," he adds, "printed too much" (*L* 8). The contents of *Personae* imply that, development aside for the moment, some accession of self-criticism had taken place. Along with seventeen previously unpublished poems, it reproduces only sixteen from *A Lume Spento*—which might mean little except that this abandonment of the other twenty-nine poems represents in most cases a permanent excision. Four of the twenty-nine reappeared in *Exultations*—"Plotinus," "The Eyes," "On His Own Face in a Glass," and "To the Dawn: Defiance"—but, even so, over half of the original collection was consigned to the comparative obscurity of collections of rare books. The process of excision continued: though *Provença* is described on its title page as "Poems Selected from *Personae*, *Exultations,* and Canzoniere," the selection represents a permanent garnering, and we find the group from *A Lume Spento* already largely stabilized; only "Camaraderie," "Ballad for Gloom," and "In Tempore Senectutis" remain to be excised to make what constitutes its current published remains. Nevertheless, nearly half of the *Personae* of 1909 consists of poems from the first collection, a fact suggesting the essential continuity of all three books, both technical and thematic.

But granted that we are to be chary of claiming to see development in books published not much more than a year apart, *Personae* and *Exultations* are exploratory in a way different from *A Lume Spento*. Certainly the two later collections were as tentative as the first: of the thirty-four new poems, only ten appear in the current edition of *Personae*, which means that they have fared slightly worse than *A Lume Spento* with its fourteen survivals from an original forty-five. Many of the poems from *Personae* and *Exultations* were omitted even from *Provença* a year later, and in *Umbra*, Pound's presentation in 1920 of "all that he now wishes to keep in circulation" from the earlier collections, the number of survivals is already down to sixteen. But this is simply editorial information; the poems themselves are ample evidence of what Pound was doing. Although even in *A Lume Spento* Pound experimented with "rules of Spanish,

Anglo-Saxon and Greek metric" (*L* 4), that first collection, compared to *Personae* and *Exultations*, was primarily an interim report—a calling card for his London appearance. Its exploratory quality makes it seem a beginning poet's attempt to find out what he can do, whereas the following three or four seek rather to find out what can be done. It is as if his confrontation by "the contemporary people," some of whom showed "what the people of second rank can do, and what damned good work it is" (*L* 8), had suddenly made him aware of how unsatisfactory his own first fruits were; for if *A Lume Spento* betrays ties of a certain kind with the nineteenth century, *Personae* and especially *Exultations* already show signs of a vigorous attempt to expand the expressive limits set by those ties.

The attempt accounts for one of the more curious differences between the first collection and at least the following two: not a lessening of perceptible "influences," as we might expect, but an intensification of them. Many of the poems in *Personae* and *Exultations* are not profitably describable except in terms of influence—and this for the simple reason that, confronted (presumably) by evidence of his limitations, of the sheltered nature of his experience of living poetry, Pound begins deliberately to expand his knowledge and his practical command of the poetically possible. For example, the attraction of Yeats and "Celticism" for Pound seems to have grown almost as much from their conducing to interesting visual possibilities as from their offering new modes of experience—although the two considerations are so closely related that even to call them considerations amounts to hedging. At any rate, experiments in this vein form part of both *Personae* and *Exultations*.

There is, to begin with, "Nils Lykke" in *Exultations*:

> Beautiful, infinite memories
> That are a-plucking at my heart,
> Why will you be ever calling and a-calling,
> And a-murmuring in the dark there?

> And a-reaching out your long hands
> Between me and my beloved?

The obviously Yeatsian rhythms in this poem and its Yeatsian "sentiments" remind us of Pound's remark that "It is only good manners if you repeat a few other men to at least do it better or more briefly" (*L* 6). If "Nils Lykke" is not better than "He Remembers Forgotten Beauty," it is at least shorter (there are only four more lines). What Pound has done is to redo a Yeatsian experience, using the master's rhythmical devices, casting over the whole a mood of Pre-Raphaelite suggestiveness, employing an eminently Pre-Raphaelite image in the first stanza, and constructing the second stanza from one image of the nineties ("The black shadow of your beauty / On the white face of my beloved") and one from his reading in Provençal ("a-glinting in the pools of her eyes"). Such a description seems absurd, but the fact is that the poem, like others in *Exultations*, simply dissolves into its literary antecedents.

Judging by the extent to which Yeats pervades *Exultations*, it would seem that Pound was now making the same straightforward study of his friend's techniques that he was carrying out with Provençal and Tuscan poetry. Hence the stage Irish of "Planh":

> Out of a new sorrow it is,
> That my hunting hath brought me.
>
> . . . . .
>
> But if one should look at me with the old hunger in
>   her eyes,
> How will I be answering her eyes?

If it were not that the theme—the poet's pursuit of Beauty—is an important one in Pound's work at this time, we should suspect that either our leg or Yeats's was being pulled. Aside from these Irishisms, which we may hope were not really

Pound's idea of Yeats's "Irish rhythms," "Planh" is a skillfully close representation of at least one of Yeats's characteristic genres—the poet perceiving strange, shadowy folk moving about in some enchanted natural setting where the faery are known to reside. "Aye!" continues Pound's speaker,

> It's a long hunting
> And it's a deep hunger I have when I see them a-gliding
> And a-flickering there, where the trees stand apart.

This is followed by a typically Yeatsian gesture, the melancholy (and here rather disattached) summation of the mood of the poem, almost the moral of the story: "But oh, it is sorrow and sorrow / When love dies-down in the heart."

Yeats is called upon with equal forthrightness in "Laudantes Decem Pulchritudinis Johannae Templi." We shall see how this poem explores as well the possibilities of Provençal stanza forms—indeed, the poem as a whole is an elaborate kind of dance, moving from one style to another, one rhythm to another, a recital performed by the poet to display his accomplishments to date. The trouble is the same as in "Nils Lykke": Pound comes too close to the Yeatsian manner as practiced by the original owner to be able to draw on it in any creative sense. His nearly outright acknowledgment of his source in part two of this poem does not help:

> I am torn, torn with thy beauty,
> O Rose of the sharpest thorn!
> O Rose of the crimson beauty,
>
> . . . . .
>
> O Rose of the crimson thorn.

This is followed immediately by the opening of part three, about "The unappeasable loveliness." And after this tribute to some half a dozen poems in *The Wind among the Reeds,* Pound takes up, in part four, the rhythm of "The Lover Tells of the Rose in His Heart":

> Pale hair that the moon has shaken
> Down over the dark breast of the sea,
> O magic her beauty has shaken
> About the heart of me:
> Out of you have I woven a dream
> That shall walk in the lonely vale.

Such undisguised excursions into the manner of Yeats are carried on throughout *Personae* and *Exultations.*[2]

This, of course, is experiment of a different—we might say lower—order from what Pound does with his "studies" of Provençal verse. A few years later he was to distinguish two kinds of literary influence: a poet might be moved to emulation, or "the sight of the work may beget simply a counterfeiting of its superficial qualities. This last is without value, a dodge of the arriviste and of the mere searcher for novelty."[3] This would be too harsh a judgment to make of these last few poems, for the imitation here, to quote the same essay, is "a closer sort of study of the original. Such study may be more 'provocative' than a casual reading, and therefore of value to the artist, so long as it does not impede him in his task of making new and original structures."

This would seem to be the real significance of all these Yeatsian gestures, and the Yeatsian exercises alternate with equally candid experiments in the usages of Decadent poetry, one of which, the opening stanza of "Laudantes Decem," is a "closer sort of study" of Dowson:

> When your beauty is grown old in all men's songs,
> And my poor words are lost amid that throng,

> Then you will know the truth of my poor words,
> And mayhap dreaming of the wistful throng
> That hopeless sigh your praises in their songs,
> You will think kindly then of these mad words.

Pound is very good here at fitting rhythm to mood, even though he does it with someone else's tools. The unobtrusive rhythm is the right accompaniment for the poem's de-energized emotional stance. The repetition of "poor words" threatens too much of a good thing, but the change in the last line to "mad words" avoids oversaturation while it preserves the limp posture of the persona. Part eight also seems to draw upon Dowson. In both cases the rhythm is his, and the low pitch of emotion reflects at least one dimension of his work:

> Because I was idolatrous and have besought,
> With grievous supplication and consuming prayer,
> The admirable image that my dreams have wrought
> Out of her swan's neck and her dark, abundant hair:
> The jealous gods, who brook no worship save their own,
> Turned my live idol marble and her heart to stone.
>
> ("Epigram," Poetical Works, 57)

We might hesitate to call such imitation as Pound indulges in here the reflection of influence, were it not that he has evidently learned at least one lesson: note how the rhythm of the Dowson passage undercuts what could otherwise be (and often was) a much stronger emotion. This "Epigram" has a studied dryness about it, as of emotion suppressed, and Pound captures the same mood perfectly. As Dowson undercuts the potential emotionality of "grievous supplication and consuming prayer" by means of deliberately muted rhythm, and as he sidesteps a possibly strong emotion by modfying *image* with the restrained and nonsensual *admirable*, so Pound deliberately saps the vigor of his throng of poets by making them *wistful* and muffles the potential noise of their praising by saying that they "hopeless *sigh* your praises." Originality aside, the poem does a good job of establishing its mood—perhaps too good, given the melodramatic wail that opens the second part with "I am torn, torn with thy beauty, / O Rose of the sharpest thorn!"

The very closeness of these studies makes them seem naive. What I have been referring to as the "mannerisms" of this poet or that are, of course, much more than that. They become mannerisms only when we detach them from the organic complexes of imagery, theme, emotional cast, diction, rhythm, and aural patterns of the poems in which they appear. Failing an absolutely perfect identification between original and imitation, the closer an imitation, the more false or superficial it will seem, for the very closeness will call up by association the other, more subtle features of the complex. At first, therefore, we are inclined to think that for Pound to imitate Yeats and the Decadents as he does in these poems is as silly as attempting to make a tree by patching together various sticks and leaves we have picked up because they seemed to be attractive aspects of trees. There are points at which this kind of tool borrowing shades over into new creation, but to "create" a couplet like "But oh, it is sorrow and sorrow / When love dies-down in the heart" implies a conception of poetry as some kind of warehouse to which a poet may repair for bricks, nuts and bolts, touch-up paint, or what have you. And something very like this underlies these experiments of Pound's, a conception similar to what underlies T. S. Eliot's warning that "To the member of· the Browning Study Circle, the discussion of poets about poetry may seem arid, technical, and limited." There were concrete, practical things that Pound had to learn, and close imitation was one kind of training. "You are out of touch," he told Williams, thereby describing his own condition upon his arrival in London. Later, when he spoke of *Personae* as the starting point of his search for self, he was not shoving the excised poems in *A Lume Spento* under the rug, but tacitly acknowledging their limited significance as only a prelude to the work which, in London, he discovered he had to do.

i

As suggested earlier, that search for the self and for the real was at least in part a linguistic search, based on Pound's continuing assumption about the relationship between idea and expression—the concept that "experience" and "form of expression" are quite separate entities which should stand one to one, the form a perfect image of the content. Now the impulse giving rise to such content is closely related to the poet's unique way of perceiving, to his *virtù* ("a man's message is precisely his *façon de voir*"). If the poet's language depends on the memorized conventionalities of a standard speech, he obviously cannot accurately express his perceptions since these are *not* conventional. "Magnetized groups"[4] of words may cloud over his very perceptions: "When I 'translated' Guido . . . I did *not* see Guido at all." Until he invents a language truly his own, the poet cannot tell even himself what his real feelings are.

The first *Personae* offers some particularly useful illustrations of this process of discovering one's native language. The characteristic failures of *A Lume Spento* stem from a loss of control in which the author seems carried away by the sheer force of gorgeous language; style and substance are all too completely in accord. The failures in *Personae* and *Exultations*, on the other hand, result from a loss of control over the relationship between style and substance; the most heterogeneous elements are yoked by violence together. In these poems Pound is perhaps not carried away enough, for they are clearly marked by what he would call "insincere" elements—modes of expression the poet has borrowed or worked up as the nearest approximation to what he needs. He tries, for example, to do what his translation of "The Seafarer" later does—to reintroduce into modern English poetry a mode of expression and sensibility no longer available.

But just as clearly as in Rossetti's translations, the transfusion is blocked and obfuscated:

> With ever one fear at the heart o' me
> Long by still sea-coasts
>   coursed my Grey-Falcon,
> And the twin delights
>   of shore and sea were mine,
> Sapphire and emerald with
>   fine pearls between.
>   ("At the Heart o' Me")

The rhythm is almost totally irrelevant to the poem's temporal pretensions, and the finicky image in the last line is no older English than Dowson's. The poem aims at the bipartite verse structure of Old English poetry, but for the first nine lines the success is largely typographical. From the tenth line to the end, the metrics are better aimed but, given the fading tone of voice, "whale-ways," "chain-mail," and "many-twined bracelets" strike one as but historical clichés collocated by a student—not necessarily advanced—of Old English:

> And thou should'st grow weary
>   ere my returning,
> An *"they"* should call to thee
>   from out the borderland,
> What should avail me
>   booty of whale-ways?
> What should avail me
>   gold rings or the chain-mail?

Even the superficial conformity of this part of the poem to some real Anglo-Saxon practices seems to deserve the stricture that a maturer Pound would later apply to Tennyson, claiming the presence of "that ineffable 'something'" which kept any suggestion of the real man out of Tennyson's works ("The Rev. G. Crabbe, LL.B.," *LE* 276). This is not a successful persona but rather a night-club act, hindered by anachronistic stage props (and not at all aided by the performer's peeping out from behind his false beard and tin-foil helmet to inform the audience in a footnote that " 'Middan-gard'[1]" is "[1]Anglo-Saxon 'Earth' "). Whether the poet's conception of the Anglo-Saxon sensibility was confounded by a Dowsonian apparatus of perception we cannot say; certainly his image of that impulse is distorted by a Dowsonian apparatus of presentation. The entire production—tone, rhythm, theme—rings false as a conception of an Anglo-Saxon anything.

A different failure of voice occurs in *Exultations*, in "A Song of the Virgin Mother" from Lope de Vega's *Los Pastores de Belen*:

> As ye go through these palm-trees
> O holy angels;
> Sith sleepeth my child here
> Still ye the branches.
>
> O Bethlehem palm-trees
>
> . . . . .
>
> Make ye no clamour,
> Run ye less swiftly,
> Sith sleepeth the child here
> Still ye your branches.
>
> He the divine child
> Is here a-wearied
> Of weeping the earth-pain.

(*E* 44–45)

This poem does not sound false so much as it fails to sound true. It is couched in Artfully Simple Language of a general nine-teenth-century sort and has little to make it peculiarly the ut-terance of the Virgin Mother or any other woman—compare the more convincing wistfulness and gentleness of the speech of the girl in "Idyl for Glaucus":

> I wonder why he mocked me with the grass.
> I know not any more how long it is
> Since I have dwelt not in my mother's house.
> I know they think me mad, for all night long
> I haunt the sea-marge, thinking I may find
> Some day the herb he offered unto me.
>
> (*P 1* 39)

The "Song of the Virgin Mother" and "At the Heart o' Me" present two kinds of falsification of expression. A third sort arises in Pound's experiments with fixed forms. We shall see in a moment that, in the disposing of words upon a given frame, Pound does a strikingly good job, judged from the limited point of view of mechanics. But from his own point of view, which is not, after all, outlandish, the adaptations in *Canzoni* are generally failures. Here is the first stanza of "Canzon: The Vision":

> When first I saw thee 'neath the silver mist,
> Ruling thy bark of painted sandal-wood,
> Did any know thee? By the golden sails
> That clasped the ribbands of that azure sea,
> Did any know thee save my heart alone?
> O ivory woman with thy bands of gold,
> Answer the song my luth and I have brought thee!

This is pretty verse, in its way, and its musical values are both obvious and pleasing. Yet if we grant with Pound that some organic congruence must exist between rhythm and meaning, we see at once how diffuse the stanza is and, from a rhythmic point of view, how inexact. The iambics are of the dogtrot sort, and filling out the pentameter line calls for numerous words—relative pronouns, prepositions, articles—whose function is merely syntactic. Pound was to conclude a few years later, after his experience with Japanese and Chinese poetry, that perceptions do not necessarily come to us neatly organized into prepositional phrases and relative clauses, any more than they come to us preorganized into iambic pentameter, so that adherence to strict forms *may* mean the importation of meaningless poetical trappings. Part of the rationale behind Imagism and *vers libre* in general was, of course, to avoid such falsification—and falsification it often was. Is the sea in that stanza "azure" because it ought to be azure or because the line needs an adjective of two syllables and of the proper sort of evocativeness? And though the poet may escape cruder degrees of semantic falsification, he is liable to be trapped into a crippling rhythmic falsification by the diffusion forced on him by a fixed verse form. What would have become of the urbane subtlety of "The Tea Shop,"[5] if Pound had spread it out into a sonnet with the iambic jog of "The Vision"?

When we speak, therefore, of falsification in these early poems we are not speaking only of a dramatic incongruity, though that is sometimes involved. It is a disparity between what the poem pretends to do and what it does, rhythmically, aurally, imagistically. What these three poems suffer from is lack of the very control Pound was working for in their writing. "The things I'm throwing out," he told his father when he was preparing the Liveright edition (1926) of the current *Personae*, "are the 'soft' stuff, and the metrical exercises. At least what I once bluffed myself into believing were something more than exercises but which no longer convince me that I had anything to say when I wrote 'em; or anything but a general feeling that it wuz about time I wrote a pome" (*YL* 778, November 28, 1925).

Yet what he sought in these metrical exercises was what every poet needs—resourcefulness and flexibility of language: "Your practice with regular metres is a good thing; better keep in mind that [it] is practice, and that it will probably serve to get your medium pliable. No one can do good free verse who hasn't struggled with the regular; at least I don't know anyone who has" (*L* 79). The experimentalism in the early books is a part of learning to bend sequences of words into meaningful rhythms and forms. Even in "A Song of the Virgin Mother," in neglecting nearly everything else in favor of the metrical scheme, Pound is experimenting with something other than a character sketch; he deliberately pursues its rather unusual metrical pattern throughout its twenty-eight lines. "At the Heart o' Me" tests the possibilities—or rather the requirements—of the Anglo-Saxon line. As early as *A Lume Spento*, the two Villonauds, besides closely approximating the meter of Villon's ballades, are severe exercises in rhyme: "Villonaud for This Yule" uses only two rhymes throughout, and "Ballad of the Gibbet" only three throughout its forty-three lines. In the original *Personae* Pound translates a canso by Piere Bremon ("From Syria") into stanzas rhymed *abbacca*, though he uses a different set of rhymes in each stanza; in *Exultations* "Piere Vidal Old" takes the stanza form *abcbdb* through a few variations, preserving the unrhymed *d* line in every stanza save one. "Laudantes Decem Pulchritudinis Johannae Templi" mingles unrhymed stanzas with a variety of rhymed forms—*abcbac, abacab, ababcdece,* and others.

All of these forms seem to have been inspired by Provençal and Tuscan examples, though not all of them quite conform to particular models (part ten of "Laudantes Decem," for example, is a slightly defective version, two stanzas long, of the Provençal *coblas estrampas*, in which the lines of a given stanza rhyme not with each other but with the corresponding lines of succeeding stanzas—*abcdefg, abcdefg*[6]). Still these are mild exertions compared to the "Canzonieri: Studies in Form" in *Provença* and *Canzoni*. In "Canzon: The Yearly Slain," which is in *coblas estrampas,* Pound manages seven stanzas without repeating any rhyme word until the envoy. In the "Canzon: To Be Sung Beneath a Window," he performs a real *tour de force* in following the stanza form of Piere Vidal's "Ab l'alen tir vas me l'aire." Vidal's canso consists of four seven-line stanzas, rhymed *abbaccd,* and Pound reproduces the form exactly in his poem; moreover, he does not simply construct four separately rhymed stanzas as in "From Syria," but follows Vidal to the letter in making four *coblas unisonans* with a single set of rhymes throughout.[7] "Canzon: The Vision," in which he adopts the stanza of Arnaut Daniel's "Sols sui qui sai lo sobrafan quem sortz," is another poem in *coblas estrampas,* this time slightly defective in that the stanzas end with a rhyming *d* line (. . . *defd,* instead of . . . *defg*).[8] The same "studies in form" mark Pound's translations of Cavalcanti, where in the ballatas, though not in the sonnets, he reproduces the original stanza forms and rhyme schemes as closely as possible.

Not all of these experiments are particularly good poems, but they did produce in Pound a considerable capability for verbal manipulation. Moreover, if they are exercises, they are also research: "Note that the English 'poet' en masse had simply said: 'these forms are *impossible* in English, they are too complicated, we haven't the rhymes.' That was bunkum . . . I have proved that the Provençal rhyme schemes are not *impos*sible in English. They are probably *inadvis*able" (*L* 179). Two relatively pertinent analogues are too good to pass by. A contemporary of Pound's at Wabash College reports: "A favorite discussion of Pound's was the theory of Rhythmics—'Rounded voice tones'—'Space words to a mental metronome'—'Strive for graceful gestures and smooth gliding stride'—'Full circle living for mind and body'— these were his slogans."[9] Some forty years later in the Army Detention Center at Pisa, the same man's daily exercises "caused quite a stir. He would engage in imaginary tennis matches, making graceful, looping forehands and backhands. He assumed fencing stances and danced nimbly about the cage, shadow boxing. 'What's he training for?' one of the trainees asked me."[10]

ii

The value of practicing graceful, looping forehands is not limited to firming up the biceps; they may help to develop particular useful qualities in one's swing. Similarly, "diagrammatic translations," as Pound described them, served for more than to exercise the poet's general ability to pour words into molds. In both the letter to Schelling and the essay on Daniel in *Instigations* (now in the *Essays*), Pound directs attention to the musical possibilities of Provençal verse. In the essay he says that Provençal verse is "an art between literature and music," and he told Schelling, "The troubadour . . . got certain musical effects because he cd. concentrate on music without bothering about literary values."[11] The effects involve setting verse to music, but not just to make the verse go tum-ti-tum whenever the music does. They involve musical effects in the verse itself— "the blending and lengthening of the sounds," Pound says in the essay, "the soft suave sound" in "Sols sui qui sai" as opposed to the staccato of "L'aura amara," and "Arnaut's system of echoes and blending." We need not go so far back as "Grace before Song" to find efforts in this vein. The fifth section of "Laudantes Decem" aims at such qualities:

> Red leaf that art blown upward, and out and over
> The green sheaf of the world,
> And through the dim forest and under
> The shadowed arches and the aisles,
> We, who are older than thou art,
> Met and remembered when his eyes beheld her
> In the garden of the peach-trees,
> In the day of the blossoming.

The echoing is obvious enough in *Red leaf . . . green sheaf . . .*

peach-trees, and the blending in the fourth line, in the collocation of neighboring vowels in *shadowed, arches,* and *aisles.*
Musical effects in a stricter sense can be felt in "Canzon: To Be
Sung Beneath a Window," which Pound describes in a note as
"fit only to be sung, and is not to be spoken." We may perhaps be pardoned for speaking it; it *is* musical and implies in its
cadence a particular kind of melody.

> Heart mine, art mine, whose embraces
> Clasp but wind that past thee bloweth?
> E'en this air so subtly gloweth,
> Guerdoned by thy sun-gold traces,
> That my heart is half afraid
> For the fragrance on him laid;
> Even so love's might amazes!

The seven-line stanzas make sizable blocks of rhyme, and their
cumulative effect is very close to music, as if one were to strike a
series of chords each of which referred closely to its predecessors.

In the letter to Schelling (*L* 180), Pound replies to a question
about two lines of a translation from Guilhem de Peitieu—

> I care not for their clamour
> Who have come between me and my charmer.
>   ("Langue d'Oc," *P* 2)

"The 'clamour' and 'charmer' are not intended to be an impression of rhyme, but of syzogy such as one finds in Arnaut's
stanzas without internal rhyme: 'comba,' 'trembla,' 'pona'
followed in that strophe by rhyme in 'oigna.'" Now these
.matters are all technical, but this does not mean that they are
always mechanical, any more than their being exploratory
means that they make for incompetent poems. This is demon-
strated by three of Pound's approaches to the sestina form. In

"Canzon: The Spear" from *Canzoni* and *Provença* Pound adapts the "equivocal" rhyme of the troubadours; he gives the device a firm shove, in his repeated use of a few words as feminine rhymes, toward sestina usage, which is what also developed in Provençal.[12]

> 'Tis the clear light of love I praise
> That steadfast gloweth o'er deep waters,
> A clarity that gleams always.
> Though man's soul pass through troubled waters,
> Strange ways to him are opened.
> To shore the beaten ship is sped
> If only love of light give aid.
>
> That fair far spear of light now lays
> Its long gold shaft upon the waters.
>   . . . . .
> Yet when within my heart I gaze
> Upon my fair beyond the waters,
> Meseems my soul within me prays
> To pass straightway beyond the waters
>   . . . . .
> My love is lovelier than the sprays
> Of eglantine above clear waters,
> Or whitest lilies that upraise
> Their heads in midst of moated waters.

But these gyrations about the sometimes hackneyed associations of a single word involve too many limp and poorly functioning images for the poem to be wholly successful. The quasi-musical chiming of *waters* does not altogether work because the meaning of the verses, or of the individual lines, has not the impact to match the aural force.

The "Sestina for Ysolt" in *Exultations* is more successful. Pound takes the term "greyness," for example and, with possibly one weak instance, carries it through a spectrum of entirely convincing associations. He speaks of rain that "wrapped men's hearts within its cloak of greyness," of his lady's eyes, "whoso look on such there is no greyness / May hang about his heart on any day"; he implies that by praising his lady's hands he can "dispel the evening's greyness," in one very subtle shift says that for one night of love "I give all nights my praise / And love therefrom the twilight's coming greyness," and then in the final two stanzas repeats the word in settings already used. But even in this poem not all of the convolutions around the "rhyme" words add much to the poem. Pound once said of Swinburne, "He habitually makes a fine stanzaic form, writes one or two fine strophes in it, and then continues to pour into the mould strophes of diminishing quality" (*LE* 292), and this is pretty much what happens in "Sestina for Ysolt."

Something similar occurs in "Sestina: Altaforte"; the speaker and topic of the poem being what they are, there is not much hope for subtle verbal exploration. *Peace*, for example, remains essentially what most of us think of when we hear the word in a political context. The best Pound can do, apparently, is to make it *foul peace, womanish peace, Peace!* and so on. Considering the energy implied by the poem, it seems strangely penned in by the elaborate Morris dance of the repeated line endings:

I

Damn it all! all this our South stinks peace.
You whoreson dog, Papiols, come! Let's to music!
I have no life save when the swords clash.
But ah! when I see the standards gold, vair, purple,
    opposing
And the broad fields beneath them turn crimson,
Then howl I my heart nigh mad with rejoicing.

II

In hot summer have I great rejoicing
When the tempests kill the earth's foul peace,
And the light'nings from black heav'n flash crimson,

But the form does tell us something about the narrator (there is no parallel function in either "Sestina for Ysolt" or "The Spear"); *crimson* first appears as the color of battle-spilled blood and becomes the color of the lightning and then of sunrise— underlining the man's obsession with mayhem. Similarly, after going through various minor transmutations, *music* ends up in the envoy as the noise made by swords. The poem is a bit like watching a street riot from a safe distance, and that is exactly the purpose of the elaborate form. De Born, the speaker, is (at least in this instance) a bloodthirsty maniac, and one function of the restraint of the sestina form is to avoid rendering the audience as bloodthirsty as De Born. Again we observe: there is no invitation to participate.

This suggests that, even in poems as early as these, the principal reason why the reader cannot enter into the emotion of the verse is that he is not supposed to. "At the Heart o' Me" and "The Seafarer," to take another pair of examples, differ in more than the verisimilitude of their Old English pretensions. The earlier poem, in using the Dowsonian devices that hinder the verisimilitude, appeals to evocative effects: the function of things like "Sapphire and emerald with / fine pearls between," and the woeful repetition of "at the heart o' me," is to invite the reader to share in the speaker's distress. '"The Seafarer" has none of this: it presents its persona for our observation only; we do not become the seafarer. What this sestina does, then, already points toward the operation of Pound's later work—toward Imagism, which centered upon showing things to the reader, not upon stirring him up about how it feels to see them, toward Vorticism, which was even freer of such "discursive" features, and toward the *Cantos*, the most violent and most lyrical parts of which we witness as in historical procession. Not that in "Altaforte" or the *Cantos* we are to feel no emotion at all; only it is not to be the emotion *in* the poem. Again, we react emotionally, but this is not the same as sighing languidly with the strangely unrobust Anglo-Saxon of "At the Heart o' Me."

The rather unimpressive images of "The Spear" culminate in one far from unimpressive image which tells us a little more about what Pound admired in the perceptive and precise Provençal and Tuscan poets:

> The light within her eyes, which slays
> Base thoughts and stilleth troubled waters,
> Is like the gold where sunlight plays
> Upon the still o'ershadowed waters.

It is a kind of image that Pound still finds attractive. The model for it (if there was a single model) seems to have been that line of Arnaut's about his lady's fair body "with the glamor of the lamp-light about it" (*SR* 34), which ten years later became (in the verse translations of Arnaut in *Instigations*), "Where lamp-light with light limb but half engages." This single line "may be taken to differentiate Arnaut Daniel from all other poets of Provence."[13] Parallels to it can be found everywhere in Pound's work, early and late. In "Piere Vidal Old"—

> Green was her mantle, close, and wrought
> Of some thin silk stuff that's scarce stuff at all,
> But like a mist wherethrough her white form fought.

In the very early "Night Litany"—

> . . . the glory of the shadow
> of thy Beauty hath walked

> Upon the shadow of the waters
> In this thy Venice.

And, the best known example (complete with "blending"), in Canto XVII: "In the gloom the gold / Gathers the light about it." In the *Cantos* especially, such effects make for some very subtle emotional discriminations. Even in the earlier poems they surpass the level of apprentice work:

> . . . Life died down in the lamp and flickered,
>   caught at the wonder.
>
>   · · · · ·
>
> Half the graven shoulder, the throat aflash with
> strands of light inwoven about it, loveli-
> est of all things, frail alabaster, ah me!
>   swift in departing.   ("Apparuit," *P* 2 68)

Pound is here depicting the poet's reward: a fleeting vision—of Beauty, we may say—out of that mysterious compendium of forms hidden in the flux of everyday events; to collect and hypostasize these visions eventually becomes the task of the *Cantos.* Its basis is in the disciplined capacity of perception and expression which enables a poet to discriminate, a discriminatory ability that enables a man first to have and then to reconstruct such a perception as *E quel remir contral lum de la lampa.* "Developing technique" is far too general a description for such exercises as those just reviewed. By reaching into the critical terminology of an earlier time, we can be more precise: they are a means of developing the faculty of *invention* in the old sense of finding figures, rhymes, and rhythms to fit the subject at hand—not a notebook of *aperçus* but devices of an alert, active intelligence in training for both a general athleticism and a skill in making specific graceful looping forehands that may some day be needed.

One more of Pound's sorties into the past is interesting, as prediction of things to come. "Guillaume de Lorris Belated: A Vison of Italy" from the first *Personae* is at once one of his most sustained masks and one of the least satisfactory. It begins with a crude kind of allegory:

> Wisdom set apart from all desire,
> A hoary Nestor with youth's own glad eyes,
> Him met I at the style, and all benign
> He greeted me an equal and I knew,
> By this his lack of pomp, he was himself.
>
> Slow-Smiling is companion unto him,
> And Mellow-Laughter serves, his trencherman.
> And I a thousand beauties there beheld.

There follows a vision of the cities of northern Italy, "Each as a woman wonder-fair"; the poet sees Verona, then "Fenice," and "then a maid of nine 'Pavia' hight." He learns that the "svelte Verona" he sees "enthroned two things: Verona, and a maid I knew on earth." He sees other cities in his vision and is finally borne to earth again by "That white-foot wind, pale Dawn's annunciatrice," having come to hate earth less because of his dream. Stylistically the poem is almost as integrated as "At the Heart o' Me" is not. Only an occasional word here seems out of keeping:

> Slender as mist-wrought maids and hamadryads
> Did meseem these shapes that ministered,
> These formed harmonies with lake-deep eyes,
> And first the cities of north Italy
> I did behold,
> Each as a woman wonder-fair,
> And svelte Verona first I met at eve;

> And in the dark we kissed and then the way
> Bore us somewhile apart.

The mist-wrought maids and hamadryads fail to harmonize, as later in the poem "elfish brows" and "so hale a draught" seem to jar. But what they fail to harmonize with is just what makes the poem unsatisfactory: the surprisingly well-sustained atmosphere of *Dante anglicé* that makes this seem the most obvious finger-exercise of all these early poems. It attempts nothing more than to reproduce as closely as possible in English Dante's manner—archaic (to us), visionary, wonder-stricken (reduced here to something like innocence). In the light of this poem, Pound's enthusiasm for Lawrence Binyon's translation of the *Divine Comedy* is easily understandable. Pound's style is a close anticipation of Binyon's:

> . . . her footsteps she retraced,
> Turning from me her eyes that wept and shone;
> At sight of which she made me more to haste.
> Thus I came to thee, as she desired, and won
> Thee from that ravening beast which would withhold
> The short way to the Beauteous Mount begun.[14]

The Dantescan style is sustained in Pound's poem; the allegorical pretensions are not. In spite of the title, in spite of the initial allegory and an attempt near the end to win by assertion the status of dream-allegory, the poem shifts almost immediately after the opening to a more visionary and generalized level. Dante does this, too, at the beginning of the *Inferno*, but his ravening wolf is not called Leering-Incontinence, and the movement from the brief allegory to the more visionary scenes is mediated by the appearance of Virgil. What is more important than Pound's failure to use allegory well is the nature of what he actually presents after his opening attempt: he fails as an allegorist by going not only beyond allegory but even beyond the metaphorical manner that is its next stage; the visions may be metaphors for Pound's subjective reaction upon seeing the various cities, but there is no more specific referent than this. And if this is the referent, then it is a collocation of feelings which evidently can be apprehended in no other terms but those in the poem. Some years later Pound was to describe the image as "the word beyond formulated language" (*GB* 102). This very position is implicit in the wordy and festooned images of "A Vision of Italy"; what remained, among other things, was to eliminate the festoons.

iii

It is clear, then, that some of the characteristics of Pound's London work represent an intensification of certain qualities in *A Lume Spento*—a use of visual effects, including color and lighting, the creation of special worlds by means of style and persona, and direct appeal to other poets' work. With Imagism on the horizon, however—Pound joined Hulme and F. S. Flint in the successor to the Poets' Club just a few days after *Personae* was published—we can see that he was not simply falling more deeply under the spell of his chosen guides, but achieving a better grasp of such of their techniques as would be useful to him. He was moving toward a poetry of his own—a more and more visual poetry, with increasingly meaningful rhythmic qualities and with increasing capacity for the accurate and compact transmission of refined perceptions.[15]

One of the more arresting developments in *Personae, Exultations,* and *Canzoni,* in fact, is a sudden increase in the use of large-scale visual effects. We have seen the use of emotionally charged details by Pound and Rossetti; the more thoroughgoing pictorialism of which this device is a part is adumbrated in *A Lume Spento,* in "Li Bel Chasteus" and in the first part of "De Aegypto." The prediction of "Famam Librosque Cano" is presented pictorially, built largely of images of detail; but as Pound presents his future, these details are presented novelistically—their import is rather thoroughly explained. In this first collection the pictorial approach is not a primary orientation and, as in "Famam Librosque Cano," it is often diluted by commentary. There is little there to compare with the careful word drawing of, say, Rossetti's "Woodspurge." What little pictorialism there is does not depart much from the charged detail, and when Pound does "make his picture" it is apt to be only briefly, as in "Invern," where the speaker claims that he

> Must take cramped joy in tomed Longinus
> That, read I him first time
> The woods agleam with summer
> Or 'mid desirous winds of spring,
> Had set me singing spheres
> Or made heart to wander forth among warm roses
> Or curl in grass nest 'neath a kindly moon.

Not until the final line do we find anything sufficiently particularized to constitute a definite visual image.

Nowhere is the new emphasis upon larger visual effects so dramatically illustrated as in the two versions of "Praise of Ysolt" ("Vana" in *A Lume Spento*). In its first published version the poem ends at the line, "Blowing they know not whither, seeking a song." As published in *Personae* the following year and in all subsequent collections, the poem adds a Rossettian account of visitations of a woman sent by the speaker's soul (much in the manner of Rossetti's "Hand and Soul"):

> White words as snow flakes but they are cold,
> Moss words, lip words, words of slow streams.
>
> . . . . .
>
> . . . in the morn of my years there came a woman
> As moonlight calling,

As the moon calleth the tides,
                    "Song, a Song."

. . . . .

. . . my soul sent a woman, a woman of the wonder-folk,
A woman as fire upon the pine woods

. . . . .

And I "I have no song,"
Till my soul sent a woman as the sun.

The presentation of the poetic impulse by the image of a woman
is important, but it is of more immediate significance that the
woman herself is presented wholly in terms of visual similes.
Whether the additional material simply had been omitted from
A Lume Spento or newly created for *Personae* matters little, for
each version is consonant with the tenor of the volume in which
it appears, and it seems likely that in using the longer version
Pound may have been deliberately trying a different, if not
necessarily new, tack. For "Praise of Ysolt" is not the only
poem in *Personae* which presents such visual effects. "Occidit"
(a thematic precursor of "Pan Is Dead") is as carefully pictorial,
and as clotted with associative metaphors, as Rossetti's most
painterly poems:

Autumnal breaks the flame upon the sun-set herds.
The sheep on Gilead as tawn hair gleam
Neath Mithra's dower and his slow departing,
While in the sky a thousand fleece of gold
Bear, each his tribute, to the waning god.

Hung on the rafters of the effulgent west,
Their tufted splendour shields his decadence,

> As in our southern lands brave tapestries
> Are hung king-greeting from the ponticells
>
>   . . . . .
>
> Wherein the storied figures live again,
> Wind-molden back unto their life's erst guise,
> All tremulous beneath the many-fingered breath
> That Aufidus doth take to house his soul.

There are, in fact—and this is the main point of interest—
a number of early poems that utilize the mannerisms of Rossetti's painting. This is to speak not of parallels of composi-
tional and dramatic effects—the general management of the
dramatic moments—but more specifically of Pound's verbal
approximations to the coloristic and lighting effects of painting. We have seen an example from "Piere Vidal Old" in the
lines about La Loba's gown, which was "like a mist where-
through her white form fought." The subtlety of perception
that Pound admired in Arnaut is very much akin to the dim and
suggestive manipulation of light and darkness in Pre-Raphaelite
painting; in Burne-Jones's "Annunciation," for example,
details, though given in abundance, are so laden with suggestive
qualification—like the "sheep on Gilead" which "as tawn hair
gleam"—that the details and indeed the entire painting seem to
emerge rather than to stand solidly forth. This effect, of course,
is the whole point about La Loba's mistlike silks, and Pound's
description of the church in "A Vision of Italy" gives the same
impression:

>   altar candles blazed out as dim stars,
> And all the gloom was soft, and shadowy forms
> Made and sang God, within the far-off choir.
> And in a clear space high behind
> Them and the tabernacle of that place,

Two tapers shew the master of the keys
As some white power pouring forth itself.

Poems like "Nils Lykke" combine the allusive tendency of
A Lume Spento with this pictorial presentation of static scenes
and with Pound's use of the very gestures typical of the poses
in Pre-Raphaelite art—all this to such an extent that some of
them read like deliberate descriptions of paintings. "Nils Lykke"
itself has much of the mood and visual suggestiveness of Rossetti's "Galahad in the Chapel," and the lines "a-murmuring
in the dark . . . And a-reaching out your long hands / Between
me and my beloved" closely approximate the poses of some
of Rossetti's and Burne-Jones's figures. So the qualities in which
Pound's work harks back to Pre-Raphaelite visual art are not
limited to those of mood and occasion, but involve technical
similarities as well. This is not the only time in his career that
he has revealed a partiality for the effects of visual art.

Personae and *Exultations* evince a greater and greater preoccupation with things seen. In the *Cantos* light becomes the
symbol of the creative Intelligence; the corollary metaphor,
seeing as a complex function of both the faculty of sight and the
intelligence, has its inception years earlier.[16] If it is first evi-
denced in what seems to be a general preoccupation with visual
effects in poetry, the development of his own work reflects
contact with progressively more modern schools of painting and
sculpture.[17]

Just as some of Pound's visual effects are taken from Pre-
Raphaelite painting, some of his coloristic devices are drawn
from the Impressionists. In "The House of Splendour," the
primary sensory appeal is based upon an Impressionist juxtaposition of colors:

And I have seen her there within her house,
With six great sapphires hung along the wall,

> Low, panel-shaped, a-level with her knees,
> And all her robe was woven of pale gold.
>
> There are there many rooms and all of gold,
> Of woven walls deep patterned, of email,
> Of beaten work; and through the claret stone,

"Au Jardin" makes a more limited use of this approach, but its appeal is occasionally similar:

> O you away high there,
>   you that lean
> From amber lattices upon the cobalt night
>
>   . . . . .
>
> But she danced like a pink moth in the shrubbery.

A few years later than these poems, "Albatre" imitates Whistler's "Harmony in Grey and Black":

> This lady in the white bath-robe which she
>   calls a peignoir,
> Is, for the time being, the mistress of my
>   friend,
> And the delicate white feet of her little white dog
> Are not more delicate than she is,
> Nor would Gautier himself have despised their con-
>   trasts in whiteness . . .

Now the color scheme of the first two examples is extremely literary; it is drawn primarily from the poetry, and not the painting, of the Pre-Raphaelites, and even "Albatre," aside from its astringent judgmental implications, accomplishes little in the way of visual effects that could not be paralleled in the poems of Wilde and Symons. But the poem is not meant to emulate Wilde's "Symphony in Yellow." The coloristic details are not its chief concern. The arrangement of whites ministers to the poem's implicit comment upon the lady's pretense to a Decadence-inspired "life in imitation of art." Pound tends to use particularly Impressionist techniques for purposes subordinate in this way to the ends of the poem as a whole; this is true even of "The House of Splendour," where the function of the color images is mainly suggestiveness. Yet there the imagery seems to attract excessive attention, as if exerting an expressive force of primary significance. And "The House of Splendour" does, in fact, anticipate a later development in which Pound seeks aesthetic values pre-eminently available through the nonliterary devices of pictorial art.

He seems to have admired Impressionism first because it stimulated an awareness of form[18] and, later, because Impressionist painters had arrived at an aesthetic concept that he himself was just beginning to explore: the expressive potentialities of form in itself. During the Imagist and Vorticist days Pound frequently quotes Whistler to the effect that "The picture is interesting not because it is Trotty Veg, but because it is an arrangement in colour" (quoted GB 98). The poems built on this rationale use devices drawn from pictorial art for effects far more significant to the whole composition than in the preceding examples:

> The swirl of light follows me through the square,
>   The smoke of incense
> Mounts from the four horns of my bed-posts,
> The water-jet of gold light bears us up through the
>   ceilings;
> Lapped in the gold-coloured flame I descend through
>   the aether.
> The silver ball forms in my hand,
> It falls and rolls to your feet.   ("Phanopoeia," I)

The purpose of such a poem, as its title implies, is merely to cast images upon the mind, to utilize the aesthetic qualities of a series of "abstract" images. The first stanza of the similar "Game of Chess" suggests more clearly the origin of the technique:

> Red knights, brown bishops, bright queens,
> Striking the board, falling in strong "L"s of
> colour.
> Reaching and striking in angles,
> holding lines in one colour.
> This board is alive with light;
> these pieces are living in form,
> Their moves break and reform the pattern:
> luminous green from the rooks,
> Clashing with "X"s of queens,
> looped with the knight-leaps.

Pound's finally limited acceptance of Impressionism[19] was based on the implications of that statement of Whistler's; Pound's assertion in *Gaudier-Brzeska* that "There is undoubtedly a language of form and colour" represents an important point of agreement between him and the Impressionists but, though he recognized their technical achievements, he rejected the passivity that the name of the school implies. He turned to the neo-Cubism of Henri Gaudier-Brzeska and Wyndham Lewis when, as in "The Game of Chess," the chief appeal of a poem was to visual values—and this fact touches upon the still point around which the seemingly chaotic world of Pound's art revolves.

The *Cantos* furnish a main clue to these issues, in their presentation of two worlds, a world of beauty and permanence and one of ugliness, perversion, and flux. A similar contrast, though of course much less pronounced, is suggested by the very form of

Pound's early poems; a striking and valuable moment implies moments less striking and less valuable. These valuable moments are not easily won, and the very fact that we call them moments is sufficient comment upon their duration—"The undeniable tradition of metamorphoses teaches us that things do not remain always the same. They become other things by swift and unanalysable process" (*LE* 431). In the face of the confusion this condition inevitably produces, only one quality enables man to function as a purposeful being and prevents his becoming an insignificant reflection of the chaos around him: the power of discrimination.

To be civilized is, as we have seen, to have swift apperception of the "complicated life of today; it is to have a subtle and instantaneous perception of it, such as savages and wild animals have of the necessities and dangers of the forest." Failure to exert the mind's discriminatory powers can have far-reaching effects—"perception" reflects "intelligence," and if one is muddled the other must be, too. Medieval asceticism, which reflects a failure to make "the dissociation that it is not the body but its diseases and its infirmities which are evil," is invariably "accompanied by bad and niggled sculpture (Angoulême or Bengal) . . . the architectural ornament of bigotry, superstition, and mess" ("Cavalcanti," *LE* 150–151). In this same essay, Pound asserts, "Loss of values is due usually to lumping and lack of dissociation." And again, "Unless a term is left meaning one particular thing, and unless all attempt to unify different things, however small the difference, is clearly abandoned, all metaphysical thought degenerates into a soup. A soft terminology is merely an endless series of indefinite middles."

The perceptions embodied in good art are one means of keeping us out of the soup, for "Art deals with certitude"—with forms, which express discriminations of particular "energies" from the surrounding confusion. Moreover, an experience transmuted into a form by art and thereby dissociated from the flux is rescued from the "swift and unanalysable process" that would otherwise sweep it away; a painting or a poem or a song is a permanent acquisition. Implicit in such an argument, of course, is the notion that the properly apperceptive man will be "more interested in the 'arrangement' than in the dead matter arranged," for of the two, form is essential—from the atom to the Empire State Building, it alone is what differentiates one lump of matter from another.

The apprehension of forms requires an exertion of the will. Experience does not come to us in neatly discrete forms, to be registered; its natural condition is chaos, and we transmute it when we organize it into intelligible conceptions. For such a process, the passivity of "taking impressions" will not do. Speaking of his well-known Imagist poem, "In a Station of the Metro," Pound says:

> In a poem of this sort one is trying to record the precise instant when a thing outward and objective transforms itself, or darts into a thing inward and subjective.
>
> This particular sort of consciousness has not been identified with impressionist art. (GB 103)

"An 'idea' has little value apart from the modality of the mind which receives it." The Imagist poem, like the "Vorticist" painting, takes a detail from the flux in which we live and gives it meaning and value by exposing it to the modality of the artist's mind. This feat, as Pound sees it, is beyond Impressionism's accurate registration of external phenomena: "The organization of forms is a much more energetic and creative action than the copying or imitating of light on a haystack" (GB 107). For Pound the formed work of art expresses a concentration of forces, forces wielded by the artist against the dead matter around him; not the play of circumstances upon the artist's sensibility, but the play of the artist's sensibility upon circumstances.

Why Pound should place so high a value upon pictorial effects in general is another question. The concept of the visible as a weak image of the invisible, of course, goes far back in the history of Western thought and obviously plays a part in Pound's choice of techniques. In fact, what seems to begin as a merely stylistic preference actually becomes the point on which concerns of style and ideology converge. On a workaday level, the use of specifically visual images simply presents the least danger of imprecision. An abstract statement of the thought or emotion the poet seeks to convey would be, for example, the least satisfactory mode of presentation; at best it would express only a limited amount of the meaning at which it aimed. The sensory image, on the other hand, is something we can know, and in presenting such an image Pound gives us pictures of "things" containing, theoretically, the emotion to be conveyed. Now, as Kenner wisely cautions, this does not mean that Pound thinks of poetry as a branch of painting. The poet's image is a combination of semantic, visual, aural, and rhythmic values. The appeal of the image to aural and rhythmic values is subordinate, though still necessary if the image is to convey a total experience. Some shade of meaning or subtle qualification of feeling which may be inexpressible in words or which might require two or three sentences to "explain" can be adequately suggested by the poem's rhythm or by its musical qualities.[20] A precisely demarcated image accompanied by its own particular rhythm and sound will present not just an idea or an emotion but, again, a total experience—the idea or emotion meaningfully particularized by the mind that first received it. It is, in other words, "that which presents an intellectual and emotional complex in an instant of time" ("A Few Don'ts by an Imagist," *LE* 4). This, Pound's earliest definition of the image (he later defined it in *Gaudier-Brzeska* as "a radiant node or cluster"), suggests its relationship to the charged detail of which I spoke in connection with Pound and Rossetti.

In both definitions of the image, Pound emphasizes its power of sudden revelation. This formulation (which has the incidental advantage of not raising the difficult question of whether the image really "embodies" the emotion) is roughly applicable to the charged detail, whose function is to capture the emotional suggestiveness of a swift but vivid perception. The charged detail is primarily a device of implication, and what it implies may be nothing more definite than a state of extreme emotional tension; as we have seen, it is usually a part of some larger composition. "In a Station of the Metro" removes the detail from its context and presents it as a perception of primary significance:

> The apparition of these faces in the crowd;
> Petals on a wet, black bough.

The poem is a "precise interpretive metaphor," and rather more complicated than the earlier device, in that it seeks to superimpose the speaker's interpretation of the experience upon his very presentation of the experience. It is literally a revelatory moment: the speaker expresses himself at the moment he becomes aware of what the perception "means" to him.

In "Gentildonna," another Imagist poem of Pound's, what looks like an emotionally charged detail actually plays back over the entire poem:

> She passed and left no quiver in the veins, who
> > now
> Moving among the trees, and clinging
> > in the air she severed,
> Fanning the grass she walked on then, endures:
>
> Grey olive leaves beneath a rain-cold sky.

This is a striking exemplification of two apparently contra-
dictory methods. On the one hand it threatens vagueness in
demanding of the reader "a fulfillment or crystallization of
beauty implied"—the impact of the poem is withheld until
we realize that it portrays a spiritual visitation and not the
appearance of a living woman; and yet it attains a kind of precision in the last line, where a single visual image both deline-
ates the appearance the ghostly woman presents and sums up
the mood implicit in the rest of the poem. This image is the
charged detail raised to the status of major significance—more
carefully chosen, perhaps, and chosen with an eye to a more
particular effect certainly, but not essentially different from
those vaguer gestures in Rossetti's and in Pound's earlier work.

It is tempting to see Pound's early search for a language as a
process of working his way free of, say, Browning or Rossetti,
or, more likely, Yeats, and to take his own metaphor as definitive
and speak of his early purgation. But such a negative image—
Marsyas losing his skin—blurs the much truer one of a man
building. Any struggle against Browningese or Rossetti-itis
or hyper-Yeatsism is really a side issue in a process of construction. The most nearly accurate image is that of a man with
immense creative gifts inspecting the practices of his predecessors, picking various useful aspects of their work, while
always reshaping and recombining them, limiting or enhancing
the effects of one with the possibilities in another, for his
own unique purposes. This would seem to be the image Pound
preferred for his early career:

> My pawing over the ancients and semi-ancients has
> been one struggle to find out what has been done, once
> for all, better than it can ever be done again, and to
> find out what remains for us to do, and plenty does re-
> main, for if we still feel the same emotions as those
> which launched the thousand ships, it is quite certain

> that we come on those feelings differently, through different nuances, by different intellectual gradations. Each age has its own abounding gifts.
>
> ("Prolegomena," 1912; *LE* 11)

His conception of poetic ability is the combination of a divine impulse and a voluntary and scrupulous cultivation of the means of expression—the poet-critic's classic definition.

Afterword:

The Ladies of Helicon

"Fool!" said my Muse to me, "Look in thy heart, and write."

—Sir Philip Sidney

IN THE BOOKS he has published under the title *Personae* Pound gathered not only his kind of dramatic lyric, but translations and "vision" poems as well. There is nothing incongruous in this gathering, for all are different versions of a single process. To the extent that the persona is a practice device, it can also be a peg to hang a poem upon—as we have seen, a form in which to embody a given experience. From this point of view the mask is essentially a focal device, a kind of image in which the feelings impelling the poet to write converge. Embodied in the poem's "account" of the persona's experience is the poet's own emotion.

In saying in the *Fortnightly Review* article on Vorticism that his translations were "a more complicated kind of mask," Pound was simply admitting to a fact that is clear enough in his work. For the translation, too, is a focal device. In the actual making of poems, the process behind the translation is almost identical with that in the dramatic lyric—the finding of poetic moments congruent with the poet's own experience. The only difference—and if the translation is viewed as one means of enriching the poet's emotional capacities, it is not so great a difference—is that in a translation the "drama" from which the poetic moment is taken pre-exists: Pound finds congenial moments, say, in Cavalcanti's poetry, whereas for the persona poems or the visions he must invent his own. He speaks through Cavalcanti just as in a dramatic lyric he speaks through Cino or Bertran de Born. The process aims at the recreation of past modes of experience and expression—this last being more than merely "style." The poet experiences a poem of Cavalcanti's at a high pitch of emotional intensity; the original is taken into his sensibility, and what emerges is a faithful poetic depiction of the translator's intense experience—not a poem *about* what the poet felt while reading, like Keats's sonnet about Chapman's Homer, but one that mirrors the poem as a subjective experience, a total emotional equivalent of the original, ideally complete with the requisite form for expression. The "experience" the translator expresses is, of course, his experience of the original experience. Like the persona, then, the translation is a central image through which the internal event is consolidated and conveyed.

The vision poems constitute a third kind of image. It would be better to call them focal-image poems rather than vision poems, for their definitive characteristic is that they present their content in terms of the speaker's contemplation of some central figure. This figure may be an object—elaborately splendid as in "The House of Splendour" or hypnotically simple as in "The Flame"—or, very often, it may be a woman, as in "Ballatetta":

> The light became her grace and dwelt among
> Blind eyes and shadows that are formed as men;
> Lo, how the light doth melt us into song;
>
> . . . . .
>
> . . . no gossamer is spun
> So delicate as she is, when the sun
> Drives the clear emeralds from the bended grasses
> Lest they should parch too swiftly, where she passes.

The image of the woman, like that of the House, is the objective embodiment of a psychic occurrence, and as such it is at one with Pound's personae and his translations. In all three kinds of poem, then, Pound is presenting his own moments of intense emotion in whatever form best fits each one, constructing now a central image, now a momentary sensibility.

Rossetti, "Dante's Vision of Rachel and Leah"
The Tate Gallery, London

"The image as a moment of awareness . . . the two figures . . .
epitomize a feeling of profound inner peace" (p. 19).
"The image of the woman . . . is the objective embodiment
of a psychic occurrence" (p. 230).

gestions. The ambiguity, of course, is a functional part of the poem; the title functions exactly as its Dantescan model functions —as part of a manner of presentation calculated to raise the lady to a level of such spiritual significance as to make the reader doubt how fleshly she really is.

"A Virginal" deals with a similar kind of experience but, as we see in its first eight lines, with the speaker's feet planted more firmly on the ground:

> No, no! Go from me. I have left her lately.
> I will not spoil my sheath with lesser brightness,
> For my surrounding air hath a new lightness;
> Slight are her arms, yet they have bound me straitly
> And left me cloaked as with a gauze of aether;
> As with sweet leaves; as with subtle clearness.
> Oh, I have picked up magic in her nearness
> To sheathe me half in half the things that sheathe her.

We may perhaps take this poem as a masculine counterpart of "Speech for Psyche." At any rate, the starting point of the experience seems clearly terrestrial. For one thing, the speaker uses similes rather than the assertive visionary description and metaphors of "Apparuit." Though the similes suggest a "mundane" reading of the event, however, there are obvious suggestions of the extraterrestrial. Any one of the descriptions of the speaker's feelings is perhaps simply a lover's hyperbolic praise; taken together they suggest an intensity of emotion that transcends the tactile and the psychological.

This same kind of ambiguity, though not buttressed by stylistic bric-a-brac, informs "Ballatetta," as we have seen in Chapter Two, but "Francesca" is probably the most successful early attempt to have the best of two worlds. When the poet anticipates the coming of the lady "out of a confusion of people, / Out of a turmoil of speech about you," he may be referring to a turmoil of speech *concerning* her as easily as to the speech that surrounds her in a crowded place; and certainly the first lines of the second stanza do not preclude our seeing the poem as the poet's vision of some ideal Beauty now being bandied about in, say, a cocktail-party conversation on Art. Or does a particular real lady stand out in a crowd of other people? Or does the third line of the poem refer to a kind of vision the speaker is used to experiencing upon contemplating a confusion of human forms? Or is the speaker, in a Pre-Raphaelite mood, musing upon those instances when the fleetingly glimpsed beauty of a girl on a crowded street suddenly seems to him a manifestation of the hidden goddess Beauty? No comprehensive answer lies in any one of these possibilities, of course, for the ambiguity of the poem transforms the lady into a reflection of a state of mind which may stem from either a visionary or a real experience and which partakes, as such things do, of the characteristics of both.

These poems are examples of how Pound was able to translate his mystical proclivities into modes of experience that do not vanish in the clear light of day. "The House of Splendour" is such a poem, with its "And I have seen my Lady in the sun, / Her hair was spread about, a sheaf of wings, / And red the sunlight was, behind it all," and its final stanza:

> Here am I come perforce my love of her,
> Behold mine adoration
> Maketh me clear, and there are powers in this
> Which, played on by the virtues of her soul,
> Break down the four-square walls of standing time.

Again, this is not poetic treatment of a real lady. Pound has described another passage in this poem as "perfectly definite visual imagination" (*L* 159)—terms that apply to the whole poem, for it is a delineation of a state of mind. The Lady is internal, and we may take the house of splendour as the poem itself.

This is to suggest, as I did earlier, that these love poems spring as much from the poet's communing with himself as the persona poems do. They represent more successful exploitations of a resource Pound first elucidated for himself in that expansion of "Vana" into "Praise of Ysolt" which appeared in the first *Personae*. The poem recounts how the speaker could not compose because "she I sang of hath gone from me," and how to replace that Lady his soul sent "a woman of the wonder-folk":

> . . . as the sun calleth to the seed,
> As the spring upon the bough
> So is she that cometh, the mother of songs.

Here is the prototype of all the visionary ladies in Pound's verse, and she is clearly an anima figure—the internalized feminine principle, or, more exactly, the creative principle in the poet himself, which he personifies as a beautiful woman of mysteriously divine origin. The poet bows not to a beautiful lady but to that in himself which enables him to make beautiful forms: these poems are analogous to—and certainly no less devout than —the addresses to the Muse of the classical poets. The poet praises this "lady" for the beauty of the praise she enables him to bestow: "Lo, how the light doth melt us into song."

In "Na Audiart" we see Pound dressing up his anima as a real historical personage—perhaps in the manner of Jaufre Rudel— and by the time we get to poems like "Ballatetta" and "Francesca," the figure has become a full-scale conceit that makes possible the "exteriorization of the sensibility."

Further, Pound is at least willing to imitate poetry in which the Lady is an actual cosmic potency. In the *Cantos* the poet's subjective states manifest themselves as goddesses (gods, we recall, being eternal states of mind). So his creative energy presents itself as an anima, synonymous with cosmic energies. At the least we may say that on this view the self and the universe are continuous, the one colored by the other—and, as we have seen, Pound's aesthetic implies that the universe can have no meaning without the poet's perceiving mind. In this general belief he is at one with the version of romanticism manifested in the nineteenth century in the Pre-Raphaelites, in the Decadents, and finally, as we have seen, in Yeats. Pound's use of this anima figure even more loudly proclaims his ties with those poets.

Thus "Praise of Ysolt" seems essentially a verse rendering of Rossetti's short story "Hand and Soul," in which a young painter, despairing over the insignificance (as it seems to him) of his work, is visited, lectured, and inspired by a beauteous lady who turns out to be his own soul. Like the woman in Pound's poem, Rossetti's lady sits for a portrait—again as in Pound, the artist is seen as depicting what is in himself. In his art as in his life, Rossetti made repeated appeal to the notion of the *femme inspiratrice*. In "The Blessed Damozel" she is presented wholly as a love object, but as she recurs, in a thousand guises, in Rossetti's work, her preliminary significance becomes plain. In "Genius in Beauty" from *The House of Life* she is the immutable focus of creative energy—"not in Spring's or Summer's sweet footfall / More gathered gifts exuberant Life bequeaths / Than doth this sovereign face." In the sonnet "Gracious Moonlight," some strikingly Poundian terminology (the Lady as celestial emanation, and a beautiful object as a "confluence of forces") accrues to this inspiriting figure:

> Of that face
> What shall be said,—which, like a governing star,
> Gathers and garners from all things that are
> Their silent penetrative loveliness?

In the sonnet "Soul's Beauty," as in the painting that inspired it, the lady becomes the hypostasis of Beauty: "I have somewhat extended my idea of the picture [Sibylla Palmifera]," Rossetti wrote, "and have written a sonnet . . . to embody the conception —that of beauty the palm-giver, i.e., the Principle of Beauty, which draws all high-toned men to itself, whether with the aim of embodying it in art, or only of attaining its enjoyment in life."[2] In "Birth Bond" the lady is again revealed as internal, as alter ego; the speaker addresses her as a kind of soul mate— "my soul's birth-partner." Rossetti could read it all in Shelley.

There is another side to her. "The Blessed Damozel" pairs with the prostitute "Jenny"; the principle of beauty has its counterpart in the evil Lilith (Adam's witch-wife) of "Body's Beauty," which follows "Soul's Beauty" in *The House of Life*; the anima figure of "Hand and Soul" pairs with the seductive *femme fatale* (literally *fatale*) of "The Orchard Pit," whose narrator describes a dream lady bent on enticing him to a death-in-love or, more exactly, a death-in-sex. Oswald Doughty mistakenly describes Lilith and "The Orchard Pit" as dealing with "the prostitute or similar theme,"[3] which is not the point: the anima and the siren are the same figure viewed from opposite sides. Attempts to find fleshly embodiments of the ideal must lead to corruption, and the long-sought-after ideal can become a corrosive torment— Rossetti could read it all in Keats, in *Lamia* and "La Belle Dame sans Merci." To pursue the ideal on its own terms is to pursue death, and to compromise with the actual is to pursue corruption. Rossetti's twisted relationship with Elizabeth Siddal is an unappetizing case in point.

The road from Rossetti to Pound is paved with versions of this anima figure. The Symons ·poem that Pound says (*LE* 367) he formerly admired uses it:

> I am the flame of beauty
> And I burn that all may see
> Beauty.   ("Modern Beauty")

Symons' work, in fact, is pervaded by trivialized versions of the

Lady-anima. For example, in his "Alla Passeretta Bruna":

> If I bid you, you will come,
>   If I bid you, you will go,
>
>   . . . . .
>
> I shall keep you as we keep
>   Flowers for memory, hid away,
>   Under many a newer token
> Buried deep—
>   Roses of a gaudier day,
>   Rings and trinkets, bright and broken.
>
> Other women I shall love,
>   Fame and fortune I may win,
>   But when fame and love forsake me
> And the light is night above,
>   You will let me in,
>   You will take me.

So in "Love in Dreams":

> I lie in the dark and see
>   In the dark her radiant face;
> She smiles, she speaks, and to me, me only;
>   She is mine for a moment's space.

This is fairly simple-minded verse and claims our attention only as an historical analogue to, and a probable model for, some of Pound's early poems. We find the theme in Pound's early "In Epitaphium Eius":

> They called him fickle that the lambent flame
> Caught "Biće" in each new-blown name,

> And loved all fairness though its hidden guise
> Lurked various in half an hundred eyes.

Dowson's Cynara belongs to the same "tradition."

To the darker side of the Lady we may link Swinburne's gallery of deadly, destructive, and sadistic women. For Swinburne as for Rossetti, the Lady is an immortal force of crucial spiritual significance (both Faustine and Dolores are immortal, and the Lady of "Triumph of Time," who had the power of salvation over the poet, has driven him into deadly sin by rejecting him). Swinburne's evil women are inversions of Rossetti's anima figures but, as the addressees of the poems in which they figure, they must be credited as the beings who move the poet to song; this means that their function in the Swinburnean scheme of things is the same as the function of Rossetti's soul images. As a matter of fact, the deadly woman does not appear much in Pound's early work; the shadow of this part of Swinburne's apparatus falls mainly upon the Circe principle (for she is not a fully realized figure) in the *Cantos*.

The notion of the Muse, whatever its true role for the poets of antiquity, is the concomitant of an inspirational view of poetic creation. It drops out of sight whenever the ideas of inspiration and subjectivity cease to be fashionable, and whenever it has reappeared in modern times it has tended to accompany subjective, often mystical poetry—in more recent times this poetry has tended to be specifically romantic, courting the transcendence of the limitations of identity, celebrating the validity of irrational modes of experience, and, sometimes, arguing for the spiritual unity of man and nature. In English poetry, at any rate, after Milton's appeal to Urania in *Paradise Lost* (even he, as an "inspired" poet, speaks with the structured subjectivity of a seer listening to God), the Muse or muse principle is seen no more as a seriously offered theory of creativity or a seriously attempted conceit—until we come to Shelley, who replaces her with anima figures in *Epipsychidion* and *Alastor*. The Middle Ages had seen the revival of this figure, after the erosion of classical mythology and the supervention of Christianity, perhaps in the person of the Virgin and certainly in the romantic verse of Provence and Tuscany, where the Lady, as we have seen, is an inspirational figure first of personal and gradually of divine significance. Dante's Beatrice fuses the two levels of subjectivity, the private and the religious.

The foregoing chapters have made it plain enough how solidly Pound is linked with this inspirational, romantic tradition: his adaptation of the anima figure is but another manifestation of the link. The fact of the relationship needs to be stated with care. Kenner's view of Pound as an unshakably objective, mimetic artist, though it flies in the face of all I have said about the true nature of Pound's poetic moments, is in its way true. But what is involved is the mimetic presentation of the inner discoveries of a thoroughgoing subjectivist. In view of the actual poems Pound has written, their shape and their style, it would not be very useful to say that he is a romantic poet. But though it is polemically convenient to see him as antiromantic, reforming the errant waywardness of Anglo-American poetry and setting our literature back upon its properly Aristotelian base, such a conception simply does not do justice to the totality of Pound's aesthetic: it ignores the neo-Platonism in his thought and obliterates the deep roots his work has in the romantic tradition—he wrote *The Spirit of Romance* presumably to show that the poets discussed there had done things of value.

Therefore, limited though it has been in scope, the evidence of the foregoing pages has touched on things of pervasive and permanent significance in Pound's work. We have detected the forming of those principles that constitute many of the major preoccupations of his later poetic career, and these preoccupations are not fatally at variance with those of romance. They are more inclusive and ultimately, perhaps, more coherent: they look to the extension of an individual psyche into a cosmological principle; they look to the establishment of a Paradise regained, a City of God not on earth but in the mind.

Notes

I. The Poetic Moment

1. In "At the Mermaid," speaking in the voice of Shakespeare, Browning again reveals the function of the poetic mask as a concealment for the artist's private inner world:

> Which of you did I enable
>   Once to slip inside my breast,
> There to catalogue and label
>   What I like least, what love best,
> Hope and fear, believe and doubt of,
>   Seek and shun, respect—deride?
> Who has right to make a route of
>   Rarities he found inside?
>
> Rarities, or, as he'd rather,
>   Rubbish such as stocks his own;
>
>   . . . . .
>
> Friends, I doubt not he'd display you
>   Brass—myself call orichalc,—
> Furnish much amusement: pray you
>   Therefore be content I baulk
> Him and you, and bar my portal!
>   Here's my work outside: opine
> What's inside me mean and mortal!
>   Take your pleasure, leave me mine!

2. Alba Warren asserts that the dramatic lyric was the fruit of Browning's effort "to unite representation and expression, to incorporate both the real and the ideal in a single poetic form"—*English Poetic Theory 1825–1865* (Princeton: Princeton University Press, 1950), p. 116. In Browning's own terms, "So write a book shall mean beyond the facts, / Suffice the eye and save the soul besides."

3. Hugh Kenner, *The Poetry of Ezra Pound* (Norfolk: New Directions, 1950), pp. 134–135.

4. W. H. Hunt, *Pre-Raphaelitism and the Pre-Raphaelite Brotherhood*, 2 vols. (London: Macmillan, 1905). Ford Madox Ford, one of Pound's closest early allies, knew the book well. See his *The Pre-Raphaelite Brotherhood* (London: Duckworth, 1907).

5. For example, in "The Prose Tradition in Verse" (*LE* 371).

6. Nicolette Gray, *Rossetti, Dante and Ourselves* (London: Faber, 1947), p. 29.

7. *Ibid.*, pp. 23–24. Miss Gray's sensitivity to the moods of Rossetti's paintings obscures for her readers the grievous aesthetic and technical shortcomings of his work.

8. All of the Rossetti poems discussed here are taken from his *Collected Works,* ed. William M. Rossetti, 2 vols. (London, 1886).

9. Miles Slatin, " 'Mesmerism': A Study of Ezra Pound's Use of the Poetry of Robert Browning" (unpubl. diss., Yale University, 1957), p. 264.

10. Revised "Conclusion" to *The Renaissance.*

11. "Conclusion: The Choice," *Studies in Prose and Verse* (London: J. M. Dent and Co.; New York: E. P. Dutton and Co., 1904), p. 290. T. E. Hulme's idea that modern poetry "no longer deals with action, it has become definitely and finally introspective and deals with expression and communication of momentary phases in the poet's mind," ("Lecture on Modern Poetry," in *Further Speculations,* ed. Sam Hines [Minneapolis: University of Minnesota Press, 1955], p. 72), and his jottings in "Notes on Language and Style" in *Speculations* ("Literature as the deliberate standing still hovering and thinking oneself into an artificial view, for the moment") both make it clear that Pound was not the only one of that group of London intellectuals to feel the influence of this approach.

12. For examples, in *London Nights* see "At Glan-y-Wern: White and Rose," and in *Silhouettes* see "An Angel of Perugino."

13. "Affirmations—II, Vorticism," *NA*, XVI (January 14, 1915), 278; a different essay from the "Vorticism" reprinted in *GB* from the *Fortnightly Review.*

14. "I Gather the Limbs of Osiris—IV, A Beginning," *NA*, X (December 21, 1911), 179; series hereafter cited as "Osiris."

15. "Osiris—VI, On Virtue," *NA*, X (January 4, 1912), 224.

16. H. A. Taine, *History of English Literature*, trans. H. Van Laun (New York, 1879), pp. 1, 19.

17. In Yeats's *Mythologies* (New York and London: Macmillan, 1959), p. 305.

18. Yeats, "Autumn of the Body," *Ideas of Good and Evil*, in *Essays and Introductions* (New York: Macmillan, 1961), p. 192.

19. Humphry House, "Pre-Raphaelite Poetry," *All in Due Time* (London: Rupert Hart-Davis, 1955), pp. 153–154.

20. Holbrook Jackson, *The Eighteen-Nineties*, (New York: Alfred A. Knopf, 1923), pp. 70–71. And in 1914, at almost the very time the remark I have just quoted was being written, Pound was proclaiming his lineage: "We turn back, we artists, to the powers of the air, to the djinns who were our allies aforetime, to the spirits of our ancestors. It is by them that we have ruled and shall rule, and by their connivance that we shall mount again into our hierarchy." "The New Sculpture," *Egoist*, I (February 16, 1914), 68.

21. From an unpublished letter to his father, quoted in Richard Ellmann, *The Identity of Yeats* (New York: Oxford University Press, 1954), p. 128.

22. Jackson, p. 144.

23. Jackson, p. 70.

24. House, p. 157.

25. *The Celtic Twilight* (London: Lawrence and Bullen, 1893), p. 6.

26. *The Wind among the Reeds* (New York: John Lane, 1905), p. 73; a reprint of the 1899 London edition by Elkin Mathews.

27. "How I Began," *T.P.'s Weekly*, XXI (June 6, 1913), 707.

28. Yeats, "Magic," *Ideas of Good and Evil*, in *Essays and Introductions*, pp. 43–44.

29. *Per Amica Silentia Lunae* (New York: Macmillan, 1918), p. 35.

30. *The Celtic Twilight* (London: A. H. Bullen, 1902), p. 108.

31. Yeats and E. J. Ellis, *The Works of William Blake*, 3 vols. (London, 1893), I, 239; quoted in Ellmann, *The Identity of Yeats*, p. 59.

32. Ellmann, p. 5. It will be helpful here to appeal to Ellmann's summary of a Yeatsian mood: "Moods and states of mind are conspicuously, but not exclusively, emotional or temperamental; they differ from emotions in having form and, often, intellectual structure. Less fleeting than a mere wish, and less crystallized than a belief, a mood is suspended between fluidity and solidity. It can be tested only by the likelihood of its being experienced at all, and being so, by many people. Ideas which occur in moods are 'lived' and lose their abstractness;

beliefs are dramatized and lose their affiliations with dogmas to take on affiliations with the dramatic speaker of the poem" (p. 57). With this last sentence, compare Pound's "An 'idea' has little value apart from the modality of the mind which receives it" ("Remy de Gourmont, a Distinction," *LE* 341). The implications of *receives* loom large in Pound's conception of the poetic process.

33. *ALSO* 14; *P 1* 57–58. Note here the echo of Balzac's distinction between the normal self and that beyond any mortal judgment, to which Yeats referred in "At Stratford-on-Avon."

34. "America: Chances and Remedies," *NA*, XIII (May 1, 1913), 10.

35. "Psychology and Troubadours," *SR* 92. If we could keep connotative values from intruding, we might say that the nice registrative abilities of the Decadents represent our kinship with the ox; one learns to respond to finely discriminated stimuli as an ox learns to discriminate between the farmer's house and the barn where feed is kept.

36. Yeats, *A Vision*, the privately printed edition of 1925 (London: T. Werner Laurie, Ltd.), quoted in Cleanth Brooks, *Modern Poetry and the Tradition* (London: Editions Poetry London, Ltd., 1948), p. 174.

II. *Thematic Geography*

1. Hugh Kenner, in "The Broken Mirrors and the Mirror of Memory," *Motive and Method in the Cantos of Ezra Pound*, ed. Lewis Leary (New York: Columbia University Press, 1954), p. 3, remarks that the title of the first *Personae* was "the first of a long sequence of efforts on his part to draw our attention to the status of the poetic process itself as the central drama of his poetry"—not always, as in these early poems, the central *issue*, but "central drama" is apt enough. As late as the *Pisan Cantos* it is there: "300 years culture at the mercy of a tack hammer thrown through the roof" (Canto LXXIV)—a point of momentary focus in a contemplative drama involving, on the one hand, the Odyssean consciousness which directs the *Cantos* and on the other an inchoate mob of "others" who do not remotely understand what sort of puma they have caged up. (At the Disciplinary Training Center, the prison camp, near Pisa, "the Trainees [prisoners] . . . considered Pound with awe, taking the reinforced cage as evidence that he was a particularly tough customer"—Robert L. Allen, "The Cage," *Esquire*, February 1958.)

2. The poet-speaker of "And Thus in Nineveh," for example, explains why maidens will scatter rose leaves upon his tomb:

> It is not, Raana, that my song rings highest
> Or more sweet in tone than any, but that I
> Am here a Poet, that doth drink of life
> As lesser men drink wine.

3. Most of the figures in that list of outcast artists would fit here, too—perhaps better: Dante, Swinburne, the troubadours, and, to replace the Decadents, Rossetti.

4. "The Approach to Paris—VI," *NA*, XIII (October 9, 1913), 695.

5. Recall Pater's "Not the fruit of experience, but experience itself, is the end."

6. In "Salve O Pontifex!":

> . . . thou mad'st canticles
> Serving upright before the altar
> That is bound above with shadows
> Of dead years wherein thy Iacchus
> Looked not upon the hills, that being
> Uncared for, praised not him in entirety

The epigraph to *Lustra*: "Definition: Lustrum: an offering for the sins of the whole people, made by the censors at the expiration of their five years of office, etc."

7. Richard of St. Victor, the twelfth-century mystical writer, was prior of the abbey of St. Victor at Paris from 1162 until his death in 1173. He was influenced by the works of Hugh, his best-known predecessor at St. Victor, by Anselm of Canterbury, and by Dionysius the Areopagite. The work to which Pound refers in his writing is *Benjamin Minor*, a treatise on contemplation that turns on an allegorical exegesis of the Jacob story. Both the *Benjamin Minor* and its later companion treatise, *Benjamin Major*, reveal a keen interest in the psychology of mystic contemplation. See the introduction to Richard's *Selected Writings on Contemplation*, trans. Clare Kirchberger (London: Faber and Faber, 1957).

8. "Affirmations—VI, Analysis of this Decade," *NA*, XVI (February 11, 1915), 409–410.

9. *Enneads* V.1.6, in *Plotinus*, ed. A. H. Armstrong (London: George Allen and Unwin, 1953), p. 70.

10. Armstrong, pp. 35–36. I give Armstrong's paraphrase because of its accuracy and conciseness. For confirmation, see *Enneads* V.1.4, V.1.11, V.9.6–8.

11. Armstrong, p. 36; alludes to *Enneads* V.9.6–8, V.3.3–4, 8.

12. In *Ideas into Action, a Study of Pound's Cantos* (Coral Gables: University of Miami Press, 1958), Clark Emery has furnished an extensive and useful elucidation of Pound's "theology."

13. Leary, *Motive and Method*, p. 14.

14. H. J. Chaytor, *The Troubadours of Dante* (Oxford: Clarendon Press, 1902), pp. xxi, xxii–xxiii. Pound seems to have thought very highly of this book (see *GK* 107). He wrote to his mother from Hamilton College (*YL* 39, March 1905), "My extra work with Bill Shepherd next term will be in Provençal, 'The Troubadours of Dante.'"

15. Remy de Gourmont, *Dante, Beatrice, et la poesie amoureuse* (Paris: Societé du Mercure de France, 1908), p. 38: "La lecture de ses poesies fait conclure que le poete ne s'adresse pas à une femme, mais à l'ideal, un ideal formé de tous ses amours, à la femme composée de toutes les perfections feminines."

16. *SR* 90–91. The context, as Pound translates it (*T* 173–174), is:

> God . . . grant that we two shall lie
> Within one room, and seal therein our pact,
> Yes, that she kiss me in the half-light, leaning
> To me, and laugh and strip and stand forth in the lustre
> Where lamp-light with light limb but half engages.

17. "Osiris—II," *NA*, X (December 14, 1911), 155, and *T* 107 (the text in *T* has been revised). The Italian, as Pound gives it in *T*, is:

> Veggio ne gli occhi de la donna mia
> Un lume pien di spiriti d'Amore,
> Che portano un piacer novo nel core
> Si che vi desta d'allegrezza vita.
>
> Cosa m'avvien, quand'io le son presente,
> Ch'i' non la posso a lo 'ntelletto dire:

Veder me par de le sue labbia uscire
Una si bella donna, che la mente
Comprender non la puo che 'nmantenente
Ne nasce un' altra di bellezza nova.
De la qual par, ch'una stella si mova,
E dica: Tua salute e dipartita.

18. "Affirmations—IV, As for Imagisme," *NA*, XVI (January 28, 1915), 349.

19. "Re / 'Heather.' The title is put on it to show that the poem is a simple statement of facts occurring to the speaker, but that these facts do not occur on the same plane with his feet, which are solidly planted in a climate producing Heather and not leopards, etc."—*YL* 439 (October 12, 1916, to Homer L. Pound).

20. Kenner, *The Poetry of Ezra Pound*, pp. 117–118.

21. Richard St. Victor, *Benjamin Major*, in *Selected Writings*, p. 137; Robert Grosseteste, *De Luce*, trans. Clare C. Riedl (Milwaukee: Marquette University Press, 1942), p. 10.

22. T. E. Hulme, *Speculations*, ed. Herbert Read (New York: Harcourt, Brace, 1924), pp. 149, 152–153.

23. *Further Speculations*, ed. Sam Hines (Minneapolis: University of Minnesota Press, 1955), pp. 72, 94.

24. "By intuition is meant the kind of *intellectual sympathy* by which one places oneself within an object in order to coincide with what is unique in it and consequently inexpressible"—Henri Bergson, *An Introduction to Metaphysics*, trans. T. E. Hulme (New York and London: G. P. Putnam and Sons, 1912), p. 7; hereafter cited as *Introduction*. In the act of perception, Bergson holds, the object, the light rays, the retina, and the affected neural structure "form a single whole; and . . . it is really in [the object], and not elsewhere, that the image of [the object] is formed and perceived"—*Matter and Memory*, trans. Nancy M. Paul and W. Scott Palmer (London: George Allen and Unwin, 1911), pp. 37–38.

25. *Introduction*, p. 56.

26. *Introduction*, pp. 69, 56.

27. *Creative Evolution*, trans. Arthur Mitchell (New York: Random House, Modern Library, 1944), p. 10.

28. *Introduction*, pp. 16ff.

29. *ABC of Reading* (New York: New Directions, n.d.), p. 19.

30. Kenner, *The Poetry of Ezra Pound*, p. 308.

31. Pater, *Appreciations, with an Essay on Style* (London: Macmillan, 1910), pp. 65–66.

32. See A. O. Lovejoy, *Bergson and Romantic Evolutionism*, University of California Chronicle, XV (October 1913), pp. 429–487; Carl Dyrssen, *Bergson und die Deutsche Romantik* (Marburg: N. G. Elwert'sche Verlagsbuchhandlung, 1922).

33. Lovejoy, p. 457. The direct line from the German romantics to Bergson was Felix Ravaisson, who attended Schelling's Munich lectures in 1837.

34. A. O. Lovejoy, "On the Discrimination of Romanticisms," *Essays in the History of Ideas* (Baltimore: Johns Hopkins Press, 1948), p. 246. On the same page: "It became a favorite platitude of German Romanticism to say that the Greeks and Romans set themselves limited ends to attain, were able to attain them, and were thus capable of self-satisfaction and finality; and that modern 'romantic' art differed from this most fundamentally, by reason of its Christian origin, in being, as Schiller had said, a *Kunst der Unendlichen*."

III. A Language To Use and a Language To Think In

1. The term is Hugh Kenner's: *Dublin's Joyce* (Bloomington: Indiana University Press, 1956), p. 28.

2. T. E. Welby, *The Victorian Romantics* (London: G. Howe, Ltd., 1929), pp. 31–32, 33.

3. Pound, trans., *Confucius: The Great Digest and Unwobbling Pivot* (New York: New Directions, 1951), p. 20. The phrase is part of Pound's exegesis of the Chinese ideograph for *sincerity*.

4. These translations are quoted from Rossetti's two-volume *Collected Works*, cited in Chapter One.

5. *The Wind among the Reeds* (London and New York: John Lane, Bodley Head, 1899), p. 61.

6. "Osiris—II, A Rather Dull Introduction," *NA*, X (December 7, 1911), 130.

7. Rossetti, I, 391: "A woman was present in his room clad to the hands and feet with a green and grey raiment, fashioned to that time." Compare the Temple translation of *Purgatorio* VIII.28–30, which Pound

quotes (*SR* 138): "Green, as tender leaves just born, was their raiment, which they trailed behind, fanned and smitten by green wings."

8. *ABC of Reading*, pp. 47–48.

9. "An image of my lady is worshiped, Guido, at San Michele in Orto, which, of beautiful appearance, true and pious, is the refuge and comfort of sinners: And he who devoutly humbles himself to her, the more he sorrows, the more comfort he has: [the image] heals the sick and drives out devils and she makes blind eyes see. She cures great ills in the public place: reverently the people bow to her; two lights adorn her from without. Her voice goes out through distant ways; but they say, the Minor Brethren, that it is idolatry, because of envy that she is not their neighbor." The Italian is as given in *T* 94.

10. Symons, "The Decadent Movement in Literature," quoted in Jackson, p. 57.

11. "Arthur Symons," *Athenaeum*, no. 4699 (May 21, 1920), 664; "Lionel Johnson" (*LE* 363)—originally used as the introduction to *The Poetical Works of Lionel Johnson* (London: Elkin Mathews, 1915).

12. Symons, *Poems*, 2 vols. (London: Heinemann, 1902), II, 118.

13. Dowson, *Poetical Works*, ed. Desmond Flower (London: Cassell and Co.—John Lane, 1934), p. 39. Compare Yeats (*Collected Poems*, p. 40):

> When you are old and grey and full of sleep,
> And nodding by the fire, take down this book,
> And slowly read, and dream of the soft look
> Your eyes had once, and of their shadows deep;
>
> How many loved your moments of glad grace,
> And loved your beauty with love false or true,
> But one man loved the pilgrim soul in you,
> And loved the sorrows of your changing face;
>
> And bending down beside the glowing bars,
> Murmur, a little sadly, how Love fled
> And paced upon the mountains overhead
> And hid his face amid a crowd of stars.

14. In another poem called "In Tempore Senectutis" (subtitled "An antistave for Dowson") in *ALS*, Pound succeeds on Dowson's own

ground. His presentation of both present and future is more vivid; yet, though he gives the joys of passion the expressive appeal they require, he does not undercut the experiential significance of that which he means to praise, the *tempus senectutis*. See *ALSO*, p. 80.

IV. Research and the Uses of London

1. *YL* 115 (September 9, 1909) to Homer L. Pound.
2. For example, "Search," the song of the "Voices in the Wind" in "Idyl for Glaucus," and "The White Stag." There is an almost direct imitation of the stories and verse of *The Celtic Twilight* in the tenth song of the "Laudantes Decem":

> The glamour of the soul hath come upon me,
> And as the twilight comes upon the roses,
> Walking silently among them,
> So have the thoughts of my heart
> Gone out slowly in the twilight
> Toward my beloved,
> Toward the crimson rose, the fairest.

3. "The Approach to Paris—II," *NA*, XIII (September 11, 1913), 577.
4. "Osiris—XI," *NA*, X (February 15, 1912), 370.
5. From *P 2* 116:

> The girl in the tea shop
> > Is not so beautiful as she was,
> > The August has worn against her.
> She does not get up the stairs so eagerly;

6. See Chaytor, *The Troubadours of Dante*, p. xxxiii.
7. For Vidal's text, see Raymond T. Hill and Thomas G. Bergin, *Anthology of the Provençal Troubadours* (New Haven: Yale University Press, 1941), pp. 97–98. For the term *coblas unisonans* and an example, see Chaytor, *The Troubadours and England* (Cambridge: The University Press, 1923), p. 160.
8. Daniel's text is in Chaytor, *The Troubadours of Dante*, pp. 52–53, and *T* 178–180.

9. Viola Wildman, in "A Pound of Flesh," ed. Jim Rader, *Wabash College Review* (Spring 1959), p. 6.

10. Robert L. Allen, "The Cage"; see Chapter Two, note 1.

11. *L* 179. By "literary values" Pound means primarily stylistic effects involving standard and nonstandard word order. The troubadours, he says, "were not competing with De Maupassant's prose."

12. Chaytor defines equivocal rhyme as "identical collocations of sound, but expressing different meanings" (*The Troubadours of Dante*, p. xxxiv).

13. *SR* 34; *T* (which reproduces the texts used in *Instigations*) 174, 175.

14. *Inferno* II.115–120, *The Portable Dante* (New York: Viking Press, 1947), p. 13. For Pound's reception of Binyon's translation, see "Hell," *LE* 201–213, where he announces that "The venerable Binyon has . . . produced the most interesting English version of Dante that I have ever seen or expect to see." See also his letter to Binyon (*L* esp. pp. 251, 255).

15. See F. S. Flint, "History of Imagism," *The Egoist*, II (May 1, 1915), 71. One is struck as well by the lucky conjunction of Pound as he was with London literary life as it was; for, undeniably useful as the strictures and slogans of men like Hulme, Flint, Ford, Newbolt, and Sturge Moore were to Pound's developing critical vocabulary, to his ability to discourse about dead English and the need for "accurate registration," the conceptions themselves clearly had guided Pound's work for some time, as this survey of his stylistic explorations shows.

16. In *SR* (150) Pound offers as the "finest of the explanatory passages" in the *Paradiso* these lines from Dante's Canto XXVIII:

> And thou shouldst know that all have their delight
> In measure as their sight more deeply sinketh
> Into that truth where every mind grows still;
> From this thou mayest see that being blessèd
> Buildeth itself upon the power of sight
> Not upon love which is there-consequent.
> Lo, merit hath its measure in that sight
> Which grace begetteth and the righteous will,
> And thus from grade to grade the progress goeth.

17. Earl Miner has made some interesting comments on related points in his *The Japanese Tradition in British and American Literature* (Princeton: Princeton University Press, 1958), chap. 5.

18. "There are two kinds of beautiful painting one may perhaps illustrate by the works of Burne-Jones and Whistler; one looks at the first kind of painting and is immediately delighted by its beauty; the second kind of painting, when first seen, puzzles one, but on leaving it, and going from the gallery one finds new beauty in natural things—a Thames fog, to use the hackneyed example. Thus, there are works of art which are beautiful objects and works of art which are keys or passwords admitting one to a deeper knowledge, to a finer perception of beauty" (SR 154).

19. "Imagisme is not Impressionism, though one borrows, or could borrow, much from the impressionist method of presentation" (GB 97). In view of Pound's critical alliance with Ford Madox Ford, it is worth noting that this "limited acceptance" entailed a selective rejection of Ford's kind of Impressionism. In "Dubliners and Mr. James Joyce" (LE 399; Egoist, July 15, 1914), Pound distinguishes between the literary Impressionism stemming from Stendhal and Flaubert, and that founded "not upon anybody's writing but upon the pictures of Monet." He adds that "every movement in painting picks up a few writers who try to imitate in words what someone has done in paint." While he was in almost unqualified agreement with Ford's praise of Stendhal and Flaubert and their concern with exact presentation and *le mot juste,* Pound felt that his friend's poetry belonged to the Impressionism that imitated in words the method of Monet and his successors. He specified the point of disagreement, as he thought, in a review of Ford's *High Germany,* in *The Poetry Review,* I (March 1912) 134: "His flaw is the flaw of impressionism, impressionism, that is, carried out of its due medium. Impressionism belongs in paint, it is of the eye. The cinematograph records, for instance, the 'impression' of any given action or place, far more exactly than the finest writings . . . A ball of gold and a gilded ball give the same 'impression' to the painter. Poetry is in some odd way concerned with the specific gravity of things, with their nature."

For more thorough discussion of Ford's place in this argument, see his *Thus To Revisit* (New York: E. P. Dutton, 1921), part III, chap. 2; also Ambrose Gordon, "Ford Madox Ford and the Prose Tradition" (unpub. diss., Yale University, 1952), pp. 218–227, and Stanley K. Coffmann, Jr., *Imagism: A Chapter for the History of Modern Poetry* (Norman: University of Oklahoma Press, 1951), chap. 6.

20. "I believe that every emotion and every phase of emotion has some toneless phrase, some rhythm-phrase to express it" (*GB* 97).

Afterword: The Ladies of Helicon

1. Jaufre Rudel, "No sap chantar qui so non di," distressingly translated by Barbara Smythe in *Trobador Poets* (New York: Duffield, 1911), p. 20. For the Provençal, see Hill and Bergin, p. 28.

2. Quoted in Oswald Doughty, *A Victorian Romantic: Dante Gabriel Rossetti* (London: F. Muller, 1949), p. 347.

3. *Ibid.*, p. 682.

Index